THE
MONEY
WARS

THE
MONEY
WARS

THE RISE AND FALL OF THE
GREAT BUYOUT BOOM
OF THE 1980s

ROY C. SMITH

T·T

TRUMAN TALLEY BOOKS
DUTTON
NEW YORK

DUTTON
Published by the Penguin Group
Penguin Books USA Inc., 375 Hudson Street,
New York, New York, 10014, U.S.A.
Penguin Books Ltd, 27 Wrights Lane,
London W8 5TZ, England
Penguin Books Australia Ltd, Ringwood,
Victoria, Australia
Penguin Books Canada Ltd, 2801 John Street,
Markham, Ontario, Canada L3R 1B4
Penguin Books (N.Z.) Ltd, 182–190 Wairau Road,
Auckland 10, New Zealand

Penguin Books Ltd, Registered Offices:
Harmondsworth, Middlesex, England

First published by Truman Talley Books • Dutton,
an imprint of New American Library,
a division of Penguin Books USA Inc.
Published simultaneously in Canada by McClelland & Stewart Inc.

First printing, November, 1990
10 9 8 7 6 5 4 3 2 1

LIBRARY OF CONGRESS CATALOGING-IN-PUBLICATION DATA
Smith, Roy C., 1938–
    The money wars : the rise and fall of the great buyout
boom of the 1980s / Roy C. Smith.
    p.   cm.
    "Truman Talley books."
    Includes bibliographical references.
    ISBN 0-525-24929-X
    1. Consolidation and merger of corporations—United
States—Finance—History—20th century.   2. Leveraged
buyouts—United   States—History—20th   century.
3. United States—Economic conditions—1981–   I.
Title.
HG4028.M4S64   1990
338.8'3'097309048—dc20   90-32257
                                               CIP

Printed in the United States of America
Set in Times Roman

To my students

CONTENTS

II

THE GREAT BUYOUT BOOM
OF THE EIGHTIES

THE
MONEY
WARS

INTRODUCTION

RISE AND FALL OF AN ERA

A hundred years after Adam Smith published *The Wealth of Nations* in the memorable year of 1776, England had reached the peak of its powers. Politically, it ruled 25 percent of the earth's surface and people. The British imperial economy was by far the strongest and most developed in the world. Its usual economic competitors were still partly asleep. France was still sorting itself out after a century of political chaos and, more recently, a war with Prussia that had gone wrong. Germany was just starting to come together as a nation and still had quite a way to go to catch up with the British in industrial terms. The rest of Europe was, well, not all that important. There was a potentially serious problem, however, from reckless, often irresponsible competition from America, which fancied itself as a rising economic power, but otherwise the horizon was comparatively free of competitors. British industry and British finance were very secure in their positions of world leadership.

English financial markets had made it all possible, according to Walter Bagehot, at the time the editor of *The Economist*, who published a small book in 1873 called *Lombard Street*, which described these markets and what made them tick. England's economic glory,

1

he suggested, was based on the supply and accessibility of capital. After all, he pointed out, what would have been the good of inventing a railroad back in Elizabethan times if there was no way to raise the capital to build it? In poor countries, there wasn't any money anyway, and in most rich European countries money stuck to the aristocrats and the landowners and wasn't made available to industry. But in England, Bagehot boasted, there was a place in the City of London, called Lombard Street, where "in all but the rarest of times, money can be always obtained upon good security, or upon decent prospects of probable gain." Such a market, Bagehot continued, was a "luxury which no country has ever enjoyed with even comparable equality before."

The real power of the market, he went on to suggest, is its ability to offer the benefits of leverage to those working their way up in the system, whose goal is to displace the men at the top. Everywhere, Bagehot noted, "small traders have arisen who discount their bills [heavily], and with the capital so borrowed, harass and press upon, if they do not eradicate, the old capitalist." The new trader, Bagehot explained, has a natural advantage in the system:

> If a merchant has £50,000, to gain 10 percent on it he must make £5,000 a year, and must charge for his goods accordingly; but if another has only £10,000 and borrows £40,000 by discounts (no extreme instance in our modern trade), he has the same capital of £50,000 to use, but can sell much cheaper. If the rate at which he borrows is 5 percent, he will have to pay £2,000 a year [in interest]; and if, like the old trader he makes £5,000 a year, he will still, after paying his interest, obtain £3,000 a year, or 30 percent on his own £10,000. As most merchants are content with much less than 30 percent, he will be able, if he wishes, to forego some of that profit, lower the price of the commodity, and drive the old-fashioned trader— the man who trades on his own capital—out of the market.

Thus, the ambitious New Man, with little to lose and ample access to credit through the market, can earn a greater return on his money than a risk-averse capitalist who borrows little or nothing. The higher return enables the New Man to undercut the other man's prices and take business from him. True, the New Man may lose on the venture and be taken out of the game, but there is always another New Man on his way up who is willing to replace him. As the richer man has a lot to lose, he risks it less, and thus is always in the game, continually defending himself against one newcomer or another until finally he packs it in, retires to the country, and invests in government securities instead.

"This increasingly democratic structure of English commerce," Bagehot continued, "is very unpopular. It prevents the long duration of great families of merchant princes . . . who are pushed out by the dirty crowd of new little men."

On the other hand, these defects are compensated for

> by one great excellence: no other country was ever so little "sleepy," no other was ever so prompt to seize new advantages. A country dependent mainly on great "merchant princes" will never be so prompt; there commerce perpetually slips more and more into routine. A man of large wealth, however intelligent, always thinks, "I have a great income, and I want to keep it. If things go on as they are, I shall keep it, but if they change I *may* not keep it." . . . But a new man, who has his way to make in the world, knows that such changes are his opportunities; he is always on the lookout for them, and always heeds them when he finds them.
>
> The rough and vulgar structure of English commerce is the secret of its life. . . .[1]

And of ours in America.

Indeed, Americans knew a lot about English commerce and the markets of Lombard Street. During most of the nineteenth century when American economic development was the wonder of the world, it was also its greatest financial magnet. Capital was extremely scarce in the United States so entrepreneurs tapped British (and other European) markets for investment funds. In the process, many were

educated in the workings of the financial centers in the principal
European cities, though none so much as London for the reasons
Bagehot supplies. The Civil War was financed there, as were the
great canal systems and railroads. And so were, by the end of the
nineteenth century, the new industrial investment trusts and corporations.

Sometime after the 1880s, however, just after Bagehot had finished his proud little book, Americans began to develop their own
financial markets. These were shaped along English lines, of course,
and many transatlantic banking connections resulted. America's economic progress was beginning to generate surplus cash: cash that
needed to be invested, preferably in promising American opportunities. The United States came of age financially around the turn of
the century, and Wall Street would soon displace Lombard Street
as the world's center of finance. As the markets came to life, with
them, predictably, came New Men with more ambitions and courage
than capital.

In 1902, for example, a thirty-two-year-old American named
Bernard Baruch took Bagehot's essay to heart and made himself the
first of many millions in a Wall Street pool buying control of a railroad
on borrowed money.[2]

About the same time J. P. Morgan organized the United States
Steel Corporation, having acquired Carnegie Steel and several other
companies, in a transaction valued at $1.4 billion, an amount worth
perhaps $20 billion today. This was the largest financial deal ever
done until the RJR-Nabisco transaction in 1989.

The U.S. Steel transaction occurred in 1902 during the first of
four large merger booms to take place in the United States. Each
of these booms was powered by different factors, but in each, rising
stock markets and easy access to credit were conditions precedent.
During each, ordinary entrepreneurs with the right idea at the right
time were transformed into enormously wealthy individuals. In each
of the booms, especially those in the 1920s and the 1980s, borrowed
money was used extensively, though the underlying financing techniques and justifications for the high debt levels were quite different.

Today, more than a hundred years after it was written, Bagehot's essay is still apropos; indeed it brings tears to the eyes of modern denizens of Wall Street. Those who maintain and administer the great fortunes from the past will weep for bygone days when they reigned undisturbed in quiet orderliness; those included among the New Men of today weep in gratitude for the opportunities of a Carl Icahn, a Saul Steinberg, or a Ron Perelman—opportunities to obtain the financing necessary to launch their bold, if risky, ventures, which in their cases tend to be takeover bids of other companies.

This access to capital they don't own is called *leverage*. In the field of mechanics, leverage permits one, by clever application, to multiply the power he has available to accomplish a particular task. The forces thus created can be powerful enough to make possible undertakings that would otherwise be impossible. Leverage in business works the same way, enabling an entrepreneur to assemble far more resources for a particular investment than he otherwise has on his own. Such resources include primarily capital, but also numerous other skills and other capabilities necessary for a successful investment: ideas, management talent, information, and technology. The rewards of leverage, successfully applied, can be great and can propel their possessor to great heights quickly, but equally leverage also works the other way around when things go wrong.

Financial leverage is not just a tool of quick-footed opportunists and scoundrels. It can, and does, produce very beneficial results for the public at large. Most Americans now own their homes, which they purchased with the aid of a home mortgage representing perhaps 80 percent of the price of the house. Some perfectly staid, conservative corporations that clearly serve the public interest use huge amounts of leverage just to run their ordinary affairs. Consolidated Edison, the electric power company serving New York City, has assets on its books valued at about $10 billion, which are almost 50 percent financed with debt and other liabilities. American Airlines, one of the most solid of such companies, finances two-thirds of its assets with borrowed money and deferred payments. Citicorp, the parent company of Citibank, has deposit and other liabilities on its books equal to 95 percent of its assets. The Prudential Life Insurance Company, the "rock of Gibraltar," carries insurance and other liabilities on its books equal to 96.9 percent of its assets. These companies have not been the subject of leveraged buyouts; the businesses are capitalized normally. On the other hand, RJR-Nabisco, which has been through a very controversial leveraged buyout, ended up with debt on its books of about 75 percent of its total assets. It is not always so clear just how much leverage is too much.

Governments borrow large sums of money too, sometimes usefully with highly positive results, as in the case of postwar Japan. Sometimes they borrow too much and run the fiscal deficit and the national debt way up, but whether or not they are borrowing to excess, financial leverage is an essential ingredient in national economic policy. Everywhere.

The powers of leverage can be misused, of course, or fall into the wrong hands, causing failures or unwanted outcomes. Failure, as in the case of a bankruptcy or liquidation, tends to be fairly absolute, and relatively unarguable. As for the other, one would have to ask, "unwanted" as judged by whom? Many of the "old capitalists" of our day (perhaps we would think of them as established management of large public companies) find much of the works of today's New Men to be quite disagreeable and controversial, just as in Bagehot's time. Others think differently, perhaps seeing some good in the effort if not in the result, or vice versa: reasonable men see these things quite differently. Failures, partial failures, and mutations are the natural outcome of periods of dynamic activity and experimentation, from all of which the whole system generally benefits.

Certainly there is a lot going on in our markets today that is dynamic and experimental. During the 1980s financial transactions abounded as never before. These included huge volumes of new issues of government securities accompanying gargantuan U.S. budget deficits, record levels of activity in stocks and bonds, in foreign exchange, in real estate, in mergers and acquisitions, in futures and options, in Eurobonds, and in every other type of financial transaction. To fuel these transactions, liquid capital had to be available in abundance, and worked overtime. It was, as a result of growing institutional wealth, of substantial deregulation and freer access to increasingly global financial markets, and of the unprecedented efficiency of the markets in making price information available and handling all the paperwork smoothly.

These markets have become substantially integrated (across borders and between different financial species) by improved telecommunications, new trading techniques, and better common financial understanding among players from all parts of the world. Competition has grown with these developments: New Men may enter the markets (at least in a particular sector) quite easily. Innovations in money-making have proliferated in the rich and fertile financial environment of the times, and many new millionaires have been created from the domain of finance in the 1980s, more perhaps than at any other time.

Success followed the bold, however, as the following tale relates.

George was the chief executive of a medium-size company, of which he owned about 5 percent of the stock. In the early 1980s he was surprised one morning from a call from somebody named Bass.

"Like to buy your company, George. In fact I already own 4.9 percent. I'm goin' to buy some more today and make an announcement. I can get quite a bit, I'm told, around these levels—20 or so. I'd be willin' to buy you out at 26. Take it or leave it. I 'recon by this time next week I'll be your biggest shareholder so you ought to be figurin' to put me on the board so I can start runnin' things."

George was stunned but recovered quickly. He had sold his own company to the one he now headed, so he wasn't really a loyal lifetime employee so like many others in the company. On the other hand, life as a CEO of a good-size company was unexpectedly sweet. He had a lot of amenities in his present job that he had not enjoyed before—a plane, a limousine, country clubs—but maybe even better than these was the regard in which he seemed to be held just because of the job he had. People were always groveling to him, flattering him, telling him how brilliant he was, asking him to join boards and special civic groups and committees. Beautiful women at parties talked to him with gleaming eyes. Only his wife reminded him that he really wasn't much good at anything but business and that wasn't all that interesting to most people. He was nice to be with in his own way, she added, but nothing for beautiful women to get all gleamy about.

Still, George liked things the way they were and was in no hurry to give them up. Besides, what would his newfound public think of him if he just curled up like a spaniel just because this guy Bass came breezing by? It was time to let them "good ol' boys" know what he was made of.

"Nothing doing, buddy. This company's not for sale. If you make your announcement and buy that stock you better be prepared for one helluva fight."

"OK, George, I just wanted to let you know. No hard feelings—this is just business, nothing personal. See you in court." The next day Bass offered $26 per share for 100 percent of the company in a cash tender offer, worth about $500 million. The offer was to be financed with bank loans that would be substantially repaid after control was passed to Bass by George's company's own money: its excess cash, real estate holdings, and numerous miscellaneous assets such as George's plane and limousine. Bass said he was acquiring the company because it was obviously worth a lot more well managed than it was poorly managed.

George said he would fight Bass until Hell froze over.

He hired an investment banker who told him that he had three options. He could essentially do nothing: arguing with the company's institutional shareholders that they shouldn't tender their shares to Bass because they would be worth more later on if they just held on to them. The banker said that it was doubtful that any of his institutional shareholders, who owned about half the stock, would go along with this. The offer at $26 was above the all-time high for the stock, and 30 percent above the current market. Bass's own reputation as a manager was not at issue; he was offering cold, hard cash, not future profits. So it was cash at a premium versus George's management record, which Bass intended to make look as bad as possible.

"Nobody wins doing nothing," said the banker, "you've got to do something. What you can do is find a 'white knight' to sell to instead in a friendly deal, at a higher price for the shareholders. You've still sold the company, though. Of course you can make it all look good and maybe work out some employment contracts. There are lots of potential white knights around, and I'm sure we could get some of them interested at a price of $30 or so.

"Or you could try to restructure the company yourself. Usually this means borrowing a lot of money to do a self-tender, that is buying-in your own stock at a price higher than Bass's. What you end up with is a company with a whole lot of debt and a very small equity base. You might be able to increase management's share-ownership in the process. What you do is turn yourself into a 'leveraged buyout.' If things work out you can pay off the debt and walk out a very rich man; if they don't you lose everything you've got in it."

"That's everything," said George, "$25 million for my stock at Bass's price. I wouldn't want to lose all that."

"Well, then go for the 'white knight'; that way you will have beaten Bass and done as well for your shareholders as you can."

"Of course, then I probably lose my job and all the trimmings. And Bass doesn't lose anything; he gets to sell his stock out to our white knight at a profit of around $10 a share. If he gets 15 percent of the stock like he said, that'll be a profit for him of more than $25 million, just for making that one phone call."

"Yeah," said the banker, "he's 'put you in play.' He now expects you to do something to yourself just to get away from him that will result in the company's being sold at a price of at least $26. The only way he can lose is for his 15 or so percent interest to become worth less than $20, which would mean the deal gets blocked by the government, or the company falls apart, or the market crashes. The government isn't going to be interested in this deal, and the other outcomes hurt you worse than him."

"Yeah, that sumbitch hasn't got a thing to lose, does he."

George put up a good fight, made a lot of serious noise, sued Bass in various courts, and flirted with white knights, none of which on closer inspection seemed much of an improvement over Bass, who might after all need George to run the business. Finally, at the last minute, Bass called George and offered $28.50 if George and his board would endorse the deal on a friendly basis. George accepted, wistfully thinking of life without the gleaming beauties.

Soon he tired of working for Bass and quit. He sat around his pool for a few months getting restless. Nobody ever called anymore except charities wanting contributions. One day he called his banker.

"I think I'd like to make a run on one of those white knights," he said. "I can put up a little money, but better yet I'm going to get ol' Bass to raise the equity for a leveraged buyout. It doesn't matter how much we'd have to pay, because Bass and his LBO investors, the banks, and maybe Drexel Burnham can put that all together. Me, I just put myself up as CEO of the company we buy, take out a lot of stock options, get a good salary, and maybe even get paid an investment-banking fee for arranging it all. Then I'll just sell off a few things and run the company for cash to pay down the debt. A few years later we sell out again, or go public, for a fantastic profit.

"Once we put all this together we just buy some stock, make an announcement and watch 'em squirm. What the hell, this time I've got nothing to lose. My money's still in the bank; Bass never puts up much of his own money—only a little of his clients' money already earmarked for LBOs. It's the banks and the buyers of those 'junk bonds' that Drexel sells that carry all the risk. As long as they're willing, we'd be pretty dumb just to sit here and let the other fellow come up with the big idea of which company to go after.

"We better get into this game while we can, before those banks and institutional lenders wise up and take their money back."

The greatest fortunes made during the 1980s were the work of industrialists, venture capitalists backing new things, and real estate developers, not financial operators per se. Of the 260 names of New Men (and Women) appearing in the 1988 *Forbes* list of the 400 richest Americans (and their numerous relatives) that were not included in the first such list, which was published in 1982, only about 10 percent were financiers. Two-thirds of the new people had gained their fortunes from industry, the rest from real estate. However, all of the New Men, regardless of the field in which their money was made, had, like George, become experts in finance and in the use of leverage as it applied to their businesses. For those people, leverage was a sine qua non, without which their success would at least have been long delayed. For society as a whole, however, the harvest of leverage is seen to be mixed.

That leverage encourages speculation, unwise investments, and waste of capital resources and perhaps imposes excessive risk on the entire financial system is as arguable today as it was in Bagehot's day. So are many of the ethical and regulatory concerns that have been expressed so often in our present day that they have become the frequent subject of pejorative comment by political, religious, and civic leaders and the brunt of many comedians' jokes.

But Bagehot's point is that however unseemly, indeed distasteful, the democratization of free capital markets has been, the good it has done in stimulating the changes and new ideas that keep us sharp is worth the price. Efficient capital markets are one of the glories of our nation, as they were of Bagehot's. In such markets the dull will be overtaken by the daring, and the slow by the quick, even if the results are the rise of "dirty new little men from the rough and vulgar crowd" who started at the bottom, and the battering that society must sometimes endure in the process of absorbing all the dynamic changes that they impart.

But what happens if things get carried too far? Nothing in Bagehot's days would have prepared him for what went on in Wall Street, and on Lombard Street too, in the crazy period that the latter-day "Adam Smith" calls the "roaring eighties." It was a time of deals. A time when American industry was transformed by real or threatened financial transactions. It was the time of a great buyout boom, when money was easy, new ideas were cheap, and the crowds cheered everything you did. A great time, but one that came to an end at the close of the decade, burned out perhaps by speculation and excess.

The end brought rough justice for some: the collapse of the junk-bond market forced the once mighty Drexel Burnham Lambert, fatally weakened by indictments and scandal, into liquidation. Some great achievements and reputations, like those of Michael Milken, were lost in criminal proceedings. Some of the principal buyout promoters like Robert Campeau destroyed both themselves and the companies they bought, companies that had stood not long before as standards for their industries. Many other glamorous entrepreneurs of the period had to struggle hard just to keep their deals alive.

Investment bankers, agents of much of the change that occurred, found their princely reputations now scuffed and battered. The literature of the times illuminated much about the lives and work of the bankers. Most of it was accurate enough, but generally nasty. You never met a character you liked, not anyway in *Greed and Glory on Wall Street—The Fall of the House of Lehman* or *Bonfire of the Vanities*, or *The Predator's Ball*, or *Liar's Poker*, or *Barbarians at the Gate*, all national best-sellers about investment bankers. The movies were just as bad, as evidenced by *Wall Street* and *Working Girl*.

There was good reason for the public disapproval. The aggressiveness of the deals, the amounts of money involved, the incredible egos of Wall Street's newest arrivals, the apparent indifference to other people involved, and of course the corruption and illegality that rose to the surface offended most people. The seamy part was pretty bad, but, alas, not unlike some of the behavior of previous boom periods.

Moralists and other judges of the times, however, need to reflect on at least one point: under the American legal and commercial system, conflicts are meant to be resolved through adversarial proceedings. And there were some big financial conflicts to be resolved during the eighties, mainly surrounding who should decide how shareholders' money is managed and invested. Management for the most part wanted to be left alone, to decide things in a patriarchal way, unburdened by ill-informed and shortsighted challenges to its authority. Others, feeding mainly on the opportunity to make money by seizing control of companies to make them run better, chose to confront management; the clashes were loud and sometimes ugly. The competitiveness of the American business economy of the future is at stake, claimed each of the challengers. But the adversarial system was actually operating at its best—with strong, competent advisers and backers lined up on each side. And the results of the confrontations have been on balance beneficial to shareholders and to business in the United States, which now has a different attitude about manager-owner conflicts and an extensive body of case law with which to adjudicate them.

The best of the legal and financial advisers were in constant demand. They were warriors of a sort, chosen because they won their battles, not because of their manners or public appeal. They were tough, smart, untiring, and eager for recognition. So were their opponents.

At the end of the eighties, the boom died out. Wall Street profits sagged, layoffs abounded, and top guys were fired. Life in the Street went on as it always has after a boom; a bit bloody, a few fatalities, some shifts in the power structure, but most of the firms survive for another day as they have before. They adjust, thin down some, and go back to work looking for the next opportunity.

This book is about finance and deal-making in the 1980s, a period of exceptional activity that exceeded everything that ever happened before. Buoyant markets, confidence, tolerance of New Men, and, of course, leverage made it all happen. The period was one of great innovation, in which such powerful (and colorful) devices as LBOs, junk bonds, white knights, squires, and greenmail were devised to effect miracles in the marketplace. It was also a time when some of the best business minds of our generation were locked into tactical combat with one another over stratagems and maneuvers, that, more often than anyone would have thought, made all the difference in the outcome. These struggles, often over amounts of money so large as to be incomprehensible, soon adopted the aggressive terminology of warfare: raid, attack, defensive positions, scorched earth defenses, poison pills, golden parachutes, and ultimately, defeat and victory. For a whole generation of Wall Streeters the merger wars, battles, and skirmishes would be substitutes for the real wars fought by their fathers and grandfathers, wars in which youthful strengths and virtues were put to the greatest test. During this period, as in real warfare, the stamina, determination, fearlessness, and arrogance of those in their thirties and early forties were among the can-do qualities most needed for operational success.

Earnest battles were certainly fought, for example, between the New Men and the entrenched capitalists of the 1980s, bitter battles that the former often won. The battles took many different forms, often resulting in complaints of inappropriate and wrongful behavior and the perennial search for the right set of rules by which such financial clashes should take place.

Battles occurred, too, between spectators—between the supporters and opponents of harsh free-market transactions. While these preserve the virtues of economic Darwinism, they can destroy great companies, the work of thousands of dedicated men and women over countless years, only to put a few extra dollars into the pockets of an indifferent pension fund manager.

And battles, too, among those believing that leverage can make anything possible and those who fear a coming collapse of a fragile house of cards—between those who believe that today's capital structures can be explained rationally and those who believe they cannot be.

And finally, highly emotional wars have been fought between those who believe greed is disgusting and those who think it's an inspiration, between those who can define it and those who cannot, and between those who feel that lust for money has corrupted our youth and taken our eye off the ball and those who shrug and assert that it's all happened before.

The Money Wars' purpose is to look at the incredible financial activities of the eighties in a manner that helps to provide greater understanding, if not resolution, of the many conflicts they have provoked. To do so the story of these years has to be put into a historical context and into a contemporary one also, so we can appreciate that all things financial, past and present—mergers, buyouts, leverage, restructurings, tactics, and bull markets and periods of euphoria—are all related. They can only flourish when markets are in an exceptional state of excitement—stock markets, debt markets, and banks' willingness to lend—and can provide the liquidity necessary to underwrite the high prices that bring out the deals.

Part 1 reviews some of the more extraordinary transactions of the early part of this century, from its robust beginning through the runaway twenties to the merger boom of the late sixties with its colorful gunslingers, Chinese money, and Saturday night specials.

The principal focus of the book, however, is Part 2, in which the merger boom of the 1980s and what lessons we can draw from it are discussed. It examines the economic rationale for the boom, the tactics of maneuver that emerged with it, and how the modern junk-bond-financed LBO became involved in the merger battles. It also illustrates these with portraits of the significant personalities and transactions, successful and unsuccessful, that shaped developments.

Part 3 examines the theoretical underpinnings of superleverage and tries to reconcile corporate finance in the 1980s with its more conservative predecessors. The issues of what sort of regulation to apply to all of this, if any, are also taken up, along with some deeper thoughts about what this great financial juggernaut, already slowing down in America, has left behind and where and when it will turn up next.

I am grateful to my many colleagues and students at the Stern School of Business, New York University, for the multiplicity of stimulations, ideas, argumentations, and perspectives that I have benefited from in undertaking this effort. My extremely proficient colleagues at Goldman Sachs, too, have played their usual role in supplying data, informed comment, and technical explanations, for which I am also most appreciative.

Finally, a literary note. In these days in which women, as well as men, perform all the important tasks and play all the roles in the dramas described in this volume, it is unfair always to refer to the players in the male gender. Unfortunately a text that constantly refers instead to him or her, he or she, and his or hers, soon makes a complete hash of its readability. This being my concern, I have left everything in male form (bowing to the majority of the players), but I wish herein to make it clear that in every case what I meant to say was he/she, or him/her, and so on.

I

ROOTS

1

MORGAN'S LEGACIES

Industrial corporations have existed in the United States for only about a hundred years, and only since about 1860 in Britain. Before their formation, going back perhaps as far as the Romans, most businesses were owned by proprietors or partnerships, which held unlimited liability for all activities of their firms. New debt capital was difficult to obtain, for a lender had to be sure that the partnership would not suffer losses or a withdrawal of equity previous to the repayment of the debt. New sources of equity capital were limited to obtaining new partners, and there was virtually no way for those partners individually to liquidate their investments except by selling them back to the other partners.

Corporations until after the Industrial Revolution were limited to special-purpose ventures such as the formation of the Dutch East India Company, or the Bank of England, or the South Sea Company (a great speculative bubble of the eighteenth century). Business otherwise was largely confined to farming, trading, banking, and to some extent retailing, for all of which partnerships or proprietorships were appropriate.

This changed after the Industrial Revolution, when manufac-

turing facilities involving major amounts of investment in plant,
equipment, and working capital began to be erected. And it changed
again when such capital-intensive activities as railroading, steelmak-
ing, electric power generation, and similar activities asserted their
massive claims on the nation's capital resources. Capital raising for
all of these new industries became a crucial task.

The Civil War in the United States was a major catalyst, as wars
seem always to be, to both advancing industrial production and developing the means of organizing requisite financing through the kind
of marketplace of which Walter Bagehot was so proud. After the
war the great westward roll of the railroads continued, making use
of both the enhanced steel- and railmaking capacity and of the financing networks that had been established. The railroads were organized into special kinds of corporations that could attract the large
amounts of financing they needed. In the 1880s, railroads dominated
finance: as much capital had been invested in railroads as in all other
industry in the United States combined.

Restructuring the Rails

The railroads were so vast and needed so much capital that many
individuals, institutions, and political bodies were involved in their
numerous and widespread operations. On one side were the managers of the rail companies, who had planned and secured the
rights-of-way, arranged for the laying of track, acquired all of the
equipment, and supervised the operational and commercial activities.
On the other side were the bankers who had organized the funds
that had been invested in the new enterprises. Most of these funds
came from Europe, and bankers such as J. P. Morgan and Jacob
Schiff of Kuhn Loeb & Co., among others, had the duty to look
after their absent investors' funds. To obtain the funds, the rail-
roaders would have to agree to the bankers' terms, including, usually,
representation on the board of directors and several of its principal
committees so they could keep an eye on things. As the companies

were in constant need of funds, management had to play close attention to the views of their bankers.

The problem with the railroads at that time was that they were the only financial game in the country, and thus they attracted every kind of corrupt and disreputable character that could somehow work himself onto the gravy train. Land and real estate had to be acquired, state permits of various kinds issued, vast purchases of steel rails and equipment made, rates set for customers, and the like. In the process of these many large and continuing transactions, room for large amounts of waste and corruption could be found. Predators, too, abounded as in our own day, though many of the tactics they employed would be gross violations of securities laws now. Still, the railroads represented the best investment opportunities available—the economic potential to be unleashed by the railroads in America was breathtaking to consider—and the bankers and their clients wanted to be involved in them despite the risks.

From the 1880s on, however, the economics of the railroad business had become very troubling. All sorts of schemes were undertaken, by financiers such as Jay Gould, Edward Harriman, William Vanderbilt, and others to manipulate the industry and, when possible, to force competitors out of business. Cutthroat pricing, predatory activities of all types, and a win-at-all-cost mentality crept into the business and nearly destroyed it. This was free-market capitalism at its worst: brutal, undisciplined, wasteful, grossly inefficient. When the great economic depression of 1893–97 occurred, many railroads thus weakened were unable to meet their debt-service payments.

At this point the bankers, led by J. P. Morgan, who was then in his sixties, stepped in to resolve the crisis on behalf of his firm's various investor clients. Morgan had been a banker all his life. He was the son of Junius S. Morgan, an American who had headed a prominent London firm of merchant bankers with many clients among wealthy Europeans seeking promising investments in America. Armed with his father's "placing power" Morgan quickly became an important factor in the main financing activity of Wall Street, underwriting new issues of railroad bonds. In time, Morgan became one of the Street's most formidable characters, whose enormous presence and banking skills made him a leading financial figure of his day.

Nevertheless, the railroad restructurings that followed are what made Morgan's lasting reputation and set him on the path toward becoming the greatest investment banker of all time.

The five-year depression of the 1890s was truly a severe one, and it resulted in the bankruptcy of 169 railroad companies, nearly 25 percent of the entire industry. Many of the failed companies were ones for which Morgan and the other bankers had sold securities and on whose boards they had been represented. Perhaps if they had acted differently as directors, the extensive mismanagement, corruption, and excessive competition of the times might have been abated. In general their role as directors was simply to be sure that the necessary payments to their clients were made; their interests in the firms (and their influence) were slight as long as the companies met their obligations on time. However, if the companies could not make the payments, then the bankers stepped in on behalf of the investors and in effect took control of the company through a voting trust into which the otherwise bankrupt shareholders would have to deposit their shares.

The trademark Morgan recapitalization would require, in addition to a voting trust, appropriate competitive rationalizations so that the future businesses of the affected railroads could be stable and predictable. Line A, for example, might have to give up its plans for a new route to Pittsburgh to compete with line B, in exchange for a concession from line B to withdraw from competition with line A on the route to Albany. That several railroads were all in the soup at the same time, all being restructured by bankers who talked to each other daily, made the complicated task easier than it might seem. Thus some effort to suppress competition occurred in conjunction with the restructuring, though without it, the problems that led to the collapse of the railroads undoubtedly would have resumed. Indeed, without being able to assure the stability of the cash flow of a corporation undergoing restructuring, the restructuring could not happen as no one would invest in it.

The typical Morgan restructuring followed a pattern that is very similar to those used in "restructuring" operations and "leveraged buyouts" (LBOs) today. First an estimate was made of the minimum annual pro forma cash flow, after whatever necessary changes to the business were effected. Then the amount of debt to be outstanding was reduced to the amount that the cash flow could reasonably be expected to service. Stockholders and banks were assessed for working capital. Then new shares of preferred and common stock, which at the time were not worth much, were generously issued all around to keep everybody happy. If the recapitalization worked, then these shares might have substantial value but not otherwise. Everybody had the same incentive: to make the thing succeed. Morgan's firm also shared in the incentives, by receiving large fees (sometimes in stock) for the advice about the restructuring and by underwriting the new securities to be issued. The voting trust, controlled by the bankers, would ensure that everything stayed peacefully the same for five years, during which time the business should stabilize sufficiently to repay some of the debt and to create some real value in the preferred and the common stock.

Morgan has been characterized by historians as having dominated the railroad industry through these competition-squelching recapitalizations as only a "robber baron" could. However, Frederick Lewis Allen, in his illuminating biography of Morgan, greatly softens the point in saying of his railroad and other industrial activities:

> it is hardly an accident that most of the Americans who at the beginning of the 20th century were charged with being monopolists had had a good look in their youth at competition at its savage and unbridled worst, and had decided to try to do something about it. . . . [Such competition] brought corruption, confusion, waste, and loss and Morgan's systematic soul detested it. Surely, he may well have thought, it would be better if instead of fighting like cats and dogs, people could

be brought together to combine forces for the peaceful and
orderly and profitable development of railroad properties.[1]

Apart from the railroads, which were the main concern of financial operators in the latter part of the nineteenth century, industrial companies involved in manufacturing of various types were
also beginning to develop. These companies, however, tended to be
small, one-plant concerns operating in one state or commercial region. There were a few large industrial companies in the 1890s, such
as Carnegie Steel (a partnership until 1892) and McCormick Har-
vesting Machine Co., which was closely held by the McCormick
family, but not many that were publicly held. Indeed, the only manufacturing company regularly traded on the New York Stock Exchange in the 1880s was the Pullman Palace Car Company. More
industrial stocks, mostly regional textile companies, then traded on
the Boston Exchange than in New York.

As the manufacturing companies grew, however, fed by all the
new technologies coming to life, they, too, developed more substantial financing needs and began to experience problems with the
partnership or proprietorship form of business organization that most
of them still retained. For some such firms, state corporation laws
made it difficult to do business in states in which the firm was not
incorporated, and one could be incorporated only in one state. For
others, the growing size of their unlimited liabilities became a worry.
For still others, the existing ownership arrangement was financially
inefficient: you had to own all the capital in your business, and there
was no way to cash in on your stake except to sell the business to a
competitor, usually at a low price.

Trusting in Consolidation

The processing industries (oil refining, sugar refining, lead smelting,
and the like) were, after the railroads, among the first industries to
"go national," that is, to transform themselves from local or regional

producers to those operating on a coordinated basis across the whole of the United States. Such a transformation was expensive and difficult and had to occur in the midst of periodic price wars, whose aim often was to drive a particular competitor out of business or into a forced sale of his business. John D. Rockefeller organized the first of many *trusts* in the processing industries to consolidate the oil refiners. Through what was in effect a large multiparty merger, the Standard Oil Trust came together in 1882, after exchanges of shares of individual refiners for new "trust certificates." The new entity would be administered by a board of trustees and operated so as to maximize the financial interests of the holders of the certificates. This meant that the board of trustees (controlled by Rockefeller) could now set prices for all of them, determining how much of their capacity would be on line and how much shut down.

In each case of the processing industry trusts, a large majority of the industry joined, thus providing a foundation for effective monopolistic control.

At the time, such a combination was not possible through a corporate form of organization, because holding companies were not permitted under any of the state corporation laws. Clever lawyers, then as now, have often found ways around important obstacles in their way. This one idea, the trust, which gave Rockefeller control of a whole industry at a very early stage in its development, may have been as important to his ultimate wealth and power as anything that he did during his whole career. Certainly it influenced others, as the other processing industries created powerful trusts of their own, which in turn precipitated two landmark pieces of legislation: the 1889 enactment of the New Jersey Holding Company Act, which permitted the incorporation in New Jersey of corporations that could own shares of other corporations, whether or not incorporated in New Jersey, and the Sherman Anti-Trust Act in 1890.

Perhaps the basic economic conditions of the oil refining industry at the time were sufficient to drive all the major producers into the trusts, but the way in which their combination occurred set the tone for all subsequent trust organizations and for the eventual wave of industrial mergers that followed them.

First, the participating partnerships had to incorporate, so an exchange of securities could take place. Second, the participants were encouraged to exchange their shares for trust certificates at a price that reflected a premium relative to the estimated value of the shares being exchanged (thereby establishing the principal of a "control premium" that had to be paid to induce a merger).

Third, the participants had to give up all interests in their own firms and to subordinate their future interests to the combination as a whole. Thus the trust had to begin to consider how to manage a large nationwide enterprise; standard (and in many cases much more rigorous) accounting and financial controls soon would be adopted by the new organization, which would also set up new national sales and purchasing departments.

Fourth, there would be liquidity in the trust certificates as individual participants offered to sell certificates to other participants, and later to the public through trading in the certificates on stock exchanges. After a while such a liquid market in the securities was regarded as an essential requirement for a combination. Without it, how could the heirs and successors of the original businessmen selling into the trust, who no longer had any real management influence in it, be able to realize the value of their investment? The trust certificates were in effect the same as shares of stock in the company, and trading in the certificates by the end of the 1880s began to outshine substantially trading in all other industrial securities on the New York Stock Exchange and the Boston Exchange.[2]

Finally, the trust permitted the organizing entrepreneurs the unprecedented opportunity to control much larger businesses than they could afford on their own with sometimes quite modest holdings. John D. Rockefeller, for example, though indeed a substantial investor, owned less than half of the trust certificates of the Standard Oil Trust, which he substantially controlled as chief executive.[3]

The trusts had a brief life in the United States—all 350 or so of the trusts that had been organized since 1882 had incorporated by 1899—but they were influential. Not only did they serve as the principal precedent for business combinations and securities trading in manufacturing enterprises in the United States, they also helped to establish the important relationships among acquisitions, corporate control, and leverage, thereby opening a very important door in the rapidly developing structure of American corporate finance.

After the passage of the New Jersey Holding Company Act, many trusts chose to be converted into corporations. The New Jersey legislature wisely foresaw, it appears, that industrial organizations were forming into trusts because such were the best alternative available at a time when holding companies were illegal. If New Jersey could provide a safe haven for these powerful but clumsy new enterprises under its corporate law, then many firms would convert themselves into New Jersey corporations, thus enabling the state to prosper greatly from the influx of incorporation fees. Also, once the Sherman Anti-Trust Act came into being, it was better not to be a trust and the comparative advantages of New Jersey incorporation increased.

In affecting the trust conversions, a matter for which bankers had to be called in, the lessons of the railroad reorganizations were brought to bear, plus at least one new idea: the utilization of preferred stock, a security paying a guaranteed fixed dividend rate that ranks in liquidation behind the debts of the enterprise but senior to the company's common stock. Preferreds had been used in railroad financing, but not before in the United States for industrial purposes. Having the preferred available meant that a trust converting to corporate form could offer a different package of securities to investors than it had originally. The original trust certificates were seen by mainstream conservative investors as bearing only risk (like common stock), and no investment value (such as preferred); therefore they didn't buy them. Only those investors with a greater preference for risk bought them, but many traditional risk investors declined the trust certificates because the investment value they contained limited the speculative potential of the investment.

Now, however, with common for the risk takers and preferred for the more conservative investors, the securities of the trust could be divided into packages tailored to the investment requirements of different investors. The result was that the market value of the common and preferred package was greater than that of the old security.

The Sugar Trust conversion in the late 1890s, as described by the historians Thomas Navin and Marian Sears, illustrates how this happened:

> The new corporation had a capital structure that was to become usual in the later mergers: half preferred and half common. Two $100 par trust certificates were to be replaced by a $100 par preferred stock and a $100 par common. The announcement of this rate of exchange had a pronounced effect on the market price, although other factors also influenced the situation. In three months the price of the trust certificates rose from $50 to the $70s. When the conversion finally occurred, the market put a value of $86 on the preferred and $57 on the common. In other words, two certificates worth approximately $100 had appreciated in market value to $143 in about three months.[4]

This discovery, that the market value of a security could be enhanced by exchanging it for a package of securities designed to appeal to specific investor groups, has been one of major importance in corporate finance, as we shall certainly see in later chapters. Recapitalizations for whatever purpose—bankruptcy, conversion, mergers, or leveraged buyouts—all can be made to benefit from value enhancement in this way. But for the enhancement to be effective, a securities market of substantial depth and diversity, from which additional sophisticated investors may be drawn, must first exist. In the 1890s such a market had emerged in the United States for the first time.

The trust movement also fathered what one particularly well-regarded observer, historian Alfred Chandler of the Harvard Business School, referred to as the era of "great corporations in American industry." Because of its subsequent contribution to large-scale organizational and modern management practices, he considered the trust movement to be "*the* major innovation in the American economy from 1880 to the turn of the century."[5] The large national corporations that would emerge in the early 1900s and serve as role models for others in the United States and Britain had the financial capacity to operate plants and marketing organizations all across the country, to invest large sums in research and development, and to engage in international business. They also had the capacity to handle war production for the United States and its allies in World War I and to exploit all of the many new technologies that rapidly came into commercial life during the early part of the new century.

The large national corporations were also, however, gradually becoming subject to increasing scrutiny and regulation by governmental authorities as a consequence of many perceived abuses attributed to "big business." Railroads had been subject to regulation by the Interstate Commerce Commission since its establishment in 1887, though no one considered the actual limitations on the freewheeling railroads significant. Price fixing and monopolistic behavior, already limited by the Sherman Anti-Trust Act, were further restricted in 1913 by the Clayton Anti-Trust Act and the Federal Trade Commission.

In early tests of the Sherman Act from 1897 through 1899 the Supreme Court came down hard on price fixing through cartels, though it allowed mergers between competing firms until 1904. Thus the court provided powerful incentives for those attempting to rationalize disorderly industry conditions or to increase their control of markets—to consolidate large segments of an industry under one holding-company roof—through mergers of competitors. Individual competitors had little choice in many cases; the cartel, as ineffective as many of these had been, was no longer an alternative to cutthroat pricing, but neither was fighting the giants in an ongoing price war.

Thus the great merger wave of 1898 through 1902, the largest in our history, was formed. This was a period in which approximately half of the manufacturing capacity of the country participated in either a consolidation (of a new industry giant) or a merger. A greater number of transactions, and more capitalized value of transactions per dollar of gross national product (GNP) took place during this intense five-year period than at any other time, including the extraordinary period of 1984 through 1988, when leveraged buyouts and extensive foreign activity were on hand to boost the numbers.[6]

Merger Mania in 1900

Ralph Nelson is the scholar most closely identified with the turn-of-the-century merger boom. (There have actually been four such booms, the others occurring in the 1920s, the 1960s, and the 1980s). During the period of peak activity, 1898 through 1902, Nelson identified more than twenty-six hundred transactions in the manufacturing sector, aggregating over $6.3 billion in value (1900 dollars). Nelson's work is firmly supported by statistics, which he uses to test the relationships between the merger activity and various economic developments in the United States that have been credited with causing it.

For example, he did not find evidence to support the notion that the wave was caused by defensive action resulting from the retardation of industrial growth following the depression early in the decade (on the contrary, the sectors doing the merging were growing). He did find the earlier growth of the national railroad system to have contributed to making national markets for products possible and therefore creating the need for national companies to serve them. He also found some motivation for increased market control, and buoyant capital markets in existence to absorb the new securities that the new mergers created. Nelson also pointed out that a very active period of merger activity occurred in the United Kingdom at the same time, though these events appeared to him hard to connect. His conclusions about what caused the turn-of-the-century merger boom, despite all of his work, seem somewhat tenuous.[7]

On the other hand, a distinguished turn-of-the-century British economist, John Hobson, an intellectual forerunner of Keynes, was more definitive in writing in 1906 that the merger booms in both the United States and Britain derived from similar economic changes, which made competitors out of companies that until recently had been strangers. Lowered transportation costs and greater access to markets and to raw materials, he said, changed the economics of competition. The United States saw much more merger activity because the advantages of these two benefits were far greater in America than in England and because powerful U.S. businessmen could get political support to protect a monopolistic position, once achieved, with high tariffs. Hobson also noted that the great days of unrestricted laissez-faire economic policies had come to an end in Britain by the last quarter of the 1800s (just after Bagehot's book was published), but they still had some time to go in the United States. Much impressed by American financial activity, he devotes almost all of a long chapter on the role of the financier in contemporary economics to American players and the rest to South Africans. Nowhere are any of Bagehot's unsleepy London crowd even mentioned.[8]

Alfred Chandler, however, rather likes the general idea that the time had finally come for important manufacturing industries to follow the railroads and the trusts and to develop their businesses on a national basis. To do so, a company, in effect, had to become large enough to be able to conduct business uniformly across a whole continent, something that had never been done before and could only be done through mergers. Chandler is a business historian with perhaps a preference for finding a "good management" reason for the mergers. Other academics, such as George Bittlingmayer, a prominent antitrust scholar, have suggested that the desire to escape Sherman Act enforcement for participation in cartels was an important factor. On the whole, however, it seems that those historians who have more forcefully suggested that the companies merging were mainly after monopoly power over large segments of U.S. industry— an early version of the unrestrained greed argument that one hears describing the 1980s merger activity—are the ones that have most succeeded in capturing the public's belief.

Clearly many factors were operating at the time, and we may never know in what proportion. We do know, however, that the merger boom really began in the early 1880s with the trusts, was carried into the 1890s by extensive mergers and reorganizations of railroads, then made its way into industrials, where it continued until 1904. In that year the Supreme Court ruled in favor of the government in the Northern Securities case, requiring the dissolution of a giant four-railroad holding company put together by Morgan and Harriman (as a compromise after Harriman's hostile takeover attempt in 1901 of the Morgan-controlled Northern Pacific Railroad failed). So although Nelson's statistics indicate a white-hot intensity to the boom at the turn of the century, the general move toward consolidation through mergers lasted about twenty years, a period sufficiently long to suggest that the effect of numerous powerful economic factors was felt.

To me, three such factors provide the most compelling explanation for the merger activity from 1880 to 1905. First, manufacturing industries were growing up helter-skelter all over the country as the Industrial Revolution passed over America. Business, mainly local, was yearning to become regional, perhaps national, but was highly disorganized, with many different small producers in each industry.

Second, capital had become plentiful in the United States for the first time. Though European investors were still highly important to American financial markets, American investors had become more important. Once organized, as they had been for the railroad reorganizations and the trust conversions, the markets were ready for and capable of more activity, provided that the bankers could impose some sort of order and discipline on the unrestrained savagery of the free marketplace. The bankers, when called in to rescue industrialists from such excesses or to discuss new financing with them, were able to influence them to consider more stable, and far more profitable, consolidations of companies into large, strong, safe, and sensible new corporations. The financial know-how needed to bring about these transactions was available, as was a new syndicate system for organizing underwriters to guarantee the outcome of their efforts by pledging their own money to support the new securities to be issued.

Third, the legal and regulatory infrastructure necessary to effect the required transformation of American industry was in place. A New Jersey corporation could hold securities of subsidiaries acquired by the merger of competitors that neither the Sherman Act nor any other regulatory body would bother as long as they avoided participating in cartels.

These factors, a perceived industry requirement for restructuring, the availability of adequate financing and skills, and the absence of regulatory constraints, generate a combination that appears in all of the merger booms of this century. These conditions had not come together before the late 1880s, and when they did perhaps there was a pent-up demand for the results they could produce. Thus some of the most remarkable transactions of the twentieth century occurred in its earliest years.

The All-Time Great Steel Deal

At the turn of the century the steel industry, buoyed by industrial growth throughout the country, had come into its own. The industry was dominated, however, by Carnegie Steel, an integrated, efficient producer that controlled prices. There were plenty of other producers, though, and these competed with each other quite fiercely. The industry had grown up in a haphazard way, was composed of numerous smallish producers, and lacked the vertical integration that it later developed. Surveying the scene in December 1900, J. P. Morgan listened to an impassioned talk on the need for consolidation in the industry by Charles Schwab, Andrew Carnegie's right-hand man. It occurred to Morgan that a new company might be formed of a dozen or so compatible steel companies, with Carnegie at the center, to accomplish just what Schwab was suggesting. He mentioned it to Schwab, organized an all-night meeting with other steel and financial men to work out details, and finally asked Schwab to mention it to Carnegie; this he did after a game of golf. Carnegie apparently had decided that it was time to retire from steel as one of the world's richest men and go into philanthropy. He agreed to sell on the spot and just as suddenly wrote down his price on a slip of paper, which Schwab later delivered to Morgan.

"I accept," said Morgan after a quick glance at the paper. There was no haggling or consultation with others. Morgan himself was doing the buying, unofficially, of course, on behalf of all of the other companies and their numerous investors and securities holders.

The deal he had accepted, just like that, was for a merger of

Carnegie's and nine other steel industry companies into a new New Jersey holding company called United States Steel. The value of the transaction, in 1901 dollars, was $1.4 billion (perhaps worth $20 billion in today's money, thus the largest merger ever until the RJR-Nabisco deal in 1989).

The Carnegie company itself, of which Andrew Carnegie owned 58.5 percent, was to receive new securities valued at $493 million, consisting of new bonds to replace extant bonds and new stock valued at 1.5 times the book value of the old stock. Carnegie himself, perhaps doubtful of the new venture's prospects, took all of his securities in the form of bonds.[9]

Morgan's role was very similar to that of Henry Kravis in the RJR-Nabisco leveraged buyout. He had to serve as the leader of the enterprise putting it all together. He had to value the constituent parts of the new corporation and provide the financial architecture for it. First, new bonds would be created; second, for those who wanted a higher yield with some asset backing, there was a 7 percent preferred stock. Finally, for those who believed in the future of the giant new corporation, soon to become the world's leading steel producer, there was common stock, with no asset backing at all: almost all of the assets had gone to prop up the other securities.

Morgan, as chief contractor, then had to see to the exchange of the new securities for those of the various companies coming in and to offer their holders not only assurance of a minimum market value for them but also some liquidity for those who preferred cash.

Morgan organized a vast underwriting syndicate, composed of about three hundred members in the United States, Great Britain, and the Netherlands. The syndicate would offer to purchase up to $200 million of the various new securities being exchanged at a minimum price and resell them to other investors. Thus a market would be available for those who wanted out, and a firm price level for the securities assured until they had been fully redistributed. Most of the underwriters in the deal were wealthy individuals and institutions, as was the practice then, though Morgan's firm and a few others joined the underwriting for amounts modestly in excess of a million dollars.[10]

The issue was a great success. Only $25 million of the $200 million of standby funds was called upon to purchase securities for which buyers in the market could not at the moment be found. Investors were captivated by the idea of the new company and its potential. The preferred stock, initially priced at $82¾, soon rose to $101⅞; the common stock from $38 per share to $55. The underwriters' commissions were paid in stock, which, when sold, netted the group about $60 million, of which Morgan's firm retained $12 million. Not bad for the days when a five-course meal at Delmonico's, where many of Wall Street's most luminous figures celebrated deals like this one, could be had for less than a dollar.[11]

The genius of the U.S. Steel deal lay in the conceptualization of a new company that would be worth, because of the economies of scale, integration, better management, and reduced competition, much more than the value of its parts. The parts themselves provided the asset backing for the senior securities; for the rest, you had to have faith—faith in the idea, the times, and the people in charge, both operating people and financiers. The same was true for RJR-Nabisco, except, in that case, the incremental value to be created (that is, the part you had to take on faith) would come from disassembling the enterprise, not from putting it together. Here the whole would be broken into parts, several of which would be sold off to others who could use them better and therefore would pay a higher price for them. Nabisco also employed somewhat more financial leverage to sweeten the possible upside return for its equity and subordinated debtholders.

Both the U.S. Steel and the RJR-Nabisco cases required a lot of careful design and precise valuation of the securities to be issued and the active trading markets to be made in them. In both cases the operatives involved were able to attract and retain the confidence of the market, and these people were very handsomely rewarded by being able to share in a small portion of the enhanced values that they had helped to create.

As in 1989, the 1901 deal attracted a great deal of public criticism from people not involved with the transaction. Numerous newspapers and magazines criticized it for being monopolistic. One in particular felt that the excessive concentrations of power in Wall Street (Wall Street, notice, not Pittsburgh) would ultimately lead the public to prefer socialism, or even "rioting in the streets," to the kind of capitalism that the Morgan transaction represented. Such combines as U.S. Steel would possess so much power, said one critic, the president of Yale University, that unless they were restrained in the public interest, "there would be an emperor in Washington within 25 years." A London paper called the U.S. Steel deal a "menace to commerce" and the "triumph of the millionaire."[12] Morgan and his colleagues and the government all appear to have ignored these complaints, however exaggerated, without comment.

Much of the same sort of negative exaggeration has been applied to the Nabisco deal, in which an important difference seems to be in the intensity of the criticism directed at the *losers* in the competition for control, Chairman Ross Johnson and his bankers, Shearson Lehman Hutton and Salomon Brothers.

Naturally both deals must answer to the judgment of subsequent results for the answer to just how good or bad they were for the economy or for the country. Most people, I would guess, think that U.S. Steel (now called USX Corp.) has made a useful contribution to American economic life over the past eighty-nine years and would be as horrified today if someone tried to take it apart as their ancestors were when it was put together. (Actually, Carl Icahn recently tried to do just that to USX, and met plenty of resistance.) RJR–Nabisco (formerly R. J. Reynolds Tobacco Co.), on the other hand, had only recently completed acquisitions of Nabisco and Standard Brands Corp., for which high prices had been paid and the strategic fits were somewhat dubious. Nevertheless, those who wanted to dismantle the company, which had just been put together, seemed to attract considerable public criticism for "breaking up a great American company."

As for the ultimate effects of the Nabisco deal on employees, management, banks, and the new investors in the various kinds of high-yield securities designed to extract the maximum enhancement in value for the original shareholders (following the Sugar Trust example), we'll just have to wait and see.

An LBO That Sprang a Leak

Even before the ink was dry on the formation of U.S. Steel, Morgan had begun work on what came to be one of his next largest deals, the formation through a series of leveraged acquisitions of the International Mercantile Marine Company, later renamed US Lines.[13]

This deal, capitalized at $170 million, resulted from the combination of several large competing U.S. and British transatlantic shipping lines into a single company in early 1903. The transaction was conceived in the high fever of the times and involved what were then alleged in the press to be greedy sellers, overly ambitious buyers who pushed the deal through no matter what, overpayment for the properties acquired, excessive amounts of leverage, large fees, and, in the end, an unsuccessful result.

In 1900, a fast-rising, thirty-eight-year-old British accountant and entrepreneur named John Ellerman who had taken control of a distinguished British shipping company, the Leyland Line, arranged to buy a U.S. shipper based in Baltimore for about $9 million. The deal came to the attention of a Philadelphia rival of the American company, Clement Griscom, who had grand ideas about the growth of transatlantic shipping in general, and U.S.-flag shipping in particular. Even then, U.S.-built ships cost 30 percent more than those built in Northern Ireland and other such places, and U.S. carriers were not all that competitive. However, Griscom believed that after the experience of the Spanish American War, which had just ended, and the evidence of the burdens of having shipping diverted from American ports to aid the British effort in the Boer War, which had just begun, Congress would be willing to grant subsidies to U.S. carriers to build up the American merchant marine. Griscom reportedly was able to break up the sale to Ellerman. In the process he offered to buy the Baltimore company.

At this point, needing money, Griscom was sent to Morgan, whose people studied the matter and ultimately suggested a bigger and prospectively more profitable deal. They urged that a large British shipping firm, the White Star Line, whose founder had just died, be included in the deal. (The White Star Line, a major operator of transatlantic passenger ships frequented by Morgan and his partners, was the ill-fated builder of the *Titanic*, which sank on its maiden voyage in 1912.) Valuations were worked on and negotiated, and apparently the Europeans considered these so very favorable to the sellers that German, Dutch, and Canadian lines tried to be included in the negotiations also, though in the end a cartel-like arrangement was worked out with these others instead. In addition to the ships being acquired, several new ships would be built and added to the combined fleet.

It took a couple of years to work all of this out, but finally, a new company, International Mercantile Marine, was formed. The company was to issue $50 million of bonds, $60 million of $100 par value preferred stock, and $60 million par value of common stock (of which $10 million would be retained in the treasury). These nominal amounts totaled $170 million, certainly worth $2 or $3 billion in today's money. For this amount of capital, approximately $110 million or so was represented by the depreciated book value of the real assets of the combined companies. However, the bankers did not expect the preferred or the common stocks to sell in the market at their par values, as each was to be discounted substantially—the expected market value of the new package was fairly close to the $110 million book value being acquired, so on that basis the organizers did not overpay, though one suspects that the press reported the situation otherwise.

The combined companies had earned an average of about $7.2 million before interest and depreciation in each of the preceding five years. In those days before income taxes, this amount was the equivalent of the company's cash flow before depreciation (in today's LBO language: earnings before interest, taxes, and depreciation [EBITD]). Total interest to be paid was $3 million, preferred stock dividends another $3 million. Fixed charges of $6 million thus were covered 1.2 times by gross cash flow, a level not too different from those found in leveraged acquisitions today. No earnings contribution was added for the new ships being built, as the bankers were being conservative and no one knew what they would earn. Not much, if anything, was left over for dividends on the common stock, whose value was almost entirely dependent on future earnings growth.

The expected market value of the bonds and preferred stock to be issued was about $95 million, the common only $17.5 million. As the combining companies had $13 million of existing debt outstanding, the combined capitalization of $125.5 million was 50 percent represented by bonds (senior securities), 36 percent represented by preferred stock (junior to the bonds), and only 14 percent represented by common stock. These ratios are very similar to those of today's large leveraged buyouts.

The deal was dependent on Morgan's underwriting the new securities to be issued, so their values would hold up in the market, and those who wished to sell could do so. Fresh from the successful underwriting of the U.S. Steel syndicate, the Morgan name was nearly magical after fifty years of princely business on Wall Street, so the arrangement of the syndicate was easily accomplished. Thirty percent was handled in London by Morgan's British affiliate, his father's firm J. S. Morgan (later to become Morgan Grenfell). In New York the syndicate was made up of insurance companies, corporations, and very wealthy individuals. It would stay intact until all of the securities bought in for redistribution were sold or until otherwise dissolved by Morgan, whichever occurred first. Underwriters were to receive shares of preferred and common stocks with a market value of 15 percent of the underwritten amounts in lieu of a commission. If all of the shares could be sold quickly (say, over two months), then the "return" to the underwriters on an annualized basis would be extremely lucrative (for example, 300 percent in the case of a two-month syndicate). Morgan's bank received additional shares with a nominal value of $5.5 million (3.2 percent of the capitalization) as a fee for its organizational and financial advisory work over nearly two years. Henry Kravis would not have been uncomfortable with the terms of this deal. It looked like another triumph, another success like U.S. Steel, in which everyone came out a winner.

But it wasn't.

Because of the many legal complexities involved, the new company couldn't be organized until October 1902, by which time conditions in the shipping industry had deteriorated sharply as a result of the surplus tonnage that had come back on the market after the conclusion of the Spanish American and Boer wars, and some rate cutting by those outside the new IMM cartel. Perhaps the most important factors affecting the industry, however, were the growing interruption of world trade caused by increasing protectionism and the increasing politicization of national shipping laws. Scheduled vessels often had to leave half empty because certain cargoes they had carried before now had to be shipped in a vessel belonging to the country of export. Trade flows along regularly scheduled routes were substantially interrupted, though cut-rate, unscheduled tramp steamers did better and ate into the regular trade of the scheduled carriers.

Public opinion also had turned against the transaction. Having British-built, British-flag ships come under American ownership was disagreeable to the British; the American side was no better because its public didn't want U.S. goods carried in British bottoms, no matter who owned them. Worse, the long-expected U.S. government subsidy to aid in building up the American merchant fleet failed to pass Congress. And, finally, the financial characteristics of the deal were strongly criticized too: some observers suggested that the deal was only being done to accommodate Morgan with yet another large fee.

Morgan toughed it out, however, and despite reservations went ahead with the deal, which was completed at the end of 1902. However, the securities couldn't be sold and were hung up. The syndicate had to be held together for *nearly four years*, an unheard-of period according to today's practices and one that must have been a record even then. All of the underwriters lost money, how much depending on when they sold out. Those who held out for a better market in 1906 were probably wiped out in the panic of 1907, which flattened prices everywhere.

It appears, in retrospect, that the International Mercantile Marine deal may have been the first large leveraged acquisition. In terms of its financial structure it is closely comparable to the deals of the late 1980s, in which of course market exposures were much shorter because things can happen much more quickly. Like many transactions today, International Mercantile Marine was the target of much public opposition, as indeed was U.S. Steel. Wall Street's role in promoting it was probably exaggerated: Griscom had gone to

Morgan for help and advice that he accepted gratefully; neither he nor any of the other principals ever blamed Morgan for the failure.

The deal, perhaps well conceived economically in 1901, was nevertheless unsuccessful because of the simple fact that deteriorating industry conditions a year or so later, caused by trade and shipping disputes among governments, were not foreseen. Perhaps they should have been but weren't; perhaps they were foreseen but not believed or considered to have such a potentially severe effect. Perhaps the deal had developed its own momentum, as often happens, and its sponsors chose not to hear the bad news. One will never know. In any case, the highly leveraged financial structure put together in a bull market did not fare well when the market turned harsh. The problem was not that the company fell apart because of poor management; it did not. In fact, one could argue that it did well in the conditions under which it had to operate.

The problem was that the changing conditions in the shipping industry affected the value of the securities that the principals had put together. These securities were based on certain expectations about the near-term future in the transatlantic shipping market, which were rapidly proving false. Payment of all fixed charges related to the bonds and the preferred stock on time became less sure, more risky. The payoff from investing in the common stock was pushed further out into the future, where it was worth less. Investors would not pay the same price to purchase the securities; indeed they offered to buy them only at a large discount. Hence the principals, the initial investors, and the bankers all lost money.

These things, however—all of them—go with the territory. All deals have risk in them, and the risks, even when provided for adequately at the outset of a deal, can increase as conditions deteriorate. Either changing conditions in the industry in question, as in the International Mercantile case, or changes in financial markets alone can cause the value of the securities involved in the transaction to alter, up or down. Financial structures involving less leverage have more "downside" protection against adversity, but that may only mean that the drop in the price of unleveraged securities will be less than the drop in leveraged ones if conditions deteriorate. On the

other hand, investors care about the "upside" potential of a transaction, too, and here, unquestionably, leveraged securities do better.

True, International Mercantile was a flop, perhaps a flop that
could have been avoided. Several lessons were learned, however.
The financing scheme worked for the company doing the deal; the
money was raised; the syndicate system functioned even for a large
transaction without the luster of U.S. Steel, one that depended much
more heavily on borrowings to make it work.

At the same time, participants also learned that even when things
go hopelessly wrong, all is not necessarily lost. The company was
restructured and survived. The bankers had fees with which to offset
their losses, which they managed to keep to a minimum anyway
through syndication. The investors lost most of what they had put
up, but leveraged investments are risky, and if you spread your
investments around, losses tend to be offset by gains elsewhere. In
any case, all parties to the deal lived to invest another day. These
lessons encouraged bankers not to abandon leveraged deals in the
future but to continue to undertake them, carefully, of course, in
order to learn how to manage the risks better.

Morgan's Legacies

Morgan's most active banking period was from 1895 to 1907, a
twelve-year period in a career of nearly sixty years, during which his
most monumental achievements took place. His knowledge of gold,
foreign-exchange markets, and foreign investors helped the U.S.
government stop a run on its gold reserves in 1895. While handling
the U.S. Steel consolidation and the International Mercantile deal,
he also had to fight Harriman for control of the Northern Pacific
Railroad, in which he was ultimately successful because he bought
up more stock at ever-rising prices than Harriman. In this transaction,
the two bidders bought more stock than existed, and the price had
run up so much that short-sellers had come in, not expecting the two
bankers to corner the market in the stock. This forced them to buy

back shares from Harriman and Morgan (to be delivered to their customers, Harriman and Morgan) at sky-high prices. A nervy, if unplanned, transaction, at the very least.

Morgan also led, almost single-handedly, the effort to halt the banking panic of 1907 that nearly resulted in the collapse of many large banks. He gathered the presidents of the strongest banks in New York in his magnificent library, locked the door, and kept them there until they agreed to advance large sums to the distressed banks. Morgan, in that role, was acting as if he were the Federal Reserve, which did not at the time exist. Only he had the prestige, the influence, and the presence to pull it off.[14]

But this man lived in an entirely different era, one whose end was prolonged only until Morgan's own death in 1913, the year in which income taxes were first collected. What legacies of his still exist today?

It is true that Morgan lived in a time when there was virtually no regulation in the field of business and finance, a period of nearly complete laissez faire. Everything was, in effect, self-regulated. If you cheated, stole, or behaved badly in any number of ways and were seen to be doing so, your peers could cut you off and you would be out of business. This happened occasionally, but more often, sharp behavior was considered smart behavior, ruthlessness was rewarded, conflicts of interest were everywhere, and integrity was hard to find. Nonetheless, the leaders of the Wall Street community, exemplified by Morgan, tried to set a standard of behavior that all could follow. It wasn't perfect, but it was a lot better than nothing.

Morgan also set the standards for professional behavior. He hired smart, hardworking people on whom he relied heavily. He probably invented, as judged by the frequency of his use of them, the all-night working session in which all the experts would hammer out a solution against the clock. Morgan was also just as quick to say "too much" as he was "I accept"; if he couldn't negotiate what he knew to be a reasonable price, he would walk away. To be so sure of oneself, one has to be confident that one's preparations have been all they could have been.

And, perhaps, most remarkably for a man who came across as

having the flair, style, and flash of a bowling ball, he was willing to look at pretty much anything if he thought a deal could be made that would fly. He was not afraid of a deal because it was too large, or too complex, or too highly leveraged. He would see whether he could make workable deals out of what he had. If so, he would support it; if not, he would drop it.

Morgan was a great believer in leverage, in maximizing the chances for success by borrowing talent, intelligence, ideas, skills, and, of course, money. He and his partners contributed a lot to the deals they worked on and expected large fees that the added value they had supplied could easily support. Morgan's standards of integrity, professionalism, and imagination, as well as his staying power, are all qualities that are highly valued and still much sought after today—our legacies from the Great Morgan.

2

ROARING TWENTIES

Morgan's was a time of westward expansion, railroads, and iron and steel. It was also a time of mass immigration, low wages, growing American cockiness, corruption, and enormous wealth accumulated by a small number of great tycoons such as Carnegie, Rockefeller, and Vanderbilt. Most of the tycoons, however, had begun life penniless themselves, and their successes were an inspiration to millions of others who, whatever the odds, wanted the same chance. A bestselling author of these times was Horatio Alger, who died in 1899 having sold more than 20 million copies of paperback novels to young men and boys who wanted to be reassured that pluck, hard work, and virtuous living were the paths to riches and fame.

Society was anything but fixed then, what with so many opportunities to rise to heady (if not unbelievable) heights. New Men of the sort that Bagehot had in mind were everywhere. There were virtually no rules or limits to what could be done in this paradise of laissez faire for those who were sufficiently determined, except perhaps for limitations on the availability of capital with which to purchase one's stake in the game.

During most of the nineteenth century, capital was scarce in

America and much of it had to be imported from London, Paris, Frankfurt, and other financial centers of Europe. Toward the end of the century, however, the balance had shifted, and capital formation in America had become sufficient to finance local requirements with substantial left over to export back to Europe, not only in the form of debt service but even in new investments in securities of European governments and municipalities. American loans had helped to finance the British efforts in the Boer War and became indispensable to the British and the French and the other Allied powers during World War I.

The new century, the one to follow the age of Morgan, would differ greatly from its predecessor. The relatively slow pace of nineteenth-century business and finance accelerated greatly as each amazing new event or discovery was succeeded by yet another. New technologies that would create new industries and countless new career opportunities were developed. Electric light and power had just become such an industry in the late 1890s. Spindletop, the greatest of the Texas oil wells, came in in 1901; the Wright brothers took off in 1903; in the same year, the first motion picture telling a complete story, *The Great Train Robbery*, was released; life insurance had become a big business by 1905; transatlantic radio communications were established for the first time in 1906; the first hotel with private bathrooms was built in 1907; the Model T Ford car was introduced in 1908; in 1909, Bakelite, a synthetic resin whose manufacture led to the development of plastics, was first produced commercially. These developments and many like them would totally change the face of the twentieth century from that of the nineteenth. It was to be the American century, and everybody knew it.

There were more than a few problems with American life in the early 1900s, however. There was considerable poverty, particularly in the immigrant communities, among whom were numerous fire-eyed radicals whose tongues and pens had been sharpened in the slums of Europe. There was an enormous disparity between the earnings of a worker and the income of a capitalist; efforts to bring these two closer together through collective bargaining were not always successful and indeed were often bloody. Government had no structure for dealing with these complex social issues and really had no wish to become involved in matters involving private property, so not much was done to address them.

The newspapers and magazines of the times (that was all there was of the media), however, began an earnest search early in the century for the American social conscience. They started with the trusts, to which popular opinion had long been unfavorable, believing that monopoly powers surely exploited consumers. Joseph Pulitzer, publisher of the New York *World*, became an ardent foe of the trusts. Frank Norris, a well-known novelist, began a series of books on big business in 1901 with *The Octopus*, a savage attack on the railroads. Ida Tarbell's uncomplimentary history of Standard Oil Company began serialization in 1902, the same year in which a sharp attack on municipal corruption by Lincoln Steffens appeared. In 1903 the "muckrakers," America's first investigative reporters, appeared, hoping to discover the truth about what was "really going on" in business. In 1906 Upton Sinclair published *The Jungle*, a scathing exposé of conditions in the meat-packing industry.

These efforts at American consciousness raising were not without some success in bringing about reforms. Congress passed the Hepburn Act in 1903, empowering the Interstate Commerce Commission to regulate rates charged by railroads. The Supreme Court forced the dissolution of the Northern Securities Co. as being in violation of the Sherman Act in 1904. The Pure Food and Drug Act was passed in 1906. The government, contrary to its traditional wishes, was being drawn into the relationship between business and the people by the force of public opinion. As in Britain during the later 1880s and 1890s, industrialization had released powerful forces that insisted on the curtailing of the laissez-faire economic policies that had guided the Republic since its birth. The tide had, indeed, turned.

And the new tide now rushing in brought with it the antibusiness rhetoric of Theodore Roosevelt; the presidential victory of 1912 by Woodrow Wilson, a known reformer; Congressman Pujo's investigation into the Wall Street "money trust" in 1912 and 1913; the establishment of the Labor Department in 1913; and the passage of the Clayton Anti-Trust Act and the creation of the Federal Trade Commission in 1914. Morgan, who died in 1913, was probably just as glad to depart such a scene, which no doubt was shocking and repulsive to him.[1]

The regulatory net-tightening continued a while longer, until the country's attention was distracted by World War I and its aftermath. However, caught up in the chain of all these events in the early part of the century were the forced dissolution by the government in 1911 of the Standard Oil Company and the American Tobacco Company, two of the largest and most dominant of the original trusts.

De-merging the Trusts

The Supreme Court upheld a lower court decision in a case brought by the government that these companies were in violation of the Sherman Act and, accordingly, would have to be broken up. In the case of Standard Oil, the market value of which was about $700 million at the time (certainly worth $3.5 to $4 billion today), distribution would have to be made to shareholders of all of the shares of thirty-three different subsidiary companies. Each shareholder of the original company, Standard Oil of New Jersey (now Exxon), would receive pro rata shares of each of the subsidiaries, which would thus become independent companies. Among the former subsidiaries thus distributed were Continental Oil Company, the Standard Oil companies of California (Socal), Indiana (Amoco), Ohio (Sohio, now BP America), and New York (Socony, which later combined with the Vacuum Oil Co., also distributed by Standard Oil, to form Mobil Oil Co.).

This was the first breakup of a corporation against the will of its principal shareholders and management. It has been instructive to us in a number of ways. First, the vast size of the enterprise seems, by today's standards, overwhelming: all of those giant companies under one roof. Its market power at the time was not only enormous—in terms of price setting, but also in terms of the threat it posed for competitors—but also corrupting.

Looking at its constituent parts draws one to wonder whether the inherent economies of scale and scope were such that the whole business ran more efficiently than the sum of the individual parts, or whether it didn't. What we know about great size today would make us skeptical that it would, unless of course the whole thing depended on the ability of the company to fix oil prices for virtually the entire industry. Such power might not have bothered anyone twenty-five years earlier, but in the new American century it did.

Standard Oil without ability to fix prices was in effect, as far as an investor was concerned, a "closed-end" mutual fund for oil industry investments.

A closed-end fund is an investment company that issues its own shares to raise funds to invest in stocks or bonds according to a specified program. An investor buys these shares, hoping the program itself, such as investing exclusively in Japanese stocks, or real estate investments, or oil industry stocks, will be a success. If the investor changes his mind and wants to sell, he has to sell the shares in the mutual fund he bought on the market, not back to the fund managers for them to redeem. Open-end funds are the redeeming type: if you want your money back, the fund manager sells some of the fund's usually very liquid assets to repay you. Open-end funds tend to trade at the market price of the combined assets.

Closed-end funds usually trade at a discount to the market prices of the combined assets held by the fund (unless these are securities that are in great demand but not otherwise available to investors), because of fees and expenses charged by the fund manager and because the investor may not really want all the securities in the fund, only some of them, but nevertheless has to take the package. Also, the funds trade at discounts because their shares may have quite limited market liquidity as compared to the securities held by the funds.

On May 14, 1911, the day before the Supreme Court ruling, the stock price of Standard Oil was $674 per share; on December 7,

1911, a week before the actual distribution, the stock price was about the same. On December 18, a week after the distribution, the price of Standard Oil was about $350 per share. The value of the pro rata distribution of the shares in the thirty-three companies as of December 11, 1911, was quoted as being about $320 per share.[2] Thus there was no real difference: the value of the package was about equal to the price of the undivided shares. There had been some arbitrage possibilities for the quick movers: the stock could have been bought for less than $674 before the Supreme Court decision, and the nearly 10 percent spread between the bid and the asked prices for the shares in the subsidiaries was large enough for a skillful trader to have sold the pieces for more than he paid for the whole. But still, the market was apparently valuing the individual holdings at about the same price as the shares in the holding company.

But the market had no way, at this stage in the proceedings, to evaluate the thirty-three companies being distributed, or the surviving parent. There had been very little disclosure by Standard Oil of financial and operating information about the companies, so it would take some time before the market was able to judge them on their own. In the long run, however, it seems most likely that the appreciation in the shares of the thirty-three distributed companies would substantially have exceeded the appreciation in the parent, Standard Oil of New Jersey.

Partly this would be expected because of the apparent undervaluation by the initial market-makers of the subsidiaries, relative to their book value. After the breakup, the shares of Standard Oil of New Jersey, the largest and most visible company in the group, were quoted at a 22 percent premium to its book value of $286 million, while the other companies, as a group, were trading at a 15 percent discount to their aggregate book value.[3] Perhaps the market believed that if the whole was worth $674 per share, then, logically, the sum of the parts must be $674. But if so, it was not attributing those industrywide qualities that enabled them to trade Standard Oil of New Jersey at a premium to the other, less well known companies. As they got to know these companies better, the market would revalue them.

The initial valuation of the market was also likely to have been distorted by the fact that all the subsidiary companies, whatever their individual investment merits, were buried under the parent and therefore could not be seen in their own light. As in the case of the breakup of the Sugar Trust, an auction market environment will bring out the highest payers for each separate security, who are likely to be different investors from those who prefer the combined package.

Thus the work of a variety of separate investors will bid the prices of the pieces to exceed the price of the combination, as long as there are no significant monopoly or other economy-of-scale factors at play. In the case of Standard Oil, the maximum nonmonopoly economies of scale had long since been achieved, and most of the companies being sold off were big enough in their own right to offer economies of scale and liquidity in the trading market for their stocks.

The point is that the value of the undistributed Standard Oil stock (in an environment not willing to permit monopolies) was probably worth less to its shareholders than the sum of the market value of its parts. The market, when it got to know all the constituent holdings better, would prove to have been treating Standard Oil as if it were a closed-end fund.

In this case, the courts, reflecting the public interest, decided the outcome. Such monopolistic power was against the laws of the country and would have to be disbanded. But at the same time the breakup revealed that there was more value in the shares of the broken-up company than in the combined company: maybe not to management or major shareholders, who enjoyed certain powers and advantages from their positions, but to ordinary shareholders, who probably were better off after the various pieces of Standard Oil had been distributed to them. No one asked them in this case which outcome they would prefer, but later in the great American century they would be asked.

With the oil industry and the tobacco industry refragmented, and watchdogs posted in Washington looking for further antitrust and

other abuses, the steady progress of Big Business took something of
a step backward, until the automobile industry, the next giant,
emerged on the scene. After an incredibly short adolescence of ten
or fifteen years, this industry had emerged fully grown and enormously powerful by the twenties. Its early days were colorful, and
its early financial history equally so.

Turn-of-the-Century Junk

Alfred Sloan retired from General Motors in 1961, after a forty-five-
year career with the company, during all of which he had been a
member of the board of directors and for twenty-three years its chief
executive. In 1964, at the age of eighty-nine he published an autobiography that has been a classic in the literature of management
organization ever since. In the book Sloan tells the story of the early
days of the company, which was founded in 1908 by William C.
Durant.[4]

Durant was one of those wonderful legendary figures from our
entrepreneurial past, totally self-made, in and out of several different
businesses during his career, both rich and broke several times over.
Durant was an opportunist, a man who had a great vision of the
automobile industry and bet the farm on it.

Nineteen eight was the year Henry Ford introduced the Model
T, the first comparatively low-price automobile that could be used
as a working vehicle and a farm machine. Other cars at the time, by
contrast, were expensive toys sold to rich people. Durant, who was
the country's largest wagon and coach builder, had bought control
of Buick Motor Company in 1904 and by 1908 was the leading motorcar producer in the United States. He had made eighty-five
hundred Buicks that year, versus sixty-two hundred Fords, but he
knew the Model T would revolutionize the industry.

Whereas Ford's approach was to do everything himself, Durant
conceived of the idea of building a large company rapidly through
mergers and acquisitions. Other companies had become giants in
their industries as a result of the great merger boom at the turn of

the century and, Durant thought, the automobile industry was now ready to be consolidated. Accordingly, Durant talked several motorcar companies into joining forces and in 1908 formed General Motors Company, into which over the next two years Buick, Olds Motors (the predecessor of Oldsmobile), Cadillac, and more than twenty other diverse automobile industry companies were merged. The combined businesses earned approximately $1.7 million (before taxes, of which there were still none in those days) on sales of $7.5 million.

Durant's vision had genius, according to Sloan. It had three parts: (1) to produce a variety of cars for a variety of tastes, (2) to diversify across all the rapidly emerging automotive technologies so as always to be on top of the winners and underexposed to the losers, and (3) to increase integration by manufacturing all of the parts and accessories that make up the "anatomy of the automobile." Sloan believed that Durant was inappropriately portrayed as "merely a stock-market plunger." Instead, Sloan believed he possessed considerable sophistication on economic matters, though "I cannot say that he was precise in the application of his economic philosophy." He also possessed "a great weakness—he could create but not administer."

In any event, a more modern observation of Mr. Durant at the time might be that he was simply buying up everything in sight, in the hope that some of what he was buying would work out big, but in the meantime he was diluting the pants off his own position in GM by issuing so much stock (he might have used cash, borrowed of course, but these companies didn't earn enough at the time to pay much in the way of debt service) and doing nothing to pull all these companies together administratively so as to enjoy the savings that would result from reductions in overhead and manning levels. He was too busy acquiring even more companies to bother with such matters when the bottom fell out in 1910, only two years after he had formed the company.

Sloan tells us the rest:

> An investment banking group . . . came in to refinance General Motors and in this connection took over its operation

through a voting trust. A loan was obtained on stiff terms,
through a $15 million five-year [first mortgage] note issue, from
which the proceeds to General Motors were $12.75 million.
The note issue carried a "bonus" to the lenders in the form
of common stock which would eventually be vastly more valuable than the notes. Mr. Durant, a large shareholder in General Motors, was still a vice president and a member of the
board of directors, but he was forced to step aside in matters
of management.

Moody's Industrial Manual of 1914 reveals that the coupon on
this restructuring issue was 6 percent. The notes were issued at a 15
percent discount from par (that is, the company only got $12.75
million in exchange for an obligation of $15 million), which means
the cost of funds to General Motors, all in, was 9.87 percent per
annum, not 6 percent.

In 1910, the U.S. Treasury was not issuing bonds in the market,
so for a comparable benchmark one had to turn to an index of yields
on railroad bonds. In 1910 this index ranged from a high of 3.87
percent to a low of 3.73 percent. These were not days of volatile
bond markets and bond yields didn't change much during the year.
Railroad bonds, usually secured, were considered top grade, and
when U.S. Treasuries made their first market appearance in 1919,
their yield was very close to the railroad yield. In any case, the
General Motors notes were offered at an interest rate *more than 6
percentage points higher than those of comparable railroads.* Plus,
the notes had some kind of valuable bonus shares attached (like
warrants), were secured, and were further protected by a voting trust
that put control of the company in the hands of the bankers.

Sloan goes on to report that the bankers ran the company "efficiently though conservatively"; they liquidated unprofitable businesses, promoted exports, and in general tightened things up,
conserving cash for the rapid pay-down of the notes. General Motors
increased its sales of cars from about 40,000 units in 1910 to 100,000
in 1915 but lost in relative market share, from 20 percent to 10
percent, to Ford, whose Model T had taken off like a rocket. Even-

tually, the voting trust was abolished when the notes were paid off and GM had returned to health. Durant, who had founded Chevrolet Motors in the meantime (apparently without concerning himself too much with the conflict of interest), merged it into General Motors in 1916 for stock, and regained control, only to lose it again in 1920, when his shares had to be sold to cover margin loans in connection with unrelated stock-market speculations.

One of today's critics of the high-yield bond market, observing the 1910 refinancing, might have commented, "This looks like the first ever 'junk bond,' and the bankers who put the gun to the company's head made off like the bandits they were then, and still are today.

"After all," he might continue, "a 6 percent spread over a Treasury-equivalent rate is an even higher spread than what it takes to sell really low-grade bonds today without a mortgage or a voting trust. On a percentage basis, the spread-over-Treasuries is even higher yet, that is, 6 percent over a 3.8 percent yield, as compared to, say, a 5 percent spread today over an 8.5 percent base for today's junk bonds. And in the GM deal, the investor got an 'equity-kicker' (the stock bonus) to boot.

"On the other hand, one has to admit that the company was in pretty bad shape after Durant's merger binge: although GM's 1910 balance sheet showed about $69 million of total assets, $7.7 million of these represented 'goodwill' assumed from the acquisitions, and $12.5 million of inventories and other unsalable assets would be written off by the bankers the next year. Meanwhile, the company was running out of cash. After the note issue, debt and preferred stock (which paid a fixed 8 percent dividend and was more similar to subordinated debt than to stock in those days when interest was not deductible) would represent about two-thirds of the company's total capitalization, common stock only about one-third.

"Still, considering the industry General Motors was in, its increasing production rate, its outlook for the future, and so forth, the terms of the notes, at least by our standards in 1990, seem a bit harsh, even for junk."

Maybe, but General Motors, or Durant in particular, didn't have

much choice. Capital for risky ventures like his was still comparatively scarce in 1910 and generally had to be obtained from the same
bankers who raised the loans that were then being threatened. Most
of these loans came from wealthy individuals, banks, and foreign
investors. When things went wrong, the bankers came in to protect
the investments of their investor clients, just as Morgan had in the
case of the railroad reorganizations. The entrepreneur in trouble had
little to say about it; if he fought too hard, the bankers would get
the courts to throw him out altogether, and he might lose his own
investment in the process of a liquidation. Bankers did not think it
prudent or proper to meddle in other bankers' problems, so it was
hard to shop around for the best deal when trying to get yourself
rescued. Durant had to go along. In this case the bankers appear to
have acted wisely, on a basis that proved to be beneficial for all.
They took charge right away, issued the junk bond (probably to
many of the existing, original investors), sold off assets, cut costs as
much as possible, and then ran the company for cash. The company
recovered very quickly, the notes were paid off early, and investors
made their real money on the bonus shares. Sloan says these were
eventually worth much more than $15 million, though we do not
know when they were sold. We do know that E. I. du Pont de
Nemours & Company purchased a 23.8 percent interest in General
Motors in 1917 for $25 million after the firm had fully recovered
from Mr. Durant's enthusiasm, so we have to assume that there were
quite a few bonus shares.

Many of these shares no doubt were retained by the bankers,
who typically, by underwriting their clients' issues, were required to
hold on to them for many months until ultimate customers could be
found. Therefore in effect they made "bridge loans" to the issuers.
The bankers would take a commission of 2 or 3 percent for underwriting issues of these types, charge some ongoing annual agency
fees, and keep a portion of the bonus shares. On the whole, the
bankers usually made quite a substantial return on their effort, but
no one seemed to question whether they earned it. Mr. Sloan didn't.

"Just about like the way they did things in the 1980s," says our
observer, "except that our investment bankers actually seemed to

be working for a bit less on high-yield transactions, even when you take the stock-purchase warrants that they often kept for themselves into account. However, our people spent their time trying to arrange the acquisitions that their clients made, and much of the financing for them involved the highly profitable issuance of junk bonds."

In the GM case, the company issued stock (not junk bonds) for its acquisitions in order to be conservative, or maybe just to avoid the bankers. But when the company got into trouble because of mismanagement, the junk bonds had to be issued. Maybe this just means that when ambitious companies with great (and not so great) visions of the future want to grow fast through acquisitions, they find that they can't get along without some kind of high-yield financing. This certainly was true for much of the 1980s, and it appears that it's been true before. But, says our observer, "I never would have thought General Motors."

Durant had been the only automobile man among his original partners in General Motors; the rest were simply investors. Bankers of course were sort of second-tier partners, who became first tier if things went wrong. Financial partners could be a problem, though. Because of them, however, one could leverage himself into controlling a very promising enterprise, maybe using the banks to leverage it a bit more. For this, certainly one was grateful, but gratitude to one's partners wore off fast as time passed and the amount of money they originally contributed lost its significance. This was especially so if the partners started to make their own demands on either the company or its principal entrepreneur.

Henry Ford's Leveraged Buyout

Henry Ford founded the Ford Motor Company in 1903 in partnership with a Detroit coal merchant called Alex Malcomson, who with Ford shared a 51 percent interest, and a dozen or so others, mostly colleagues of Malcomson. At the time, the company only assembled cars from parts made by independent contractors. Among these were John and Horace Dodge (the Dodge brothers), two Detroit machinists who capitalized seven thousand dollars of materials and added three thousand dollars of cash to purchase 100 shares between them for a 10 percent interest. The company's Model A, after a nervous start, did very well, and all of the stockholders got their initial investments back in dividends after only one year.

By 1905 the company had more orders than it could fill. Ford and Malcomson then had a falling out over marketing and pricing policies. Malcomson wanted to make high-grade, expensive, fashionable cars for the well-to-do, as all the other car manufacturers were then doing. Ford disagreed. His contribution to the automobile industry, probably more than anything else, was the extraordinary vision of a mass market for inexpensive cars that anyone could buy. The company would constantly expand its production, and in so doing, it would be able to lower the price of the vehicle further. Each of the partners was adamant. A showdown was inevitable.

Before it came, however, Ford announced that he would form a totally new company, Ford Manufacturing Co., that would produce the cars that Ford Motor Co. would sell. The new company would have a different shareholding from the old one, and Malcomson would be excluded. The expected growth of Ford Manufacturing (where the large capital expenditures had to be made) would, of course, limit the amount of dividends that Ford Motor could pay out, because funds would be reduced either by the loans from Motor to Manufacturing or by the pricing practices used to sell cars from Manufacturing to Motor. The directors, however, were told by Ford that, as soon as the matter with Malcomson was straightened out, the two companies would be combined. Malcomson soon recognized that he had been outmaneuvered, and, after a bit of outraged protest, he and several of his colleagues sold their stock to Ford, leaving him with a 58.5 percent and controlling interest in the company.[5]

In 1908 the Model T was introduced, to great acclaim. The Dodge brothers grew concerned that they were overexposed to Ford's business, he being their only customer, and decided to go into the car business for themselves in 1913. Dividends from their Ford stock, which totaled $1.4 million in 1914, financed the new venture, which was to make low-price cars to compete with Ford's. In 1914 Ford manufactured 248,000 cars and captured 42 percent of the U.S. market. In 1916 it made 524,000 cars and earned $58 million, though its market share had declined to 32 percent. During the year Ford turned down a proposal for recapitalizing the company at $500 million.

By 1916 Ford had begun to publicize a number of his strange ideas and was coming to be seen as something of an eccentric. Among his odd business notions—or so they were considered at the time— were a tractor manufacturing company that would be run rather like a commune and a giant new production complex that would permit total integration of all of Ford's manufacturing operations. Ford wanted to own and control the entire manufacturing process from raw materials to finished product, all to be housed in a new manufacturing facility located on the River Rouge outside Detroit. Ford told his shareholders that he wanted to stop paying special dividends on the stock, reverting to a nominal dividend only, in order to have the funds to invest in these new projects and in further rapid expansion. Under the new plan shareholders would be cut back to about 10 percent of the dividends they had been receiving. This would be an unacceptable hardship for the Dodge brothers, who suggested that Ford buy them out, which he said he did not want to do.

The matter lay quiet for a while until the day following the wedding of Henry's son, Edsel, in November 1916, when the Dodges filed a suit against Ford that complained of mismanagement and unreasonable retention of income. Despite the ambitious plans that Ford had described, the company still had a substantial cash balance.

The suit moved through the courts at the usual slow speed. Ford said he would never buy out the Dodges, nor would he run the company to maximize profits; he just wanted to make cars affordable to common people and give them jobs. Nineteen seventeen came and went, another record year.

Then late in 1918, Ford, then fifty-five, quit. He resigned as president in favor of Edsel (though he remained on the board) and

went to California. There, in February 1919, he received the news
that the Michigan Superior Court had thrown out all of the Dodges'
arguments in the lawsuit, except the one about the unreasonable
retention of earnings. The company was required to pay out nearly
$20 million in dividends to its stockholders, an amount substantially
less than what the Dodges had asked for, but still a very substantial sum.

Was this a radical decision? Are the courts supposed to establish
dividend policies of corporations? What of the "business-judgment
rule" that seems to have its origin in English common law and, in
essence, asserts that as long as the board of a company is acting in
good faith, legally, and not in order to line its own pockets at the
expense of the other stockholders, the courts will give management
the benefit of the doubt in cases where their collective or individual
wisdom is being challenged. Should not management, rather than
outsiders, decide how much, if any, dividends should be paid (subject
to board approval) in the light of expected plans for expenditures,
competitive conditions, business policies, and so forth? The judge
said that normally, yes, but in this instance he was convinced that
Mr. Ford had acted unreasonably and therefore had required the
payment. The Dodge brothers were delighted with their victory but
still thought they should sell their stock, knowing that future dividends would be kept to a bare minimum once the $20 million was
paid. They turned down an offer of $18,000 per share, however, just
after the verdict was announced. After all, 1919 looked like yet
another record year.

The next month, however, Ford, claiming he was unable to work
with minority shareholders who so limited his ability to do what was
right for his company, announced that he was going to found a new
car company that would be several times larger than the present one,
to which he would devote all of his energies. He didn't know what
would happen to the old company, he said.

Subsequently, Ford asked his bankers to try quietly to buy up
the minority interests through the purchase of options on the shares
on the basis that Ford would buy only all of the minority interest or
none of it. The initial offers were at $7,500 per share, but the sale

was finally agreed at $12,500 per share for a total of $105.8 million, which capitalized the whole company at $255 million. This was an extraordinarily large transaction, by the standards of the day, not to mention that the whole thing was done by just one man.[6]

Ford, of course, had screwed his minority stockholders, all co-founders with him of the original 1903 company, right to the wall. First by quitting the company, then by starving them of dividends and refusing to buy their shares, then by threatening to abandon the company in favor of a new one, he squeezed them to accept a much lower price for their stock than they otherwise might have received. Ford had learned his lessons from dealing with Mr. Malcomson well.

Although 1919 was a difficult year for the economy, which suffered from labor unrest, rising inflation, and subsequently tighter monetary policy, Ford was doing well. The company had regained its 40 percent market share and produced over 750,000 cars. The River Rouge plant had come on stream, and by the end of July the company had a backlog of 2.5 million vehicles. *Moody's Industrial Manual* shows that Ford earned $75 million for 1919. Surely under these circumstances, a purchase price of 3.4 times earnings would seem a bit on the low side, but what could the others do? Ford had not decided to tender for the minority interest at a price designed to be fair and reasonable, the way such things are done today. He threatened to abandon the company and to go into competition with it unless the minority sold to him at a fire-sale price, as they did. Just a few years later, Ford turned down an offer of $1 billion for the whole company, four times the price at which he had bought the minority out.[7]

Ford financed approximately $75 million of the purchase price through a one-year syndicated credit arranged by Chase Securities Corp., Old Colony Trust Co. of Boston, and Bond & Goodwin Co. The credit was funded by the issuance of ninety-day commercial paper with three renewals.[8]

The loan was backed, of course, by the shares of Ford Motor Co., which had no other debt at the time, $155 million of cash and receivables on its books, a large cash flow (most of which had been earmarked for reinvestment into the company or for the River Rouge project, however), and a healthy and growing business. The new debt (called "temporary debt" on the company's balance sheet) represented only about 25 percent of Ford's combined debt and equity capitalization. It did not look like a terribly risky loan.[9]

Still, to finance a stock buyback on a one-year credit is a flagrant violation of the old banker's principle of never borrowing short (term) to invest long. As it was, the latter part of 1919 turned very blustery, and 1920 was a terrible year for the economy, and for the automobile business. In the midst of it, Ford decided to reduce prices further, to protect its volume, but at great cost to its cash flow. There must have been a few nervous bankers that year, though the loan was repaid on time.

The Ford buyout was highly leveraged of course, to the extent of 70 percent of the purchase price, but the relatively low price paid for the stock, and the enormous balance sheet behind it, not to mention Ford's private assets, made the loan a comparatively safe and unremarkable one, at least by the standards of today, when merger and buyout loans are common.

What was remarkable about the transaction was the extent to which Ford chafed under the burden of having stockholders other than himself whose interests he had to consider and the ruthless way he went about getting rid of them.

"Well," says our observer, "the Dodges in particular hadn't contributed anything to the company for years, and they had gotten to be pretty rich for a couple of country blacksmiths. You might be able to see how Ford had lost all his patience with them.

"And you certainly have to admire the way he went about getting rid of them in the end, rather the way you'd admire a Sicilian Mafia chief's eliminating a particularly troublesome rival. You might admire it, but you probably couldn't get away with it.

"The Dodges apparently were so happy to get their dividends, which, however hopeful they might have been, they surely couldn't have expected, that they blew their main chance. That would have been to get right back in there before the same judge and claim that

Ford was acting equally unreasonably in not buying back their shares at a fair price. If outside experts had valued the company then, they would have come up with a much higher price—of course, the beauty of the Ford scheme was the way he threatened to abandon the company, which pushed the price down. Tactics not altogether unworthy of our day, though today the courts believe in protecting the rights of minority shareholders so that they are not forced out at bargain prices."

Like Durant, Ford took on his partners when he had no money and couldn't talk the banks into lending him any. He outgrew them, and no doubt he resented how rich they had become for doing so little. He decided that he had to undo the initial equity leverage he had started out with, replacing it with borrowing from the commercial paper market. He realized that *leveraging with equity*, that is, diluting one's own interest in the company by issuing shares instead of borrowing, can be extremely expensive. Leveraging with debt, though initially more difficult and expensive, is much cheaper in the long run, as long as you don't have Mr. Durant's experience along the way and have to let the bankers take over.

Ford's buyout occurred about the time the Dow Jones Industrial Index (DJII) reached an all-time high of about 120. It didn't stay there long, however, as the expected postwar recession began in early 1920 and lasted for about a year and a half. During the slump, which was much milder than many had thought it would be, the DJII bottomed out at about 70, thereafter beginning a long, continuous rise only to end with the crash of 1929.

There was a tremendous confidence in America's economic future. The country had survived history's most brutal war with hardly a scratch and had been greatly enriched by its support of the victors. In Europe, winners and losers alike were flat on their backs economically, and the United States had become the world's leading economic and financial power. The American century, one that would improve the standard of living and the quality of life for all Americans, had now truly begun.

Life in the 1920s took on a giddy quality amid all the enthusiasm—flappers, goldfish swallowing, jazz and pop music—but underneath it all was optimism, at least among the better off.

However, a third of all wage earners still earned less than two thousand dollars a year during these years of rising prosperity. During the twenties there were a number of difficult labor disputes, and the decade had begun with a furious bomb blast in front of the offices of J. P. Morgan on Wall Street.

The dominant feeling, nonetheless, was well-being, and this feeling, as it tends to do, entered into the financial markets. A land boom had begun in Florida. Retail brokerages were setting up branch offices all over the country, doubling their number during the decade. Interest rates were low, and credit relatively easy. And lots of people were doing pretty well in the stock market, which rose between 15 and 20 percent per year, on average, from its low point in 1921 to mid-1928.

The middle-class salaryman had no prior experience in the market. It was yet another sign of the new prosperity that an "ordinary" person could play the market and make money in it, just like the tycoons. It was heady and thrilling, and it seemed to work. It certainly seemed to be working for one's neighbors and relatives, whose killings in the market were invariably reported by one's wife.

"Did you know that the Browns are moving?" asks the wife. No, one didn't.

"They're moving to Larchmont, where they've bought a lovely new house that Jerry earned the money for in the stock market. Something called RCA? [*Pause.*]

"Don't you ever hear about these things?"

Not only was everybody else doing it, all the government leaders and economic hotshots seemed to think it was OK; they actually seemed to be encouraging people to invest. And what was best, perhaps a new, inexperienced investor thought, is that I can invest directly in the enterprises of the world's smartest and most skillful business and financial operators.

*   *   *

There was a lot going on; the country was enjoying the second great merger boom in the century. This one was centered on public utility companies (that is, electric, gas, water, and bus companies) and on chain stores like Montgomery Ward and Woolworth. Whereas in the first great merger wave, competitors joined together to form large nationwide firms, sometimes in search of monopoly powers, on this occasion entrepreneurs sought to link together noncompeting companies in the same business, all to be run efficiently by experienced managers. The market thought this was a great idea that would lead to great cost savings and economies of scale, so the stock of any company thought to be acquiring others became hot.

This environment convinced some business promoters that they were smarter than they were, and they decided to reach out a bit further and to increase the leverage they were using by acquiring control of company A through a minority interest, then having company A acquire control of company B in the same way, and so on, through the alphabet.

Insull's Pyramid

In 1881 a twenty-two-year-old Englishman crossed the Atlantic to great adventure. Samuel Insull had worked as an operator on the Edison telephone exchange in London and managed to get himself hired to serve as the great man's private secretary and expediter. Edison was then in the process of commercializing his system for providing electric power and light. From small offices in Manhattan he had accumulated a couple of dozen customers, including Pierpont Morgan, who had a feeling about the future of electricity.

Edison's enterprise was to branch off in several directions. The Edison General Electric Company was formed in Schenectady, New York, in 1889 to manufacture turbines and other power-generating and transmission equipment. Insull, then thirty, was made vice president. Three years later, Insull volunteered to go to Chicago as president of the Chicago Edison Company, then one of several small

power-generating and marketing companies in the area. Edison's
General Electric Company was about to merge with another manufacturer, Thomson-Houston Electric Company, to form the General Electric Company, and Insull thought he might be overshadowed
by the new talent coming in.[10]

Soon after arriving in Chicago, Insull recognized two interre-
lated problems of the business. First, the generation of electricity
was too capital-intensive to support several small operators in one
area. These operators would have to consolidate. However, consolidation would undoubtedly produce monopoly charges. The Sherman
Act had just been passed, cartels were being denied in the courts,
and, worst of all, there was much talk at the time about having the
government own the electric power industry as it did in most other
countries. The consolidation that was so badly needed would probably occur sooner or later, but Insull, who saw the industry's potential
as clearly as anyone, wanted to protect it for the private sector.

His contribution to the industry was an enormous one. He has
been given much credit for his role as manager and builder in the
early days of large power stations and networks. He did a great deal,
too, to sell the idea of safe electric power to consumers and make
people comfortable with it. However, his most important contribution, perhaps, was his devising the notion that electric power companies should be owned by the private sector, but with any
monopolistic powers that might result from industry consolidation
curtailed by strict regulation of prices and other competitive conditions by state or local authorities. Insull supported the regulated
private ownership idea with an enormous uncorking of propaganda,
and with a substantial flow of bribes and payoffs to politicians from
both parties. In time, Insull's approach was accepted and became
the standard used throughout the country.[11]

By 1907 Insull had acquired one of his principal competitors in
Chicago; he renamed his company the Commonwealth Edison Co.
Soon it became the dominant producer of power in the region. In
1912, he formed a holding company, Middle West Utilities, that
owned or controlled several regulated utility companies in the region.

In forming the holding company Insull anticipated expanding
his operations, not just in the Midwest but all over the country. Thus

at sixty-two, he passed into his second career in public utilities, one in which his role would be that of a financier and promoter.

While working with Edison, Insull had met a former naval officer who had also been drawn into the inventor's web, Sidney Z. Mitchell. About the time that Insull had left for Chicago, Mitchell left for the Pacific Northwest. In 1905 Mitchell set up a holding company called Electric Bond and Share Company, that would become the largest of the utility holding companies, and its most durable: it paid dividends on its common stock through the mid-1930s.[12]

Mitchell was something of a financial genius, who first saw that once a power company was up and running, you could expect a steady, and indeed a steadily increasing, cash flow from it. Initially, most of the cash flow would be needed to service debt and preferred stock, but as the company grew, more of it would be available to the common stock. If you set up a company that would raise money to acquire all of or a controlling interest in several utility companies, you could have a very profitable, diversified investment, which could be made even more profitable by borrowing some of the money to be invested in the stocks.

The secret, according to Mitchell, was to buy companies cheaply and then shore up their management so the expected cash flow does materialize, issue bonds and preferred stock against the cash flow to raise all of the money needed for the acquisition, and let the holding company keep the common stock, which ought to represent 20 to 25 percent of the company's capitalization, to capture all of the future appreciation—not very different from Morgan's railroad recapitalizations.

Insull started off, it appears, following this approach. However, before long the enormous potential of the power business had become widely known and several other operators were following Mitchell too. In fact, if one wanted to grow and to become big, significant, and powerful, one had to get moving and acquire companies before the other fellows did. Financing was no problem: the markets would take almost anything. So, when America's second great merger wave began in the 1920s, it was heavily concentrated in the public utility sector.

The electric power industry had blossomed during the first thirty years of the new century. During this time United States electric power generation increased from 2.5 kilowatt-hours to 79 billion, and the book value of plant and equipment from about $500 million to $12.5 billion. Profits, too, had grown considerably. Though they were regulated, most companies did not find the constraints on rate increases too severe. They were, of course, on close terms with the regulators.

During the same period nearly 80 percent of the entire industry became part of a consolidated holding company structure, though most of these were more operating than financial companies. A dozen or so large publicly owned financial holding companies existed by 1930, however, and most of these, like Insull's, were highly leveraged pyramids with hundreds of thousands of individual investors and small institutions providing the money to fuel the escapades of a small handful of highly competitive tycoons whose control embraced virtually the whole industry. The market, of course, thought these tycoons were wonderful. They were the "smart operators," the skilled managers whose coattails ordinary folks could ride on to get rich.

Insull, who was certainly ambitious, wanted to be the most powerful man in the industry, indeed the most powerful in all industry. Accordingly, he overdid it. He paid almost anything to buy the companies he wanted and ended up with a great deal of expensive "goodwill" and other intangible assets on the books, mystifying the Federal Trade Commission when it later conducted a three-year investigation of his empire to find out "where the money had gone." He issued huge amounts of stock in his companies to pay for the businesses he acquired, promoted, and traded in these stocks in the market. He regularly reported the value of the upstream holding companies in terms of the market value of the stocks of the downstream companies. It all worked wonderfully for quite a while and came to a peak, as everything did, in 1929. Insull was generally considered a financial genius: one Chicago journalist claimed, "It was worth a million dollars to anybody seen talking to him in front of the Continental Bank."

When the crash came, his stocks collapsed, of course, like all the others. But underlying them were the steady cash flows of the power companies, which on balance were very little affected by the Depression. These cash flows kept most of the holding companies afloat, but not Insull's, which proved to be too hyped and stock-watered to last. The common shares of the holding companies started to drop, and Insull started to support them in the market. To make matters worse, Insull found that a rival predator, Cyrus Eaton, had been buying shares in his best companies. Eaton offered Insull a "greenmail" package ($56 million to buy back $50 million of stock whose market value was declining), which Insull, surprisingly, accepted. This purchase was financed with short-term bank loans. Before long it became clear that Insull could not service this debt, and by 1932 he was forced into bankruptcy.

Middle West, his largest sub–holding company, which owned or controlled 239 other companies, and 5 other giant sub–holding companies all failed: 19 of his companies altogether. Investors lost between $500 million and $2 billion. Insull, told he was to be indicted for fraud, fled the country, remaining abroad for two years before returning to the United States in 1935, when he was tried on federal and state charges of mail fraud and acquitted. Broken and contrite, after his trials he returned to Paris, where he died in 1938 at the age of seventy-nine.[13]

Insull's trusts became as much a scandal as their collapse was tragic. Based on a reasonable idea of the regulated holding company, they became infected by two familiar viruses: hubris—Insull's passion to control a giant empire that pushed him beyond good judgment—and madness—in the markets that believed anything he said and paid whatever price he asked for his paper. The patient, however, did not survive the infection.

Unfortunately, during the once-thought fail-safe twenties these viruses were not only rampant but widely regarded as harmless. As a result, we have another, even greater, example of the disease in the "investment trusts," which Galbraith described as being "the most notable piece of speculative architecture of the late twenties,

and the one by which, more than any other device, the public demand
for common stocks was satisfied."[14]

Leveraged Investment Trusts

Leveraged investment trusts were closed-end investment companies,
which issued their own stock and bought common stocks in the market with the proceeds. Under ordinary conditions, as we have seen,
the shares of the trust sell at a discount from the aggregate value of
the shares in the trust—not, however, when hundreds of thousands
of investors, knowing little about the market themselves, push their
money onto Wall Street's most renowned investors to manage for
them. They were willing to pay a higher price under such circumstances just to have someone competent manage their money for
them.

For example, a new issue of shares in an investment trust that
would own $100 worth of stock would be sold to the public for $104,
the $4 premium being the investment bankers' compensation for
underwriting and distributing the shares to the public. The trust
manager, often an enterprise owned or affiliated with the same investment banker, would earn a fee for managing the fund, often one
that was based on the performance of the trust: if it went up, the
fee would be greater.

The trusts were first launched in substantial quantity in 1927,
when about $400 million of new issues were launched, approximately
one-third of the total amount of new security issues for the year. By
1929, more than five hundred of these trusts existed, with total assets
under their control of about $8 billion, almost all of which had been
invested back into the market.[15]

The trusts were often highly leveraged with preferred stock and
with debt. A $150 million trust, for example, might have one-third
of the funds supplied by common stock and one-third each by preferred and debentures. If the market drove the common stocks
owned by the trust up by 50 percent, as it did from early to mid-

1929, then the market value of the assets would be $225 million. Subtract $100 million for the value of the preferred and the debentures, which did not participate in the appreciation of the assets, and $125 million was left for the investors in the trust's common stock, for which eager new investors, wanting some of this success for themselves, might be willing to pay a further premium of another $5 or $10 million. Thus an investment of $50 million had turned into one worth as much as $135 million, in only six months.

Needless to say, if the market value of the stocks held by the trust decreased, then the leverage worked in reverse.

The roaring market began in the summer of 1928, when the DJII was about 200. By the end of the year it had reached 300. By August 1929, it peaked at 381. Those who had bought into trusts were making a fortune. However, it didn't last long: by the end of October the DJII had collapsed by more than 30 percent to 199. A postcrash recovery actually got the index up to 300 again by March 1930, but afterward it slid further and further downward to bottom out at 41 during the summer of 1932.[16]

The effect of the leverage was devastating to those trusts that employed it. In the preceding example, if the investor bought in to the trust in late 1928 when the stocks in it were worth $100, by October they were worth only $67, the very amount needed to redeem the debentures and the preferred stock. The common stock, for which the investor had paid $104 less than a year before, was now worth nothing.

One of the firms most active in promoting investment trusts during this period was Goldman, Sachs & Co., which had gotten into the business rather late, in 1928. It sponsored several of the more disastrous funds, the Goldman Sachs Trading Corporation, the Blue Ridge Corporation, and the Shenandoah Corporation. Most ended up worthless. The firm was disgraced and spent years recovering its good name. The managing partner at the time, Waddill Catchings, was sacked and replaced by Sidney Weinberg, an extraordinary man who became a legendary figure in Wall Street, largely for the dedicated rebuilding job he effected over the following forty-five years as head of the firm. Weinberg had started out as a porter's assistant in 1909 and worked his way up to become the head of the firm, but it would be years before the stigma of the investment trusts would pass.

One investor in the Goldman Sachs trusts had been the comedian Eddie Cantor, who never failed to take the opportunity during his performances to ridicule the firm.

After Cantor died, the firm thought it might have some peace and the memory of the funds could be buried. Not so. As some readers may recall, the closing episode of the long-running Masterpiece Theatre serial "Upstairs, Downstairs," aired in the late 1970s and early 1980s, featured the sad figure of James, the son of the house who hadn't been able to get his act together after World War I, who finally came into his own with a stroke of long-buried genius. He had caught the rising market in New York and had made a fortune—until the crash, of course, which wiped it all out. He then proceeded to shoot himself, almost but not quite on screen, after announcing to his father and others in the final episode that he had "lost it all in Goldman Sachs."

Some memories die hard.

3

CHINESE MONEY

It took several years after the signing of the Japanese surrender document in Tokyo Bay for things to get back to normal in the United States. Nobody quite knew what would happen to the economy—all that pent-up demand for consumer products, housing, automobiles, and so on, ought to create some serious amounts of inflation, but at the same time the huge amount of government spending for the war effort was no longer being poured into the economy and the boys were going to take some time getting home and back to work, so maybe a recession was ahead instead.

Though most rationing and price controls were removed in 1945, there wasn't much inflation after all. The economy was sluggish but not depressed. There was plenty of money in circulation at the time: the lowest interest rates in the history of the United States were recorded in 1946, when a new issue of government bonds sold to yield as little as 1.93 percent.[1] The Dow Jones Industrial Average closed at about 170 on V-J Day and ended the year (1945) at about 200, the highest level since a short-lived peak in 1937. The rest of the 1940s was a time of adjustment and reorganization.

The United States had many new and vitally important responsibilities in the world for which policies had to be established and
implemented. Atomic energy had to be controlled and contained.
Europe had to be reconstructed, a new international monetary system put into effect, and communism had to be contained and indeed
opposed. Housing and educational assistance for returning GIs had
to be provided. Corporations had to reconfigure their production
lines to the manufacture of goods for a civilian economy. A presidential election had to be fought in 1948, a recession year. Americans
were reestablishing their lives, beginning families, starting to plan
for their futures.

It was difficult to know what sort of future one might look to
at the end of the forties. For nearly twenty years life had been hard
for most Americans, requiring much in the way of sacrifice and
patience. During that time, the government had become enormously
large in everyone's life, controlling so many things then that it hadn't
in the twenties. People had become used to looking to the government for solutions to all sorts of problems. The government, too,
had become comfortable with all of its recently accumulated powers
and didn't appear eager to give up many of them.

Then in the 1950s the Korean War began, a terribly discouraging
event for war-weary Americans wanting to get back to ordinary,
peaceful lives. The cold war that accompanied it, with the knowledge
that the Russians, too, had nuclear weapons and that communism
was now our deadly enemy, further chilled the spirits of those who
had borne the Great Depression and World War II and would now,
it seemed, have to endure this as well.

General Dwight Eisenhower was elected to the presidency in
1952, as a kind of supreme protector to sit outside our doors at night
while we slept. Eisenhower, one of the few people in the world whose
prestige equaled General MacArthur's, was admired for his wartime
achievements and for his symbolic representation of strong, steady,
quiet, conservative values. Eisenhower was probably as popular a
president as Ronald Reagan. Their appeal was similar: they were
each reassuring when the country needed reassurance.

The rest of the fifties included the outlawing of segregation by the Supreme Court in 1954, the Russians' successful launching of *Sputnik* in 1957, a serious recession in 1958, continuing labor-management disputes culminating in a long steelworkers strike in 1959—and the largest rise in the Dow Jones Index since the late twenties, from just under 300 at the end of 1952 to 616 at the end of 1959, the year before John Kennedy was elected to succeed Eisenhower.

The contrast between the two presidents was as great as any we have ever had. The contrast, however, was almost entirely one of style, outlook, and image, not really of substance. The outgoing president, at seventy, had come of age in the twenties and couldn't help looking over his shoulder at the grim and difficult days behind him; the incoming one who, at forty-three—if he had come of age at all it had been only recently—looked to the future and articulated dreams that had very wide appeal, especially to those of his own age or younger. The generation gap between the two was enormous, almost a continental divide. The Kennedy election was a major dividing point in our modern history, a time when the gray and gloomy baggage of the past was left behind. The future was now, to be gathered in by the spirited, the confident, and the brave.

Also by those who, like Kennedy, no longer wore hats to work or confined themselves to white shirts and dark ties. And by those who couldn't wait for their turn at the top, who believed in growth and opportunity, even if the folks currently in charge did not.

On Wall Street the generation gap was physical, not just representational. Indeed, a whole generation of bankers and brokers was missing. Very few had come to work there after the crash in 1929: the thirties didn't represent much opportunity. During most of the forties, of course, the place was manned by a skeleton crew of those too old for the draft. Not until the late forties did the firms start hiring again. In 1960, those who had been there in the 1920s were now in their sixties and seventies, and those hired after the war were in their thirties and forties and starting to take over many of the key operating positions in their firms.

The emphasis in the sixties was on growth, not safety; on performance, not conservation: a Kennedy approach, not an Eisenhower one.

*   *   *

Before the sixties investment advisers were mainly guided by the "prudent man" rule, in which a court years ago had prescribed that a manager of someone else's money would not be liable for losses incurred under his stewardship if he could demonstrate that the investments he made had been prudent ones, ones that he might have made with his own funds. For most of the century, the largest aggregation of funds under management had been those placed in trust accounts by individuals. Now, however, new sources of funds were finding their way into the hands of professional money managers, known as "institutional investors": insurance companies, banks, pension funds, and a comparatively new figure on the scene (not seen much since 1929), the investment company, or mutual fund. These institutions in aggregate had controlled $9.5 billion of investments listed on the New York Stock Exchange in 1949; on election day in 1960, however, the total was about $70 billion, representing about 20 percent of all listed securities.[2]

After all, the stock market had doubled in the Eisenhower years, despite Korea, the cold war, Senator McCarthy, and everything else. This meant an investor, despite only a 2.5 percent overall U.S. economic growth rate, could have made a compound return of somewhat more than 10 percent on stock-market investments during the period as compared to an average of about 3 percent on government bonds. And, investors had been reassured, the market had been subject to strict and efficient regulation since the thirties, and what happened before couldn't happen again.

The institutions that managed the funds were paid a fee based on the total value of the funds under management: the original funds plus the market appreciation since investment plus new money coming in, minus, of course, any money going out in redemptions. They had to compete for the business (the business of managing new, enlarged pension funds, for example) if they wanted it, as there were plenty of managers like them. The basis for competition was performance: growth of the assets under management.

"The prudent man ought to have at least some of his investments in the stock market; otherwise, in this environment, he's not being very prudent, is he?" points out one fund manager on a marketing call.

"And our research indicates that investors such as you ought to be into stocks to the extent of about 30 or 40 percent of your total assets. Good stocks, of course, but stocks of companies that are growing, benefiting from the new technologies and markets that have developed since the war.

"Here you will need to think about a manager for your stock portfolio, an experienced firm whose research and market activity puts it right at the center of what's going on. Someone who can select the right stocks and know when to buy and sell them for you. A firm who can get you top performance in today's markets, as indeed it has been doing for its clients for the past several years.

"Someone, for example, like us."

Competition among the fund managers for business led to competition among brokers and dealers for the business of supplying the stocks the fund managers had to perform with. As the institutional assets under management had sextupled during the fifties, there was nothing of even remotely comparable importance going on in Wall Street. Those firms with a natural interest and capability in the "wholesale" end of the business went after it very strongly. As important as the old-line investment bankers in these firms had been, in the fifties and sixties the new block traders and institutional salesmen became their equals.

Soon the competition among the brokers led to competition in providing investment ideas and in supplying execution services. The minimum commission structure then existing on the New York Stock Exchange had never envisioned trades in such large amounts, thus it provided a substantial reward for transactions in "blocks" of stock (10,000 shares or more). This structure forced on investors the same commission per share whether the trade was 100 shares or 100,000 shares. Commissions on blocks were large enough to pay for a firm's research costs and to cover any trading losses, while still providing an excellent return.

Fund managers were tough customers for the brokers. They

wanted the best ideas they had, the first call, the finest executions. They yelled and complained a lot and carried on just to let the brokers know who was boss. They also liked to get tickets to sporting events, and the latest shows, and to eat out a lot. They rewarded performance, they said. If a broker had a research idea they used, they would either give the broker the order to execute it for them or select another house which was better at large block executions and tell it to send part of the commission to the broker with the idea. They paid out a lot of commissions, and they had a lot of clout.

The market had turned optimistic in early 1961, buoyed by the Kennedy spirit perhaps, but certainly buoyed. It floated right over the Bay of Pigs fiasco in April and the construction of the Berlin Wall in August. Older folks might have been worried, but the New Men were not. Such things, they thought, were just politics. What really counted were electronics, computers, new technologies, and business ideas. The newly proclaimed glamour stocks soared, companies like IBM, Litton Industries, Texas Instruments, Polaroid, and Xerox. Price-earnings ratios soared, too, as investors discounted not only the future but, as many said at the time, the "hereafter as well." The rally was fairly sudden, and sharp. The market rose from a DJII in the low 600s to reach nearly its all-time high of 735 by year's end, a 20 percent return in just one year. Soon afterward, however, the market developed a hangover from its excesses and started a steep, unexplained decline that lasted until late May, when after a breath-grabbing plunge of 35 points on May 28, it bottomed out at 575. The next day, however, as if purged by the last of the sell orders, the market recovered and began a protracted and nearly continuous rise to over 1000 in early 1966, nearly doubling the DJII in only three and a half years, an average return for the three-and-a-half-year period of more than 20 percent.

These were the "go-go years" of the "Soaring Sixties." These years included the Cuban missile crisis, the Kennedy assassination, and the beginnings of both the Vietnam War and its subsequent inflation and the great American civil rights movement. But the market wasn't worried about these things. It was *a go-go*, a name taken from a new, freeform, wild and wavy kind of dance being performed in all the trendy nightclubs at the time. This was the market of the New Men of the Kennedy generation: the optimists, the believers in growth of corporate earnings and prosperity, the opportunists.

The market's gains engorged pension funds, college endowments, foundations, and other institutions with unexpected wealth, which soon came to be taken for granted. The University of Rochester had become the fifth-richest university in the country because of success with Xerox shares. The University of Richmond similarly benefited from shares in A.H. Robins. The new head of the Ford Foundation, former Harvard dean and Kennedy aide McGeorge Bundy, complained that the foundation's support of universities might be cut back for those who failed to capitalize on the opportunity to manage what money they had aggressively. "We have the preliminary impression that over the long run caution has cost our colleges and universities much more than imprudence or excess risk taking," he said. In other words, the prudent man should not be so cautious as to miss all the action.

The idea got around that the best professional money managers could produce superior investment performance year in and year out. Similarly, the general notion came to be that managing money, like using computers, had experienced a kind of intellectual breakthrough. But only the young, highly intelligent, talented new fellows, many trained at fine business schools in the latest financial and management techniques, were capable of applying the new science; the old guys from the gloomy Depression era were too old-fashioned or burned-out to really perform. They couldn't compete and thus had to move out of the way.

But like many highly talented people, these new managers were a little hard to take, a bit too cocky, too independent, too impulsive, disorderly, even rude. "Adam Smith" in a 1967 best-selling description of the money and investment science, called *The Money Game*, christened this new breed the "gunslingers."

Gunslingers of the Sixties

The gunslingers were the portfolio managers of the large institutional investors. They worked under the loose supervision of a senior investment manager, but basically it was a sink-or-swim business. They started off with a small portfolio to manage. Their performance was evaluated in relation to that of other managers and the DJII. They were entirely on their own, them against the world. If a portfolio did really well, then its manager was given a bigger one to manage, and a bigger one after that—if the manager was still around, not having gone off to "run some money" on his own.

They were quick; they caught the market's moves (which were mainly up). They traded almost everything they owned. They could turn over an entire portfolio during a year, some even more often. Other managers sponsored special funds, called *hedge funds*, which were free to trade on margin and to short stocks and to trade in other kinds of securities: they were supposed to offset their long positions with their shorts so as to be hedged, but often they weren't.

All the gunslingers were fast on the draw; they believed in acting quickly on information culled from the "market," that is, from talking to each other. Their motto seemed to be to "invest before you investigate"; otherwise the opportunity might be missed. One could always investigate later and sell out if what he learned didn't check out. They had nerves of steel, as they had to, being exposed to such intense competition. On the surface anyway, they were unbelievably self-confident. "Adam Smith" gave madeup names to real people in his book, like characters out of *Guys and Dolls*, colorful names like "Odd Lot Robert," "The Great Winfield," "Poor Grenville," and "Scarsdale Fats."

They were quick to act and bold, but they were professional too. They read the long research reports published by the new firm of Donaldson, Lufkin & Jenrette, founded by three young men right out of Harvard Business School in the early sixties: solid, thorough research reports that their business school professors would be proud of. Detailed. Full of facts and figures of all types. Explaining the "concepts" behind the stocks.

Some relied more on what they heard on the telephone and spent most of their working day talking on it. Many had special angles that they used in investing, but all of them were looking for growth stocks. Growth stocks were stocks that went up. There were quite a few of these around in the 1962 through 1966 bull market, causing a skeptical John Kenneth Galbraith to comment, "Genius is a rising market."

In *The Money Game*, "Adam Smith" refers to a mid-1960s interview with the dean of all money managers, the proper Bostonian Edward C. Johnson II, known only as "Mr. Johnson," who had headed the (then) $3.5 billion Fidelity group of funds since 1939, when its assets were only $3 million. His group was then, and still is, the one everyone else tries to beat. "Smith" was hoping to distill into print Johnson's simple formula for doing so well but wasn't able to do so. Johnson seemed to think everything was relevant but couldn't be pinned down other than to indicate that he agreed that psychological factors played a major role in driving markets. Perhaps his most useful observation about the market in the sixties was "The dominant note of our time is unreality; all times of 'crusading spirits' are times of unreality."[3]

It is true that there were several crusades going on in America at the time, a cold war in Europe, the early days of Vietnam in Asia, one in the civil rights arena in the United States, and the crusade for growth then present in the financial markets. In the latter case, the indestructible bull market theme was familiar; indeed, the theme had been almost exactly the same in the twenties. Buy growth stocks, technology stocks; get rich easily; let the young professionals show you how; buy mutual funds; and invest in pyramiding industrial assets.

Still, Mr. Johnson's advice was a little vague. Were "unreal" times good or bad? What stocks do you buy in unreal markets? Do you buy the unreal stocks, hoping to sell them to someone else later at a higher, more unreal price, or do you buy the not unreal stocks that nobody wants, hoping that someday in the not too distant future, when reality returns, he will?

One of Mr. Johnson's most outstanding disciples, a Chinese-

born, highly visible whiz named Gerry Tsai, was the manager of one
of Fidelity's largest go-go funds. He decided in early 1966 that as he
was not likely to succeed Mr. Johnson at Fidelity, he ought to have
a little fund of his own. He thought he could raise $25 million or so
through a public offering that Bache & Co. had offered to lead for
him. The incoming orders, however, astonished everyone. They totaled $274 million on just the first day. Within a year the new vehicle,
called the Manhattan Fund, would attract more than $400 million in
assets. Gerry Tsai had become *the* star gunslinger almost overnight.
He received star treatment everywhere: unreal treatment.[4] In later
years, however, the star would fade, and reality would resume. The
Manhattan Fund held its own in 1967, but when the market started
to soften in 1968, it did poorly. Tsai seemed to have lost his magic
touch. So he sold out to CNA, an insurance group, for $30 million,
enough to stake him in later years when he acquired American Can
Co. (which has since become Primerica Corp.) in order to become
a latter-day corporate gunslinger during the 1980s.

Sometime during 1968 I remember attending a meeting at an
important fund manager, Standard & Poor's InterCapital Corp., for
which my colleagues at Goldman Sachs and I were trying to arrange
a Eurodollar financing. I was surprised to encounter a friend and
business school classmate, Brock Stokes, at the meeting. I was further
surprised to learn that Brock was the guy in charge of the offering
for S & P InterCapital, for which he was a senior portfolio manager.
He, on the other hand, seemed not surprised to find that I was the
juniormost person among the investment bankers, just along to carry
the bags and to fill out forms. Brock knew that at the time the smart
guys went off to manage portfolios, and the dull clods stuck it out
in the pits of investment banking.

Even though I, too, knew all this, I was amazed to see Brock in
action. He started off in a large open room filled with stock-market
machinery telling us what he wanted, between phone calls from brokers and analysts, then sat back for a while to watch the tape, placing
orders every so often. He seemed like a Wellington at Waterloo,
taking everything in through the haze of battle, issuing commands,
and requesting information right and left. Periodically he would

return to our group to ask how we were getting on, chatting amiably.

Then, rather quietly he said to me in an aside, "Have you ever heard of this guy Milton Friedman at the University of Chicago?"

"He's a monetary economist," I replied with dull-clod precision.

"Right, well one of my sources just now told me he may be the key to understanding these markets. Apparently he says that it's money supply that counts; it's what really drives things. You watch the money supply and you can make a killing.

"Well, I guess I'd better go see him. You guys get along OK without me for a while?"

He left the room, shouting to his secretary to get him a seat on the next flight to Chicago and to call Friedman's office to set up an appointment.

He'd been out of business school less than three years at the time.[5]

The real story of the sixties markets was their institutionalization: the domination of trading markets in stocks and bonds by professional managers. Assets under professional management would continue to grow during the next two decades, and the influence of these managers would increase further. But until the sixties, individual investors, in the aggregate, had been the principal day-to-day investors, trading for the most part infrequently and in small quantities. With the professional managers came the need to service them, and brokers and dealers had to change to accommodate them.

The gunslingers of the sixties were simply the first of these institutional managers to come to town. None of them knew any more about investing in the stock market then than anyone else, but the first wave cleared the air and got things going. Few from this wave of managers would survive the bear market of 1969, or the much worse one to follow in 1973–74. Overexposed to growth, their performance was shattered when the market turned. But the institutionalization, the stock-market research, the block trading, and the performance orientation that they inspired did survive and continues today.

Though the soaring sixties market fell sharply in 1966, it recovered later in the year, and thereafter the DJII traded between 750 and 1000 until the end of 1972, after which it fell off into the "slumping seventies."

In 1967 riots broke out in several cities; 1968 was a dreadful year, when both Bobby Kennedy and Martin Luther King were killed. The Vietnam War was coming to its peak, drawing out student unrest and conflict all over the country. Antiwar protests had turned ugly and divisive. Drugs were coming into widespread use. Money was being tightened to control inflation. There was a lift in 1969 when Neil Armstrong landed on the moon, but even that monumental achievement couldn't offset all the rest.

But throughout these years, the markets, though rocky, were active and volume was very high by contemporary standards. Because of the volume and the inability to process the avalanche of paper associated with it, many Wall Street firms suffered back office problems, several terminally, having lost control of their securities delivery and record keeping activities. The volume and price levels, both periodically at record levels, provided the financial environment necessary for substantial corporate activity—the next great merger wave.

The Conglomerates

One legacy of the thirties that had not changed even during the probusiness Eisenhower years was the attitude of the government toward antitrust enforcement. It had become holy writ that concentrations of economic power that were not in the public interest (as evaluated by the Justice Department and the Federal Trade Commission and ultimately determined by the courts, which usually seemed to back the government) could not be allowed. Certainly combinations of companies in the same industry would not be permitted if their prospective market share appeared to be anticompetitive. Nor could vertical integrations be permitted if too much market power resulted. This pretty much ruled out mergers within one's own industry as a way to growth. And growth, of course, was what the market was looking for: growth in sales, earnings, earnings per share, and corporate visibility—one's ranking in the annual *Fortune* magazine list of the 500 largest U.S. industrial corporations.

There was a way, however, to grow by acquisition: the acquisition, that is, of businesses in unrelated businesses, ones that posed no antitrust conflicts. If a company could borrow money, the after-tax cost of which is comparatively low, to buy another company with decent earnings at a reasonable price, then the purchaser's earnings per share (eps) could be increased, or at least not decreased. These transactions were mainly a matter of mathematics: at a given cost of borrowing, and given earnings for the two companies (buyer and seller), there was a maximum purchase price a buyer could pay for the seller without decreasing (or "diluting") the buyer's eps. Dilution of eps was a bad thing—that was not the road to growth and a happy life ever after with the institutional investors—the market did not like to see companies experience dilution of eps in connection with acquisitions, except in rare, exceptional circumstances, and even then, not for long.

The minimum price that could be paid would be the current market price. The actual price that would be negotiated would have to be somewhere between the maximum and the minimum prices if the buyer were to be able to show an advantage, that is, an increase in its eps, and if the seller were to be able to pocket a nice premium over the market price of his shares.

Of course, other factors apart from price are important, too, in an acquisition: the historical growth rate of the company being bought, its size, the debt it already has outstanding. If a seller's historical growth in its eps is greater than the buyer's, then the acquisition will help to increase the buyer's prospective growth rate, a good thing. If the seller is a company with little debt on its books, the combination of the two will create additional debt capacity, which initially may be employed in financing the acquisition itself. The size of the acquisition relative to the size of the buyer is really limited only by these factors; that is, will the combined debt-carrying capacity of the two support borrowing the amount of debt necessary to accomplish the acquisition on a nondilutive basis? One can stay up all night figuring out all of the different permutations possible in such transactions, and many people did just that during the sixties.

So far, no mention has been made of the fact that substantially different businesses might be joined together, just to take advantage of the mathematical consequences. How can the market be persuaded that a combination of very dissimilar businesses—a brickmaker, a lingerie manufacturer, and a chain of hamburger restaurants, for example—makes sense? Such persuasion is a key task of the buyer, who must in such circumstances become a promoter. If the buyer fails to convince, then his existing shareholders may dump his stock on the market, knocking its price down, which is definitely not the object of the exercise. If this happens, he has to cancel the deal or suffer the consequences. To prevent it from happening, he has to polish up his pitch, his "rationale" for the transaction, and show how this deal fits in with his overall "concept" of the company.

"Folks, this acquisition does three important things for our company.

"First, it continues our present thrust into new areas of countercyclical growth so as to achieve our overall corporate objective of 15 percent annual growth in eps, which we believe is achievable more or less indefinitely under our modern management practices.

"Second, it offers us many attractive opportunities to benefit from the synergies inherent in bringing our new friends in under our management. We can expect cost savings to result from the use of our centralized administration and control systems, from integrated long-range corporate planning, and from rigorous application of a common strategic doctrine.

"And, third, it repositions our company among the most important corporations in America. We expect that this acquisition will enable us to move up considerably on the Fortune 500 list, and of course, we can expect that such a move will bring with it many new opportunities in the future because of our increased visibility and prestige."

The chief executive might go on to add that each company in the group will continue to operate its own business, and that the small central staff was essentially a group of highly experienced and respected *financial* managers whose objective was to make money for the stockholders by increasing the growth of the assets owned by the company. "We are no longer in business just to make bricks, brassieres, or burgers, or whatever: we are in business to make money!"

The market bought it: buzz words like *synergy* and *systems* and all. The gunslingers signed on. The growth potential in these stocks was theoretically *unlimited*. The investors were after growth, and these new creatures, the "conglomerates" as these new multi-industry, diversified companies were called, seemed to be offering it. After all, where else was one going to find 15 percent after-tax growth in an economy that even in the best of the soaring years averaged growth of only about 5 percent? Things did, of course, depend on the man in charge and just how good the market thought he was.

The earliest of the conglomerates (a somewhat pejorative term that none of them liked) were born under the banner of necessity. Royal Little, a feisty New Englander, wanted to shelter wartime profits from his small textile company, Textron, against income taxes by consolidating with money-losing companies that he might be able to turn around. There were not many such losers in the textile industry (which had been at full capacity during the war years), so he had to step outside the industry to find what he was looking for. He found and acquired several such companies, then several more. These companies then did pretty well, whereas the textile businesses didn't. In the fifties, Little decided to forget the textiles and concentrate on the diversified investments that had done so well. Then he devised a "strategy" that embraced the decision he had already made. He regarded skillful mastery of the mathematics and tax laws and good operating horse sense essential to success in this unusual business. Being an experienced operating manager himself, he was good at sorting out the incoming acquisitions into compatible groups. By 1966, several years after Little's retirement, Textron had acquired and sold hundreds of companies and had combined sales of over $1 billion.[6]

In 1959 Harold Geneen became president of ITT. He was re-

cruited from Raytheon, where he had risen before the age of fifty
to become an executive vice president. He was an accountant by
training and very, very good with numbers. ITT's problem at the
time was that more than 80 percent of its business consisted of telephone companies located abroad, one of which had just been con-
fiscated by Fidel Castro. Geneen was pessimistic about overseas
business and wanted no further foreign "surprises." In 1963 he presented a paper to the ITT board titled "Acquisition Philosophy,"
which set forth the objective of rapidly reducing the company's dependence on foreign earnings. This would be done by increasing the
American part of the business through the acquisition of growth
businesses of various types. Within five years he wanted ITT to have
at least 55 percent of its earnings coming from America instead of
the 18 percent that these earnings then represented.[7]

Over the next several years Geneen acquired a hundred or so
very diversified companies: Avis Rent-a-Car, the Nancy Taylor Fin-
ishing School, a car parking company, Cleveland Motels, a pump
manufacturer, a speedwriting company, Bobbs-Merrill publishers,
Pennsylvania Glass Sand, Levitt Homes (the builders of Levittown),
Rayonier (a maker of chemical cellulose and a major timberland
owner), Continental Baking, Sheraton Hotels, and Hartford Insurance, among many others. He also made an unsuccessful effort to
acquire the American Broadcasting Corporation.

There were many other conglomerates on the move in the 1950s
and 1960s. Litton Industries, one of the earliest, had been founded
by the former Ford Motor whiz kid Charles ("Tex") Thornton in
1953 to invest in diversified technology and "systems" companies,
though after a while its collection of companies resembled ITT's. It
was an early favorite, producing steady growth in eps for fourteen
years until it missed a quarterly earnings increase in 1968 and fell
from grace. A former Litton executive, Henry Singleton, founded
Teledyne Corp., which was also successful as a technology and systems "concept" company. U.S. Industries was organized to acquire
literally hundreds of smaller companies, to preserve their original
entrepreneurial spirit. Even in the United Kingdom the conglomerate boom was on; a great favorite there was Slater Walker & Co.

Ltd., which rose high into the heavens before collapsing in the bear markets of 1973 and 1974. By the end of 1969, *Moody's Industrial Manual* listed dozens of "diversified industry" companies. Virtually all of them had been put together during the past ten years, during the twentieth century's third and largest merger wave so far, one that resulted in the disappearance of more than twenty-five thousand companies during the sixties.

Leveling the Playing Field

The conglomerates provoked a lot of controversy. Some, like ITT and Gulf + Western, seemed voracious and dangerous. Gulf + Western was nicknamed "Engulf and Devour" on the Street. Northwest Industries attracted much scorn and disdain from the corporate establishment for its hostile takeover bid for old blue-chip B. F. Goodrich in 1969; the bid was ultimately unsuccessful but many similar bids were not.

In those days (before passage in 1968 of the Williams Act, which attempted to "level the takeover playing field") an aggressive conglomerate could sneak up on a larger, more established and conservatively run company and launch a sudden "tender offer" for it. These offers, tendered directly to the shareholders, not to the board of directors or the management, were called "Saturday night specials," after the name given to cheap, lethal handguns used in robberies and muggings. Such an offer would be at a 15 to 25 percent premium over the current stock price of the target company to induce shareholders to sell for a quick profit. Sometimes the offer would be for only 51 percent of the stock, with the assumption that the remainder would be forced into a merger through an exchange of securities after the acquirer had gained control. If a shareholder wanted cash, instead of a low-grade convertible debenture or preferred stock, he had better accept the tender offer while he could. Such securities issued in merger transactions were called "Chinese money" by the market because they were inscrutable, i.e., never what they seemed to be. The securities always traded at a discount from par value. Tender offers were accepted on a first-come first-serve basis (in the terminology of the eighties these offers would be "two-tiered, front-end loaded" offers).

The whole thing could happen very quickly. After secretly buying up a small stakeholding, the tender offer would be launched to expire after fourteen days, as permitted then by the rules of the New York Stock Exchange. By the time a target company got its act together, a large portion of its stock might already have been sold in the market by its fast-moving institutional stockholders. The buyers were speculators willing to acquire the stock at a discount from the tender-offer price in order to be able to tender the shares themselves later. Such speculators are called "risk (or, merger) arbitrageurs." They are mainly Wall Street broker-dealers and block traders, who offer to make a market in the shares of companies subject to bids for those institutions who want to take the money and run. Their role in takeovers, then as now, was formidable and controversial.

The advantages in the takeover game during most of the sixties clearly favored the aggressor company. It could plan an attack without anyone's knowing, then spring it suddenly with a tender offer to shareholders that was set to expire within two weeks, and then wait for Wall Street arbitrageurs to buy up enough shares from institutions who wanted to lock in a sure profit (but not take the risk that the deal would fail) so the tender could be a success. The arbitrageurs usually did very well for their trouble, but sometimes when a deal fell apart unexpectedly—as in the case of ITT and ABC—the results could be disastrous for them.

The best defense under such circumstances was for the target company to keep cool but to act quickly to turn on the public relations and legal departments. The PR folks would run full-page advertisements in major newspapers claiming that all shareholders must rally together to repel this villainous raid on their old and distinguished company by disreputable corporate scum whose purpose was only to rob them of the company's true value. By tendering they would be acting disloyally and aiding and abetting a terrible national pestilence. A defender would also make every effort to arrange meetings with its large shareholders to persuade them to hang on to their stock.

At the same time, the defender's lawyers would try to gain badly needed time by seeking legal injunctions against the transaction any way they could. There would also be an effort to call in all the corporate chips to bring antitrust or other federal or state regulatory factors into play to foul up, complicate, or delay the other side's attack. It could also revise its earnings estimates, raise its dividend, and stagger the election of directors to its board to deter the attack.

This environment in general, however, especially favored the attacker who had little to lose. Therefore many cheeky "David over Goliath" deals were attempted. These included such unsuccessful efforts as the attempt by Resorts International (a gambling casino company) to take over Pan American Airways (then in good shape), and the most unthinkable of all such deals, the effort by Leasco Data Processing Equipment Company, an eight-year-old computer-leasing operation owned by thirty-year-old Saul Steinberg of Great Neck, Long Island, to take over the $9 billion Chemical Bank New York Trust Co., one of the ten largest banks in the country. Steinberg's efforts failed, but certainly they were taken seriously by Chemical, and in any case, they resulted in a lot of no doubt beneficial publicity for him. Later Steinberg succeeded in capturing the much larger Reliance Insurance Company.

In this time of great activity it is difficult to select one or two star conglomerators, ones who stand way above the rest. One name, however, that would be on everyone's short list is James J. Ling, founder and chairman of LTV Industries, who started with an investment of $2,000 and ended up in control of the fourteenth-largest corporation in the country with annual sales of $3.8 billion—all through acquisitions and extremely fancy financial footwork.

Jimmy Ling's Illusions

Jim Ling is a high school dropout from Oklahoma who, after wartime service as a navy electrician, scraped together the $2,000 to start an electrical contracting business in Dallas. He was ambitious and hard-working and the business prospered. But he wasn't satisfied. In 1955 he decided he needed to go public to raise some money to go after greater things. He talked some local underwriters into offering 450,000 shares of his company at $2.25 per share and was launched.

By 1960 Ling had acquired Texas Engineering and Manufacturing Co., a medium-size aircraft manufacturing company. The new company, renamed Ling-Temco Electronics, thus appeared for the first time on the Fortune 500 list, an achievement of great importance to Ling. In 1961, Ling-Temco successfully made a quick, hostile raid on Chance-Vought Aircraft, one of the country's leading aircraft companies. The deal was done by issuing new 5.5 percent convertible debentures, convertible into shares of the combined company, re-named Ling-Temco-Vought (LTV), at $34.80 per share (that is, for every $34.80 of bonds held one new share of LTV stock could be converted, or every $100 bond could be converted into 2.87 shares of stock).

Chance-Vought was big enough to propel the combined enterprise into 158th place on the prestigious Fortune rankings, but the company had a lot of problems that Ling overlooked in his eagerness to acquire it. "I wanted it because it was big," he said. Afterward large writeoffs had to be endured and the company fell out of sight for a while.

After the 1962 stock market decline, LTV stock was trading at about $15. By this time Ling was devoting almost all of his time to the financial side of the business. Early in 1963, he launched one of his more original transactions, one he would use repeatedly in the future: an exchange offer of new LTV securities for outstanding LTV securities.

In this case, Ling wanted to reduce LTV's outstanding debt and interest cost. So he offered holders of outstanding $100 par value 5.5 percent convertible debentures the opportunity to exchange each debenture for $100 par value of new securities consisting of a $60 par value 5.5 percent *nonconvertible* debenture and a $40 par value 4.75 percent convertible debenture, convertible into LTV stock at $18 per share. *Par value* is the value paid to the debentureholder on redemption; the market value in all these instances was much less. For the exchange offer to succeed, the market value of the original convertibles would have to be significantly less than the expected market value of the two other securities, as it was. The original securities were depressed in value because of the great difference between the market price of the LTV shares (about $15) and the conversion price ($34.80) of the debentures. The nonconvertible debenture was at a discount because the 5.5 percent interest it paid was well below the market at the time, and the 4.75 percent convertible was below par (though probably not too much below) because the coupon rate had been lowered from 5.5 percent, although the conversion price of the stock had been lowered, too. Chinese money for Chinese money.

Ling had launched the exchange offer because he expected the stock price to rise again after some tightening up of the company's operations, which was then under way. It did, and when it passed $18, he called the new 4.75 percent convertibles for redemption, forcing their holders to convert them into their underlying LTV common stock instead. The result was that through these operations the company reduced its outstanding interest-bearing debt by half, was recapitalized more favorably, and paid a small premium to those LTV security holders who had participated in the exchange. Also, by issuing low coupon nonconvertible debentures, Ling was setting them up to be repurchased by the company over the next few years at a discount from par, which recovered discount could be taken into ordinary income as earnings.

Smoke and mirrors? Maybe, but Ling would maintain that frequent restructuring of the company's liabilities was healthy and both the debentureholders and the stockholders benefited, so everybody won.

In 1964 Ling still thought that LTV's stock was underpriced, even though its earnings outlook was weak. So he applied some of his talent for financial engineering to another exchange offer, but this time one that would reduce the number of common shares outstanding. The move would thus help to shore up the price of the stock in the market and increase eps by reducing the fraction's denominator. He offered to redeem up to 1.5 million shares by exchanging for each one $15 in cash plus a new $3 dividend preferred stock (convertible into 1.25 shares of common stock). About 800,000 shares were repurchased through the exchange offer and another 200,000 from the market to enable LTV to reduce its total number of common shares outstanding by about a third.

The first exchange offer had the effect of deleveraging the company, that is, reducing its debt to equity ratio; the second had the effect of releveraging it. Through his exchange offers, Ling was micromanaging the company's balance sheet, particularly the stockholders' equity account.

Ling was still just getting started, however. Later, in 1965, he took the equity exchange offer one step further. In an exercise that enabled him to coin the term "redeployment of assets," he reorganized LTV into a holding company with three corporate subsidiaries: LTV Aerospace, LTV Electronics, and LTV Altec. Then he asked LTV shareholders to turn in some of their shares in exchange for a package of cash and some of the shares in these three new companies, which were becoming publicly owned, majority-controlled subsidiaries of LTV. The deal, though complex and difficult to explain to shareholders, was moderately successful. More important though, the combined market values of these new subsidiaries would, buoyant markets continuing, exceed the market value of the parent, thus increasing the total market value of the properties controlled by Ling simply by an exercise in reshuffling.

Ling was only applying the principle that was demonstrated in both the incorporation of the Sugar Trust in the 1890s and the breakup of Standard Oil in 1911: under the right circumstances the sum of the market values of the parts can exceed the market value of the whole. The right circumstances include the opportunity to provide increased visibility of high-grade properties that might otherwise be hidden, greater marketability of poorly traded securities, and enhanced opportunities for investors to select the exact portfolio of the company's securities that suited them best, for which privilege they ought to be willing to pay something.

By 1965 LTV's stock reached nearly $60. Other acquisitions had been made, some directly by the publicly owned subsidiaries. In 1966 Ling noted that the company was actively looking for "targets of opportunity." Late in that year he found one: Wilson & Company, Inc., the meat packers.

True, LTV already had some mundane businesses wrapped in with its aerospace and electronics companies, but nothing like a meat packer. Though the third-largest company in its industry, Wilson, like the other packers, earned only a small return on sales and assets. Management had attempted some restructuring, however, and had developed its by-products businesses, Wilson Pharmaceuticals and Wilson Sporting Goods, into successful companies.

Wilson put up a halfhearted defense to Ling's cash offer for 53 percent of the company, and control was acquired for just over $81 million, all of which was borrowed (most in Europe). The remaining Wilson shares were exchanged for $115 million par value of preferred stock.

Then, its assets were redeployed as LTV's had been. Wilson was divided into three companies, and each sold some shares to the public, raising about $44 million from the exercise, which was used to reduce the debt incurred in the acquisition. Again, however, the unbundled pieces of Wilson scored a higher market value than the whole of it did as a unit. By autumn 1967, the market value of LTV's majority interests increased to about $250 million, for which Ling had incurred $37 million of new debt (net of the repayment) and issued $115 million par value of new preferred stock to the old Wilson shareholders.

The Wilson deal was a remarkable one for Ling. On the surface it seemed totally implausible, wrongheaded, and foolish. But, according to Ling's biographer, the business journalist Stanley Brown,

The success of the Wilson move indicated to Ling that any corporation, no matter how established and vulnerable, could be considered a redeployment target if its shareholdings were widely dispersed and if it were in a diverse group of industries and markets. In fact, it didn't have to be a very good company.

With confidence flowing, Ling next set out to hunt some real game: Allis Chalmers Manufacturing Co., one of America's largest heavy machinery companies. Allis Chalmers was a venerable Milwaukee company, part of the traditional American corporate establishment, but it was ailing underneath and not at all well managed. Ling offered $55 per share to the board and said he would proceed only with its approval. Allis scurried but could only come up with a next-best offer from General Dynamics of $32.50. Ling didn't want to fight the establishment, however, so he withdrew his offer. The Allis Chalmers stockholders didn't seem to mind, though the arbitrageurs and gun-slingers among them surely did.

Ling's next move was to acquire a Texas company that he knew well, Greatamerica, an owner of insurance companies, Braniff Airlines, First Western Bank and Trust Co., National Car Rental Co., and some real estate developments. This group of companies cost LTV about $500 million in debt. Later in 1967, he, too, made a pass at American Broadcasting, which was rejected.

Ling was aware that by 1968, the word *conglomerate* was becoming a dirty one in all of the uppermost business circles in which he deeply wanted to be included. Before the effort with Allis Chalmers, he had decided not to make any more unfriendly offers and indeed would bend over backward to ingratiate himself with future targets to ensure their friendly acceptance of his offers.

The next target was, unbelievable as it seems today, Jones & Laughlin Steel Company. LTV's board, thoroughly tamed by now, seemed to have no objection to an offer of $85 per share for 63 percent of J & L, which would cost $425 million in cash and which would be deposited into a voting trust controlled by J & L executives for three years. The market price of J & L at the time was about $50 per share, so the tendering shareholders would receive a premium over the market of about 62 percent for their shares. The cash tender offer would be the largest ever made.

The J & L offer was extremely generous and accordingly it was quickly accepted, in a suitably friendly way, by the upper-crust J & L board members from the top of Pittsburgh society. Ling was delighted.

So was the Street. The deep-thinking firm of *Wunderkinder* Donaldson, Lufkin & Jenrette put out an "action recommendation" to its clients to purchase the stock, then selling at 120. So did other firms. The stock then went to 135 briefly.

J & L, however, was an old, tired, integrated steel company being creamed by imports and needing to downsize its operations substantially. The integration of its works made dividing it into redeployable pieces very difficult. And, having given up control to the voting trust, J & L didn't have to do anything that Ling wanted, good or bad, for three years. Meanwhile, the cash part of the deal had to be financed, just after the company had taken on $500 million of debt to take in Greatamerica. It was the beginning of the end.

The one outfit that appeared not to like the deal at all was the Justice Department, which filed an antitrust suit seeking the forced divestiture of J & L that took several years to settle. This was the first major action by the government against conglomerates. The rationale for the Justice Department's suit was that the acquisition would cause LTV to become so large and powerful that it had the "potential" to control markets in restraint of trade. Bigness per se was to be suitable grounds for denial; similar suits would be brought against other conglomerate acquisitions, notably the ITT takeover of Hartford Insurance.

Ling found himself trapped but didn't want to acknowledge it. On one side, the government's case had to be fought. He believed the suit was wrong and unfair, and he was unwilling to back away from the deal that he had found so satisfying (for its bigness, and its entrée to business' top echelons) and promising. On the other side, he had to produce some fast financial footwork to "redeploy" Greatamerica and J & L assets so as to reduce the debt load, which was more than his present operations could service. But, the J & L assets were tied up, both through the voting trust and by the government suit. The less flexibility he had with J & L the less he had with

Greatamerica, whose assets now had to be sold quickly to raise cash.

In 1968 the conglomerates in general were starting to lose some of their magic with Wall Street. After Litton announced its lower quarterly earnings, all of the conglomerate stocks dropped. LTV recovered nicely after the J & L deal was announced but started to drop again in the second half of the year. J & L's earnings proved to be very disappointing; the Greatamerica redeployment was too. In early 1969, LTV announced that its consolidated earnings for the full year 1968 would be down, relative to the preceding year, for the first time since 1963. The stock dropped, and dropped, settling at about $65 at the end of February. Late in the year it would be below $25.

Ling was not to survive at LTV. Too many of his fellow board members were being squeezed by the decline in the value of LTV securities, and in the end a palace revolt occurred that forced Ling out in 1970. The stock was then $16; it had been as high as $170 only a few years earlier. New management would spend the next several years trying to get out from under the huge rock that J & L turned out to be and to deconglomerate the company. But nobody there will ever forget James J. Ling.[8]

The whole of the soaring sixties market lasted until late in 1972; however, the years after 1968 included the period when the soarers come suddenly down to earth, the less happy part. The year in which the first man walked on the moon, 1969, was a terrible one for the market. The DJII dropped from around 1000 to nearly 750, then after a brief recovery down to 630 in mid-1970. Subsequently it returned to around 1000 by the end of 1972, not to exceed that level for a decade. In 1970 the Penn Central Railroad, itself a product of a "synergistic" merger, collapsed and declared bankruptcy, nearly causing a national banking crisis. In 1971 the gold standard was abandoned by the United States, which thus unilaterally moved the world to floating exchange rates, about which much anxiety existed. Inflation was rising, money was tighter, and markets tougher, but deals went on, though it was getting much more difficult to believe in growth-stock scenarios. What soarers there were left crashed in the great bear market of 1973 and 1974 with its sudden oil price rises, inflation exceeding 10 percent, failure of the Franklin National Bank—then the biggest in history—and the Watergate scandals and subsequent resignation of President Nixon. In the bear market of those days many of the gunslingers would be shot down and carried out, and the conglomerates would drop out of sight, until the time came to take them apart again. But the sinking market snuffed out the third great merger wave and bull market of the twentieth century, just as their predecessors had been killed by the panic of 1907 and the great crash of 1929.

What the Ledger Brings Forward

At the end of every accounting period the books are closed and what remains in each account is brought forward to open the books for the next period. In closing our books on the sixties, we bring forward lessons and experiences from the past—all the way back to the turn of the century, and to Walter Bagehot's period even before. Each period is unique, of course, and shaped by events in its own time, yet lessons from other periods still apply, if only one is able to find out or remember what they are.

Merger waves and bull markets seem to go together, in a mutually enhancing way. They tend to last for many years, all told—from buildup to die-out—not just the three or four years that economists pick out as their peaks. Apart from each other, the two seem to require some additional stimulation from either a need for some form of industrial reorganization, which occurs periodically, or some change in government regulatory policy, or both.

However dominant of the financial scene at the time merger waves and bull markets have been, they have never involved more than a relatively modest amount of the GNP, even at their peaks (about 7 percent, for example, for the peak year in the 1980s boom).

Each successive boom, however, has deepened the market for

the sale of companies. The boom of the sixties was quickly resurrected in the latter seventies and eighties, and even during its off years thousands of deals were made, many involving privately owned companies looking for a buyer. Today, as a result, there is a highly liquid "merger market" with its own price structure, rules, and accessibility, like all other markets.

The presence or absence of government policies concerning both mergers and securities markets appears to make a considerable difference. The trust and corporate merger boom from 1882 to 1906 was affected, first by no policies regarding business concentrations at all; then by restrictions only on cartels, not on mergers; then finally on excessive concentrations in whatever corporate form. In the 1920s the acquisitions of regulated utilities were so plentiful because they were permissible as other large concentrations were not after the bust-ups in 1911. Also there were few restrictions on the brand-new investment trusts that bought all the pyramided paper.

In the sixties, the antitrust guardians were on full alert, ready to pounce on any significant concentration, vertical or horizontal, that industry might produce. Only acquisitions of dissimilar businesses were possible; so that is what occurred. As conglomerate transactions became larger and more troublesome, the government tried to rule them out, too. And through their LTV/J & L and ITT/ Hartford Insurance lawsuits, the Justice Department was moving to prevent any large deal that *might* lead to excess market control through sheer corporate size, not through concentration of actual market share. Many conglomerators complained that the Republicans in office, whom they all supported philosophically, were overtly favoring (by protecting) establishment businessmen over newcomers like themselves. Then government decontrol became fashionable under President Carter, and when President Reagan almost totally abandoned antitrust enforcement, no one seemed to notice.

Both antitrust and securities laws, however, lag the times. They are changed after the fact, and usually not so effectively that clever lawyers can't find ways to do what they want while abiding by all the laws. Even when the laws change substantially, things still get done.

Wall Streeters often say that the stock market oscillates between two fixed points, total fear and total greed. Some of their more exacting colleagues might elaborate by adding, "fear being expressed by panic selling, greed by mindless optimism. And there is also a dreadful dead center in the spectrum in which nobody does anything; such times can be just as bad for us."

Nowadays, most of our corporations and institutional investors are run by professional managers, not start-up entrepreneurs as in the past. Professional managers, alas, however well trained by modern business and law schools, are often careful folk. They try to avoid or minimize risk, not to seek it out. However, every so often a new business fad or investment vehicle comes along and goes through the roof. These investors invariably participate, not wanting to appear to have missed out. For a time, it all works out well. Impressed with the only results available, that is, those compiled over too short a time, the investors label the performers as stars, even demigods, though usually they are not. The Greeks have warned us about what happens to demigods such as these—most will ultimately be severely humbled, if not totally destroyed. This happened to many of the characters of the sixties—gunslingers, conglomerators, hedge fund operators, and others. It has since happened to Real Estate Investment Trust operators, S & L entrepreneurs, Collateralized Mortgage Obligation originators, and junk bond investors, and has already begun to catch up with some of the most celebrated leveraged buy-outs. Fads may be based on good ideas, but they don't last when they attract too many emulators.

In the sixties, management's job was to produce growth, even if the results could only be achieved by acquiring, faster and faster, increasingly useless, low-grade assets with no staying power. If a fund manager's job then was to "beat the market," quarter to quarter, then the only way he could hope to do so was by buying the securities that the acquirers put out.

Both kinds of managers suffer the burden of having to perform in this way and of being limited by the kind of market they are in. In a rising market, a fund manager can shovel in the coal, maximizing his exposure to it, and look good; but when the market turns he finds himself maximally exposed to losses, not gains.

One senior Wall Streeter I know, who is a director of several corporations and often appointed to the committee supervising the pension funds, says, "Every time we look at the performance of the fund managers, once a year or so, I always say fire the one that's done the best. He's almost certainly not going to repeat the performance and he's probably too stretched out in this particular market to survive a change in sea conditions." Usually, however, his advice is not taken seriously.

Still, it is these performance-oriented professional corporate and investment managers who have given us our most valuable laboratory experiments in finance. Many of the most brilliant of the real geniuses, however, perished in the flames of an experiment gone wrong: Durant, Insull, the investment trust men of the twenties, the gunslingers, Ling.

But their experiments have been very instructive: experiments in corporate leverage, in the added value derived from putting things together, in the added value derived from taking them apart, in the management of a company's balance sheet by redeploying its assets, through exchange offers of Chinese money.

These have been lessons in financial engineering, that marvelous ability to get the maximum performance out of a fixed amount of assets: like learning how to make a sailboat go faster by repositioning its sails or changing its course slightly, or, if these don't work well enough, by changing the parts of the boat or the equipment utilized on board.

The eighties, as performance-oriented a time as any other, put all of these engineering lessons to work. They were also a time of financial sophistication and of the fine-tuning and perfecting of some of the experiments of the past. And the eighties hosted many new market experiments of their own. Some of the most successful of these, such as leveraged buyouts and high-yield bonds, were also among the most controversial.

In fact, they probably were just as controversial as the big mergers and their tycoon bankers at the turn of the century, the pyramids and trusts of the twenties, and the gunslingers and conglomerates of the sixties.

Success in finance is almost always controversial.

II

THE GREAT BUYOUT BOOM OF THE EIGHTIES

4

THE MERGER WARS

"It's just plain greed," she said firmly, "and it's ruining the whole country."

My friend Ruth was giving a dinner party at her home, during the time of the RJR-Nabisco transaction. She was speaking to me as we were walking into her dining room to take our places at one of several attractive tables she had set up. A few minutes earlier, she had asked me what was going to happen in the Nabisco situation.

"My husband [a prominent lawyer in the state] does some business with Nabisco, and we know several people in the company quite well. What's going to happen to them?" she asked. I said it was still the early stages in the deal and impossible to predict the outcome.

"Except you can be sure of one thing," she responded. "A great American company is going to get all torn apart, no matter who wins, and a lot of nice people are going to be out of work, their families disrupted, with who knows what prospects for reemployment. And why? To introduce a new laborsaving technology? To close down inefficient plants? No. The whole thing is just to make a small number of corporate executives and their investment bankers a lot richer. No other good comes out of it. It's all just because of greed!"

I had reached my place. She was sitting at another table but had not gone over to it. The others were sitting down. She waved me down, too.

I noted that there were many factors at work motivating the large acquisitions and leveraged buyouts that were then taking place. "It's all rather complex," I added, reassuringly.

"Acquisitions I guess I can understand," she continued, "but these leveraged buyouts: what good do they do? Breaking up companies for no purpose just so a lot of guys on Wall Street can make a lot more money than they already have.

"It's disgusting, but what's worse is that all our kids want to do nowadays is get their little snouts in the trough too."

Everyone was starting on the first course. Ruth was still intent. The subject was important to her. It worried and upset her.

"Is that really what we want our best and brightest to be doing, getting rich off LBOs that don't do anybody any good? Who's working on making this country competitive again, anyway?

"It's crazy. It makes no sense at all. And it's all you Wall Street people that are making it happen."

Then she smiled and turned to take up her place, adding, "See what you can do about it."

The merger boom of the 1980s was a dramatic and highly visible one. Between 1982 and 1988, more than ten thousand transactions were completed within the United States alone, aggregating over $1 trillion of capitalization. Another thirty-five hundred international transactions, totaling $500 billion, also occurred during this period. This boom differed from those that preceded it in several ways. One was the extent to which same-industry mergers occurred in the oil and gas, foods, drugs, finance, and numerous other industries—such concentrations had not been allowed since the early days of antitrust enforcement at the beginning of the century. Another was in the extent to which transactions included divestitures of corporate subsidiaries and divisions: some companies would buy others, often very large ones, then pare down again by selling off parts of either their original company or the newly acquired one. Finally, the eighties were different from earlier booms because of newly developed, sophisticated financing techniques that permitted players whose ambitions were greater than their bankbooks to enter the fray. The key buzz words of the 1980s came to be *restructuring* and *going back to basics* by *focusing on core businesses*, frequently through the employment of *leveraged recapitalizations*.

The eighties were distinctive in the number of studies of mergers and acquisitions conducted by academics and regulators to attempt to determine whether or not they "worked," that is, whether evidence could be found to establish whether companies were better off having acquired others or being restructured than they would have been if they had not. There were lots of data for the studies and powerful computers to sort them out. Neither had been available to the same extent in earlier booms, so for the first time we were to get the word: Were mergers good or bad?

For the most part all the studies agreed that mergers benefited the stockholders of companies that were acquired. They received a big premium for giving up control, 30 to 50 percent according to Professor Michael Jensen, a Harvard Business School expert on mergers, a premium that progressively increased as additional competitors came in to join the bidding. Most also agree that the process of maximizing the value of a target company has been made more efficient by the various tactics and stratagems employed to fend off raiders. Indeed the cost of defense often proves to be a very good investment for the defending shareholders.

The studies also seem to agree that finding the value added in the transactions for the acquiring company is difficult. In fact, though some early studies showed value increases for shareholders of acquiring companies based on the difference in their share prices in the period beginning before the deal was announced and ending after it was completed, these increases rarely exceeded 4 percent, and in more recent years rarely exceeded 0 percent. Jensen and Richard Ruback also looked at the performances of acquirers in terms of stock price differentials over a full year after the transaction and found "post-outcome negative abnormal returns," or worse results than expected. The British economists Julian Franks and Robert Harris found similar results in a study of 1800 British acquisitions from 1955 to 1985. A different sort of study by David Ravenscroft and Frederick Scherer, which aimed its attention at the changed profitability of particular lines of business, concluded that mergers were not on the whole successful because the "merger-makers suffered from massive hubris" and "seriously overestimated their ability to integrate, motivate, and effectively control the companies they acquired." One further study by two senior economists at the SEC concluded that after poorly thought-out acquisition strategies bidders ultimately became targets themselves. "In part," they argue, "the proliferation of hostile takeovers in the mid-1980s had its genesis in the failed acquisition strategies of many large corporations."[1]

These studies are helpful in providing a better understanding of the overall effects of a great merger boom and in this context shed light on public-policy issues that derive from the boom. However, they suffer from a serious defect that limits their usefulness. Scholars, of course, want their studies to be academically and statistically sound, and this they cannot be if they rely too much on individual cases, what they call empirical, or anecdotal, evidence. They prefer to take all the deals they can get data for, strip them into mathematical parts, and grind out conclusions based on the averages (and the standard deviations) of their calculations. This process tends to lump smart acquisitions in with stupid ones, and often to treat all kinds of different financing techniques in the same way. In the end, it is true that a lot of acquisitions diminish, rather than increase, the wealth of the acquiring shareholders, who must sit quietly by as their highly self-confident managers press ahead with one ambitious deal after another, but some do produce the results intended. The important point is that every attempted acquisition is launched with the full confidence and support of the company's supposedly most knowledgeable representatives, its management and board of directors. Their aim is to invest the company's excess cash or credit capacity in a new venture that will increase shareholder wealth in the future—even the distant future. Management's job is after all the enhancement of shareholder wealth, which for many companies requires a whole lot more than just sitting there. Whatever the result of the acquisitions of other companies, all start with the same motivation—and probably the same degree of confidence—to do right by their stockholders. In a highly liquid market with minimal government interference, many will adopt acquisition strategies. They do not believe that they will fail where others have. Obviously some do fail, at least in terms of how the scholars measure success or failure. Their method is to compare the acquirer's stock prices over relatively short periods of time, usually less than a year, which may be the most practical method of measurement, if not the most useful. One result of using this method of measuring success or failure is that those that succeed after a few years of effort are counted as failures instead and they bring down the averages. But if it is true, nevertheless, that those that fail are rewarded by a takeover themselves, maybe the premium those shareholders get should be averaged in with rest of the results.

The Boom in Buyouts

Many of the transactions in the 1980s were "leveraged buyouts," in which a group of financial entrepreneurs, often in competition with other bidders, succeeded in acquiring a company through an auction process—and thus unavoidably for a full price—the funding for which was almost completely provided for with borrowed money. In such transactions the large amounts of debt required to finance the initial transaction usually would be provided, first from a group of banks, then by the sale of low-grade, high-yield "junk bonds," an important financial innovation of the times. Proceeds from the sale of the junk bonds, together with the sale of parts of the company, would reduce the banks' exposure to more reasonable levels. What survived of the acquired company would then be run to maximize the amount of cash generated by the business. The outstanding debt would be further reduced by the application of excess cash flow, and in a few years the company would go public again, markets permitting, enabling their sponsors to cash in on their vested interest.

There was plenty of money available from the banks and in the capital markets to finance these transactions, but as competition for them increased, the acquisition prices paid for successive deals rose to levels that many players considered too high. Large acquisitions with offering prices representing control premiums averaging 40 percent or so above market prices became common by 1986. The premiums increased well above this level in 1987 and 1988. On the other hand, LBO operators were no longer playing just with their own money: they were now managing large quantities of money entrusted to them by others, by investors who (as in the 1920s) eagerly sought out Wall Street's most skilled and knowledgeable investors to let them into the game.

One contribution made by the LBO movement, however, was to increase the number of participants who could become involved when a particular company had become the target of an offer. Soon it became necessary for corporate bidders when planning moves and setting initial offering prices for takeovers to consider the possibility that an offer would draw out previously unknown LBO bidders. A number of large deals, Philip Morris's acquisitions of General Foods and Kraft, for example, might have been accomplished at lower prices had not Philip Morris known that an LBO group would almost certainly have emerged at any price less than a fully competitive one, despite the large size of the transactions (Kraft was acquired for $11 billion in 1988). In the latter years of the eighties virtually every deal, friendly or unfriendly, generated at least three or four LBO workups. The original bidder had to know what a competing LBO competitor could pay for the target. The target had to know that, too, in case it decided to encourage one or more such bidders or to undertake a management-led self-restructuring. Other, unseen, competitors did their own calculations, so did banks, arbitrageurs, securities analysts, and institutional investors. The simple possibility of an LBO ensured that market forces were in effect, no matter what kind of deal was originally put forward, whether board-endorsed or not. These forces would spring into effect immediately upon the announcement of any kind of takeover attempt, thus limiting management's ability to get themselves out of play but nonetheless delighting the target company's shareholders.

Landmark of the Eighties

The landmark transaction of the period was the leveraged buyout of RJR-Nabisco Corp. by an investor group organized by Kohlberg, Kravis, & Roberts (KKR) in late 1988 for $24.7 billion. This was the largest corporate reorganization ever completed and one of the nastiest.

In October 1988, RJR-Nabisco's chairman F. Ross Johnson suddenly announced to his board of directors that he had tried everything he could since becoming chief executive two years earlier to boost the stock price of the company without much success. The market, dominated by institutions looking for something else, just wasn't responding to his efforts. No matter how well the foods and other brands did, the market still valued them as tobacco company assets. Therefore, he thought it best if he and a group of colleagues, including the investment bankers Shearson Lehman Hutton, put together a bid for the company at $75 per share. The stock had previously been trading at $55, so the offer represented a 36 percent premium. "After all," said Johnson, "the shareholders already know it's a lot goddamn harder to launch a new cigarette than to go out and borrow money at the bank."

The Nabisco board, surprised by this development, announced Johnson's proposal to the public and appointed a special committee of its nonmanagement directors, which promptly hired its own legal and financial advisers, to consider the proposal and any alternatives. Though it had not previously had any intention of doing so, the board's actions "put the company in play."

A few days later an alternative was presented: KKR, which also had discussed an LBO with Johnson within the last couple of years and was up-to-date on the company, offered to pay $90 per share in cash for 87 percent of the Nabisco shares. The special committee then solicited bids from any other interested party, and a few tentative proposals came forward. The committee said it was also considering certain self-recapitalization and restructuring moves. It then asked for all final and highest bids to be submitted by November 18. On that day three bids were received: from KKR, the Johnson group, and a group organized by First Boston Corp. A group of industrial corporations organized by Forstmann Little, another buyout firm, and advised by Goldman Sachs joined together for the purpose of bidding but in the end chose not to. The bids were all quite different; the Johnson group valued its bid at $100 in cash and securities, the highest of the three. The special committee met often with each group to clarify features of the bids, then decided—to ask each to bid again.

The last and final bids received from the two sides were effectively tied—the Johnson group's bid had a face value of $112 per share, but it had to be discounted because the terms of some of the securities offered in the package were inferior to the securities offered in the KKR group's package valued at $109 per share. Felix Rohatyn of Lazard Frères, senior adviser to the nonmanagement directors, explained to them after an all-night effort to value the two bids:

> Both bids are between 108 and 109. When you get that close, and you are dealing with securities in amounts that have never been dealt with before, in my business judgment, these offers are essentially equivalent. They are both fair from a financial point of view. They are close enough that we can't tell you one is clearly superior to the other.

To help the board make its decision, Rohatyn pointed out a number of differences between the two bids. KKR had promised to leave 25 percent of the stock in shareholder's hands; management offered only 15 percent. KKR promised to sell only part of Nabisco, Johnson would sell it all. He was also inflexible on guaranteeing certain employee benefits, such as moving expenses. Johnson wanted these matters to be negotiable with the ultimate buyers of businesses to be sold.

The directors made their decision based on their assessment of the intangibles, by no means the least of which was the outraged reaction of the press to the "greed" of the Johnson group, which had deeply colored general public opinion of the deal. The board was certainly leery of being seen as a captive of Johnson, whose many favors to the outside directors had been fully reported at some embarrassment to them.[2]

Henry Kravis explained his view of the outcome in an interview in *Fortune* (January 2, 1989):

> I think Ross Johnson made a number of mistakes. When he made his first offer, a management buyout at $75 a share, my first reaction was to think that RJR was in play—and at a price substantially lower than its real value. Was he actually putting up a For Sale sign on the company? Or did he really want to own it? If the latter, the one thing we were very certain of was that the management group was stealing the company.

The accepted bid was nearly double the stock price of RJR-Nabisco before the original Johnson proposal. The whole deal had been put together and concluded in less than three months.

It was stunning. Such a large deal, nearly $25 billion, and done so quickly. There was a great deal of fierce competition between the groups, and personal animosities were often evident. Ross Johnson, who had become CEO of RJR-Nabisco only in 1987, acted at times as if the board would do whatever he wanted, at other times as if he were the single most important party to the transaction and without him any other bidder would be at a serious disadvantage. KKR offered at one point to allow Johnson to join their group, but he rejected this offer.

Johnson knew that no other large LBO had been done without management on board and well taken care of. After all, management not only could point to some success at having already run the company, which would be an important comfort to the lenders; it also had the benefit of inside knowledge of the company to use in shaping its bidding strategy—it would know just how much cash could be squeezed out of operations to service debt. Accordingly, Johnson believed that he could call his own shots in the deal. He could dictate the terms, and the investment bankers would have to take it or leave it.

Several bankers had proposed an LBO to Johnson, though he had been noncommittal until late in 1988. Shearson Lehman Hutton and Drexel Burnham Lambert seemed to be the most aggressive. Each firm was willing to follow Johnson's lead into the deal, or at least they told him they were.

Finally, Shearson was picked, and Johnson submitted his version of a management agreement, which he claimed was not negotiable. Shearson (joined later by Salomon Brothers) would put up about $3 billion in equity, but Johnson and six management colleagues were to get 8.5 percent of the equity, complete with a tax-compensated loan from Shearson to pay for it. There were several earnings performance bogeys to be met, which if management met them all, would push the group's stake up to 18.5 percent. The management package might be worth as much as $2.5 to $3 billion over the coming five years. In the meantime, the group would share annual income of $100 million. Johnson would also receive a veto and control over the board, unlike any major LBO ever signed. On the whole, the management agreement was a fantastic illusion, something Johnson insisted on while he was negotiating with Peter Cohen, Shearson's chief executive, but which would fade away quickly once the buyout offer had been announced.

Cohen badly wanted to manage the transaction, as any investment banker at the time would have wanted to do. It was the sort of high-quality transaction on which reputations could be built, which would attract many future deals, and would be enormously profitable. However, if Cohen had sat down with Johnson in the old-fashioned way and said, "Look, Ross, there's no way the people putting up the money for this deal can let you take so much out of it—you'll have to do it our way, or get someone else," he knew what the answer would be. Maybe Johnson would hear the same story at the next place, but then he'd be talking to somebody else, not Shearson. So Cohen said, "Fine, Ross," only he held out that the agreement would have to be renegotiated if their group had to bid more than $75 a share, their opening shot, as he thought it quite likely they would.

Johnson, thinking $75 was a full price that would be hard enough to raise the money for, was satisfied. Thus he could argue that he had extracted an unusually favorable deal for the management group (therefore confirming his good judgment in selecting Shearson to run the deal and binding him to the firm). Cohen could equally argue (as indeed he did when Salomon challenged him on the agreement) that it was all meaningless: once the company was in play, Johnson would have to go along with whatever Shearson and Salomon wanted to do; if higher bids had to be made, they would be paid for by squeezing Johnson's deal. If no one else appeared on the scene, there was enough juice in the relatively low $75 price for the investors to pay Johnson what he wanted and still have a lot left over. By the time of the final bidding the management group's share interest (now forced by adverse publicity to be spread over a greatly expanded group of managers) was down to 4 percent from the original 8.5 percent.[3]

It wasn't long after the announcement of the buyout before Johnson's management deal leaked to the press and became the focus of attention, which then grew into a greed-bashing hysteria. *Time* magazine ran Johnson's picture on a cover announcing a story about greed in America. According to *Time* (December 5, 1988):

> Seldom since the age of the 19th-century robber barons has corporate behavior been so open to question. The battle for RJR-Nabisco seems to have crossed an invisible line that separates reasonable conduct from anarchy.

Time never did make clear how "anarchy" was to fit into the transaction, just as the press reporting in J. P. Morgan's day were unclear about why "rioting in the streets" should follow the U.S. Steel deal, but what was clear was the strong adverse reaction by the press to the deal and to Johnson himself. According to Henry Kravis, "Ross Johnson turned out to be the best thing we had going for us because of all the adverse publicity he was collecting."

The transaction would also generate $700 million in fees to bankers and lawyers involved in the transaction, 2.8 percent of its total value. Some of these fees were for legal and financial advice in structuring and negotiating the deal, but most were for arranging and providing commitments for the substantial amount of financing that was needed. It was a difficult and complicated transaction and the technical advice was necessary—the financial engineering had to be exact for the highest bidder to have any chance of making money on the deal—and organizing financing of almost $25 billion in very short order was a large and crucially important task that only the most experienced banks could handle.

In the end the RJR-Nabisco shareholders received a large premium on the value of their holdings and retained a small carried interest in the new company. Capital gains to the prebuyout shareholders would exceed $13.3 billion.

The KKR group would have the opportunity to restructure the company, which, though founded in 1875 by an itinerant goods trader, had only been put together in its present form in 1985 when R. J. Reynolds Tobacco Co. acquired Nabisco Brands (itself the result of a 1981 merger of Nabisco and Standard Brands) to become the nineteenth ranking company on the Fortune 500 list with 1988 sales of $16.6 billion. It was a very profitable corporation, with a 1988 expected operating cash flow of about $3.5 billion. The tobacco business generated a substantial surplus cash flow with which to service debt, and the hundreds of branded food products could be sold off for high prices as part of the restructuring that would follow the acquisition.

The KKR group, however, had to stretch its bid to the group's outermost limit in order to win. After the tender offer and subsequent merger had been completed, the new company (that is, RJR-Nabisco after KKR had financed its acquisition) would have $23 billion of interest-bearing debt outstanding, and only $7.8 billion of equity and equitylike securities holding it up. Total debt would account for 80 percent of capitalization, and annual interest costs would only just be covered by annual cash flow.

The beauty of the transaction lay in its capitalization structure. There were three tiers, each designed to appeal to the investment interests of particular types of investors.

Banks would supply the largest piece of the financing, a commitment of nearly $15 billion, of which 65 percent was provided by Japanese, European, and Canadian banks. The bank facility would be "senior" debt and have first claim on the assets of the company in the event of a bankruptcy. In addition to the banks' debt, the existing debt of RJR-Nabisco that was outstanding before the acquisition, about $5 billion, would be included in this senior tier for a total of $17.5 billion. Before the acquisition, the book value of all of the company's assets was slightly in excess of this amount, and the market value was very much higher. In other words, taking a leaf from the railroad reorganizations of the 1890s, the amount of debt (senior debt in this case) to be used would be set at the amount that would have full, but not generous, asset backing and reasonable prospects for the payment of all debt-service costs out of the company's existing stable operating profits. After the expected issuance of "permanent" bonds to replace the short-term notes and "bridge loan" facilities (offered from two investment banks) to finance the tender offer, and some immediate sales of assets, bank debt was expected to be reduced to less than half of the total capitalization of the company. The bank loans would have a six-year life and be subject to rapid mandatory repayment. The bank facilities were designed to provide substantially more asset and cash-flow coverage to the banks than most leveraged buyouts, and the interest rates payable on the loans, and the fees paid to the banks for providing their commitments, would be somewhat higher than what was normally received in large LBO transactions. The banks would also share arrangement fees of $380 million.

The bank debt, however, was thought to be illiquid. There were restrictions on selling down participations in the loan to other banks, not that there were very many banks in the entire world that had not already been offered a piece of the deal at the outset. The liquidity consideration, and the negative publicity that the deal was attracting, dissuaded many banks from participating.

The next tier in the capital structure was $5 billion of "subordinated debt," which was junior to and ranked behind the senior debt. The subordinated debt was provided by the sale of several issues of long-term, high-yield, noninvestment-grade "junk bonds" to the market (in the largest such offering ever done). This tier was roughly equivalent to the preferred stock used in the nineteenth-century deals, that is, the middle tier of the capital structure. The subordinated bonds were sold to pension funds, insurance companies, mutual funds, and savings and loan companies all across the country, and some were sold abroad. They, too, offered generous interest rates, approximately 5 to 6 percent more than U.S. Treasury securities at the time they were issued.

The final tier consisted of an even more junior ranking level of debt (provided by KKR), two types of "payment-in-kind" (PIK) securities, and common stock, the latter of which involved less than $2 billion, or less than 8 percent of the total capitalization of the company. The PIK securities, one a convertible debenture, the other a preferred stock, paid interest and dividends not in cash but in more of the same kind of securities for several years. Like the common stock tier in the railroad deals, these securities were designed to have very little value at the outset but possibly substantial value later on. Investors in this tier could make money only if future operations succeeded, either through growth or through sale of properties at high prices and/or further recapitalizations at more favorable financial terms.

Altogether the KKR group invested less than $2.5 billion in the transaction, approximately a tenth of its market value. And the $2.5 billion was not KKR's own money; it came from investment funds managed by KKR, whose investors were state and corporate pension funds, college endowments, insurance companies, banks, and savings institutions, most of which had invested in other KKR deals and done very well. These investors would be taking the financial risk of the transaction. In the final analysis, Henry Kravis and George Roberts (Jerry Kohlberg was no longer associated with the firm) had put up virtually none of their own money but had personally secured control of one of the largest and most profitable companies in America in a little over three weeks. From control of such a company, the opportunity for very substantial fees and equity participation profits would be very considerable. J. P. Morgan would have been impressed.

Ross Johnson and his losing group of managers did not really lose very much. Each of them walked away quite wealthy because of shareownership and severance arrangements—Johnson's golden parachute alone was worth $53 million—though nowhere near as wealthy as they might have been had their group won. Apart from the departing Johnson group, most of the management of the company would remain. Severe cuts in manning levels did not follow the buyout, though some businesses were sold and most staff functions were cut back rather sharply. A large number of the old-time employees were shareholders and enjoyed their windfall like everyone else.

Ruth's friends, having survived two traumatic acquisitions before the company was sold to KKR (the sale of Standard Brands to Nabisco and of Nabisco to RJR), might very well be better off being sold to yet another company that badly wanted to keep them.

Even the IRS ended up ahead on the deal: what it would lose in income tax payments from KKR (which would have substantial tax deductions on incremental interest charges) would be more than made up by capital-gains taxes and the increased taxable income of LBO creditors and advisers.[4]

The main losers in the deal were the preacquisition RJR-Nabisco bondholders who found the paper they owned substantially downgraded in the market. The outstanding RJR-Nabisco bonds, rated A ("investment grade") by the rating agencies, were suddenly downgraded after the original announcement of the LBO to BB (a "below investment grade," or junk bond, rating), thus becoming in the terms of the market "fallen angels." The downgrading caused the market price of the existing bonds to drop about 15 percent, and institutional investors in these bonds suffered an unrealized loss of about $340 million.[5] This loss so incensed one bond investor, Metropolitan Life, which had already lost millions on other fallen angels, that it sued RJR for breach of promise; the suit was subsequently dismissed. Some of the bondholders, however, had hedged themselves against downgrading by takeover by also investing in RJR shares. For these bondholders what was lost on the bonds was more than fully made up from the capital gains received on the stock.

In dining rooms all over America, however, people like Ruth were trying to take it in. It was such a large amount of money, so much wheeling and dealing. People were talking about earning hundreds of millions, even billions, from their equity positions or from fees. Management had so many perks and special deals that shareholders were never told about. It all seemed to be totally out of line; such enormous amounts could only be "earned" by screwing other people, the other stockholders, the employees, and the residents of local communities, for example: the little people. They were also uncomfortable in appraising a financial transaction that didn't seem to do anything except rearrange things. Should people get paid so much money just for that? Jim Ling had called that kind of fast financial footwork "redeployment of assets," and though it worked for a while, in the end he brought LTV, then the country's fourteenth-largest company, down with it. Is all of this RJR stuff just another case, to quote Yogi Berra, of "déjà vu all over again"?

Folks were also asking whether all that money might have been better used for something else: investment in new technologies to keep up with the Japanese, for example, or reduction of the national debt, or shelters for the homeless, though how shareholders' wealth was to be transferred to such undertakings without confiscating it was not very clear.

And, unlike in Morgan's day, everything was on page one of the newspapers. The fees paid to the banks and investment bankers, the various payouts to the corporate executives, communications between the competitive parties and the target company, financing plans of the bidding groups, and every other detail of the transaction were a matter of public record. So, too, was every little snipe made by one side or the other, as rivalries were magnified by the press and refocused into terms familiar to regular watchers of the TV serial "Dallas." No transaction had ever been commented on so extensively by people not involved with it, almost always adversely.

Untrained readers following the story of the deal in the press might not understand many of the complex details, but they could tell that $3 billion of payments to RJR-Nabisco's chairman and a small group of executives was a lot. And it didn't seem right to them that the chairman and a few cohorts should have secretly plotted to put the company in play with a management buyout offer at a price far below what the KKR group, without the benefit of inside knowledge of the company, bid only a few days later. And the approximately $700 million paid out by management in fees seemed incredible. The public smelled a rip-off.

But that wasn't all. The public had some other worries.

For example, what about the banks? Already suffering from a decade of bad loans and continuing Latin American exposure, they were now going to lend as much as *$14.7 billion* to the winning KKR group so it could complete the deal. Americans had just been told of the extent to which the government would have to bail out the federally insured savings and loan industry (which most Americans thought were banks too), whose reckless lending practices would cost the taxpayer at least $300 billion over the next few years.

Not only that but there were reports of some large investment-banking firms' lending amounts in excess of their entire capital to LBO operators in the form of short-term "bridge loans," supposedly to be refinanced when the firms sold junk bonds for the LBO later on. The RJR-Nabisco deal alone would require $5 billion of junk bonds to be sold to replace such bridge financing.* What if the junk bonds couldn't be sold? What would happen to the investment banks then? Who would be called upon to bail *them* out?

And who bought all of these junk bonds? S & Ls, insurance

---

*Actually, in the RJR case, the $5 billion bridge loan offered by Merrill Lynch and Drexel Burnham was not drawn down because Drexel had substituted $5 billion of lower-cost Increasing Rate Notes, a new form of short-term junk notes that were successfully sold to the market.

companies, and pension funds, all supposedly fiduciary institutions, many of them regulated (if not guaranteed) by government agencies. So if a large LBO goes wrong, the repercussions could be felt from the banks, to the brokers, to the regulated institutions, and then could spread rapidly through the whole financial system right back to the taxpayer, just as in the S & L case.

"Exactly," said Ruth, "don't you think you're overdoing things, when you leverage the whole financial system up to the eyeballs so that a major collapse in one place can spread down the line, as it did in the thirties? Shouldn't something be done to protect the system before it is threatened with collapse? Are we so devoted to the spirit of free enterprise that in order to allow Henry Kravis and Ross Johnson to get even richer, we would expose the already very well stretched fabric of our financial system to the possibility of catastrophic failure?"

Finally, there was all this immorality in the financial field. Insider trading, S & L scandals galore, apparently countless violations of securities laws, and senior officers of distinguished firms being indicted and convicted for all kinds of fraud and market rigging. "America has had enough," claimed Robert Reich, a well known critic of free-market capitalism, in an article in the Sunday *New York Times Magazine*. "Even by the cynical standards of the 1980s, Wall Street is giving greed a bad name."

It is difficult to remember when greed had a good name. Or a time when controversial transactions were not said to be motivated by greed. There seems to be little question that when the rewards are large in a fully competitive free-market environment lots of people will cut corners in their efforts to capture them. Their misbehavior is an added cost to society, along with those other costs derived from excessive behavior that many observers have attributed to free markets. Many people began to wonder whether free markets were all that they had been cracked up to be during the Reagan era. The more we get to know them, they thought, the less we like what is dragged in with them. Many wondered whether the benefits of free markets were worth the cost. If so, was the government justified in further regulating the behavior of participants to improve the net result? Shouldn't regulations be tighter and enforcement tougher?

Ruth had simplified all of these concerns into three: was there too much greed; had the restructuring movement of the eighties become, after seven or eight years of unrestrained deal-making, more destructive than it was constructive; and had the extent of all the new financial activity finally reached the point where it simply didn't make sense?

Just Plain Greed?

Greed and avarice are the same thing. Defined as an excessive desire for money or power, avarice is one of the seven deadly sins. Laws against usury and upward mobility (in several religions and ancient societies) derive from a desire to avoid the sin of avarice. However, as Barbara Tuchman reminded us in her history of the fourteenth century, *A Distant Mirror*, medieval man rarely complied with such laws and rulings by the Church as it was totally contrary to his nature. Apparently, it still is.

Greedy figures in literature have always been objects of scorn, even if almost always portrayed with exaggeration: King Midas, the Merchant of Venice, Scrooge. In their cases there has been little doubt about just how warped and unlikable the greedy can be. Ambition for high office or power hasn't done much better, with role models such as Richard III, Robespierre, Hitler, and others like them.

But in real life, things aren't quite so black and white. Greed is "excessive" desire for money, or other things. Excessive relative to what, and according to whom? Are characters out of Horatio Alger, known for their hard work and righteous ambition, also, at the heart of it, greedy because their desire to "get ahead" exceeds that of others? Is a fiduciary trustee or a director of a public company trying to get the best deal for his shareholders greedy if he acts aggressively to negotiate the best possible price? How differently would any of the journalists reporting on the actions of Ross Johnson have acted in his situation? Greed lacks a common standard by which to measure it.

The Michael Douglas character in the movie *Wall Street*, Gordon Gekko, at one point in the film gave a speech titled "Greed Is Good," allegedly based on a similar episode in the real life of Ivan Boesky. What Gekko meant was that ambition and the desire to succeed (which in Wall Street means making money) were as powerful incentives as there are. If "greed" was wanting to succeed more than most other people, that was good! Most employers today would agree.

Henry Kravis, however, never thought to be lacking in ambition and desire to succeed, claims, "Greed really turns me off," meaning mainly that he cannot condone actions that are illegal (or only questionably legal) in pursuit of a business objective. Greed in this context is like cheating. Clever Henry figured out that the better public relations position was to be against greed, not for it. What is seen to be greedy and to attract volcanic reactions from the press, and what is not, is often just a matter of how it is presented.

Most people seem to feel that the process of pursuing an economic opportunity is not a dishonorable activity, as long as all the laws, that is, the rules of the game, are obeyed. Indeed, is it not an element of economic law that when an opportunity exists it will be exploited as naturally as apples fall to the earth when let loose from the tree? Not every opportunity will appeal to everyone, but those who are not attracted are simply replaced by others, like Walter Bagehot's New Men, who are. And not every opportunity will be pursued with equal grace and charm. There is a lot of room in life for people to behave obnoxiously while still operating within the law. We may not like such people enough to have them over to dinner, but we may do business with them, and even when we don't, we know that others will. We acknowledge that people like that have always been around and are probably no more plentiful today than at any other time.

Wall Streeters are used to accepting that successful business people are good at what they do because they care about making money, they don't mind haggling when they have to (some even like it) and they regard being tough in negotiations as a virtue. Bankers expect their clients to take the path that leads to the maximum value of the deal they are trying to do. No one is expected to leave anything on the table; everyone has fiduciary obligations to get the best possible value in every transaction. This value is usually determined by the point at which the other side walks away, not by formula written down for fair transactions.

Greed is a sin, not a crime. It is a temptation to do wrong, not the wrong itself. It is one of many temptations that affect humans. Being humans, we shall always find greed, and the other sins, among us. We can't as a society shake it off. But as far as anyone can tell, greed is no more or less present today than it ever was. It has been present during our other boom periods and during the slack ones, too. Those like Morgan, Carnegie, Rockefeller, and Ford who achieved great financial success in their own times were often referred to as greedy, yet none was ever accused of violating the laws of his day (admittedly skimpy), and each contributed millions to charities and left great and responsible corporations behind them.

However we address greed objectively, if such is possible, we are left with the fact that we can't get rid of it. But should we attribute to greed, an ever-present human condition, the role of a primary cause of the merger and LBO boom of the 1980s? This boom was not formed by greed any more than, or any less than, any other boom was.

Other factors had more influence.

Economic change was one: change that required restructuring. But was restructuring, on balance, good or bad for the economy? That is the big question.

Does Restructuring Really Do Any Good?

The money wars were fought throughout the eighties over this issue. On one side are the defenders, corporate managers who, now in their middle to late fifties, entered the business world in the Eisenhower years. Most of these are strong-minded men who have worked their way up to the top spots they hold through a series of management jobs in industry. Most are experts at managing a large semi-bureaucratic institution with a substantial culture of its own, in which to be selected as CEO one has to have at least some diplomatic skills and regard for company ways. Most also have an idea about what they want to accomplish during their years as chief, after which they expect to retire and turn the reins over to a successor. Few own more than a modest percentage of the total number of shares outstanding in their company, though usually most of what these CEOs do own is tied up in their company's stock.

For the most part these defenders are professional managers, who do things the way they have been trained to. Few among them are innovators, or radicals, or reformers. They are solid, dependable, conservative men whose deepest feelings involve the preservation and protection of their companies for the future. They are not inclined to propose to their directors actions that would bankrupt the company if they fail. Of course, they also try to be hard drivers who crack the whip to make sure the profits hold up and to ensure that the stockholders are happy, or anyway, happy enough.

The stockholders, however, are predominantly indifferent, performance-oriented institutional investors acting as agents for their clients, the true owners of the companies whose securities the institutions hold. The institutions thus act as "holders," not as "owners." They almost never debate decisions made by management. They are not on the board of directors and have no direct influence on management. They do not monitor management's performance closely enough to affect events or scream and yell when they aren't happy. Instead they just sell their stock, an action that management tends to regard as based on misunderstanding rather than disapproval of the company's strategies. They tend to sell into takeover bids to capture the gain without any regard for whether or not management has been doing a good job. This kind of indifference is very frustrating to managers who find themselves actually or potentially on the receiving end of a takeover. They feel there is virtually nothing they can do to win the kind of loyalty from their shareholders that they had enjoyed only a few years before.

Managers, however, are subject to very few restraints on actions they might take as managers. Institutional investors are passive monitors of managerial behavior at best. Also, in a market in which a large number of managers behave similarly, the choice open to the investors is a narrow one. Bankers are not a strong restraining influence either: most are eager to make loans or perform other services for the company, whose business has to be won in competition with other aggressive banks. It does not pay to be a scold in such situations. Investment bankers are today much less frequently represented on corporate boards of directors or as representatives of powerful absentee investors, in which cases their advice and judgment might be heeded as in Morgan's day. Their influence on clients has been reduced to the value of their ideas or opinions in an environment in which the fellow with the most useful opinion gets hired. The only real monitors of corporate management during the eighties were the board members whom management themselves had appointed. Frequently, these board members were well plied with perks and comforts and special compensation packages that kept them tame. Mostly such directors only start to think for themselves when a takeover situation comes along and their lawyers are telling them what to do.

One consequence of the continuing lack of restraining influence has been the increasing institutionalization management of large corporations. A barrier had developed between the ultimate owners of the business enterprise and its hired managers. The barrier, in some cases, prevented the owners of the business from realizing its fullest value or from performing in the most competitive ways possible. Conflicts would develop among management and owners over such vital issues as what should happen to excess funds that had built up in the enterprise. Should the enterprise be run to maximize profits in the short run, or should it make plans and investments to maximize long-term success? How much should the agents entrusted with management functions be compensated for their efforts, and how should such compensation arrangements be decided? How extensively should management be allowed to change the enterprise without seeking explicit consent of the owners? These conflicts between owners and managers became increasingly frustrating to all who had to deal with them. The most efficient way to resolve them was through a takeover struggle, in which shareholders could decide for themselves.

In opposition to management (and supposedly therefore on the side of shareowners) are those seeking to replace them by seizing control of the company. This number, of course, includes the management of other large corporations, which are seeking to make strategic moves of one kind or another. It also includes the New Men, who have little to lose but possibly much to gain in discovering situations where restructuring a company would create added value for its owners. These people are for the most part individuals who act for themselves and are unafraid of stepping on toes if that should be necessary to make their point: men like T. Boone Pickens, Carl Icahn, William Farley, and James Goldsmith. They may or may not be good managers; they have made their way in the world not by managing companies but by owning them (or at least seeking to) and structuring and restructuring them to their maximum advantage. Most of these men are self-made, egotistical characters who were totally unknown during the last merger boom. They are a group of fast risers, usually of humble origin, with great ambitions and a desire for success and attention. Farley, for example, who burst on the big-time scene only in 1985, is said to have contemplated a bid for the presidency of the United States. Most of these New Men will not last until the next cycle; indeed, many will be ruined by the collapse of companies they forged together during the wondrous days at the peak of the 1980s cycle.

They are well-to-do but not terribly rich. They do not have as much money to spend on acquisitions as large corporations have.

They are therefore highly dependent on their ability to borrow funds for their deals and generally willing to pay virtually any cost for enough chips to sit at the high-stakes tables. Many of them got their start with financing arranged by Michael Milken of Drexel Burnham, who found buyers for the high-yield, high-risk junk bonds they issued.

These people, the "raiders," are interested in buying into companies whose market value is significantly below what they think (or are willing to wager) that the value could be if a restructuring were accomplished.

In many companies values have become misaligned as a result of the many dramatic changes in the underlying economics of their businesses, competitive conditions, technology, and the cost and availability of finance during the past decade or so. Alan Greenspan, chairman of the Federal Reserve Board of Governors, attributes the bulk of the 1980s merger boom to market corrections of these many and substantial misalignments. Once the market makes the adjustments that it must and macroeconomic policies are implemented to stabilize the conditions in the economy that have created the misalignments, the merger boom, he says, will end.[6]

Other companies, of course, have misaligned themselves through ineffective management or unsuccessful acquisition or diversification programs. Often these have been older, more inertia-ridden companies that are unable or unwilling to take the steps necessary to effect the realignments that must be made or to correct mistakes of the past. Or as Carl Icahn has put it:

> The takeover boom is a treatment for a disease that is destroying American productivity: gross and widespread incompetent management. Takeovers are part of a free-market response, working to unseat corporate bureaucracies, control runaway costs and make America competitive again.[7]

Naturally the managements of companies said to fall into this category dispute all the charges made against them in this vein.

One close observer of this scene, Harvard professor Michael

Jensen, notes that takeover and restructuring premiums paid by acquirers in the current period average about 50 percent over the market value of the shares of the target company (before the takeover effort), as compared to premiums of 15 to 20 percent in the preceding merger wave. Thus, he says, "Managers have been able to destroy up to 30 percent of the value of the organizations they lead before facing serious threat of disturbance." Jensen has also estimated that acquisitions and LBOs created (perhaps he should have said restored) more than $400 billion of value for investors in the period from 1975 to 1986. But the greatest value, he adds, may actually be in the increases affected by managements of companies that have not been taken over but feared that they might be and acted accordingly.[8]

In any event, there have been many misaligned companies out there for opportunistic restructurers to pursue. Those seeking to restructure companies rely on two principal methods of doing so. First they deconglomerate the company: selling off separate businesses, divisions, or other properties so their true market values can be realized. Money liberated by such sales is then returned to the investors or used to reduce debt.

The second thing the restructurers do is to increase the amount of financial leverage used by the company to increase its return on investment. There are simple reasons for this. It increases the possible rewards for investment in the business enterprise by increasing the risk somewhat. Growth in the underlying enterprise, though welcome, is not necessary for an investment to be successful—it can be successful just by changing the risk-reward ratio. Also, borrowed money is tax-efficient: it is more effective to distribute excess cash to banks in the form of tax-deductible interest or to pay down high-cost debt than it is to give it to the stockholders as a taxable dividend.

Also, the restructurer, being an individual or a small group of investors, doesn't have much money of his own to use, so access to borrowed funds becomes necessary if sizable deals are to be done. Such restructurers are usually more accustomed to operating with larger amounts of borrowed money than the restructuree and are able to put it to better use. And, most important, large amounts of money have been made available to finance aggressive, entrepreneurial restructurings during the eighties, from banks and investors in junk securities.

A restructuring is not without its risks, however. The estimated values of the constituent parts may have been misjudged or may prove to be unobtainable as a result of a subsequent slump in market prices or because the new management team is unable to harvest the anticipated quantities of redeployable cash from the operating parts of the enterprise. A sharp rise in interest rates or a decline in the economy while the debt levels are still high could result in severe financial distress, maybe even bankruptcy.

So, as in Morgan's day, the restructurer tries to learn as much as possible about the company beforehand. Operating experts as well as financial experts have to pore over every available detail about the company's business before an offer can be made. Frequently the restructurer seeks to have the participation of top management in his deal before he can be comfortable enough with the feasibility of his restructuring plan to proceed with it. The higher the price that must be paid for the company in a competitive bidding, the more difficult the execution of the restructuring plan becomes: there is less room for error. Sometimes mistakes are made, which are usually only evident at the end of a cycle, when several restructured companies get into trouble all at the same time.

Some companies attempt to restructure themselves, either to prevent someone else from doing it or because they see the financial opportunities themselves. In the long history of corporate finance, however, there are very few cases in which established corporations have leveraged up or sold off major subsidiaries and distributed the cash to stockholders, unless they were forced to do so in connection with an unwanted takeover attempt or the fear of one. There are plenty of recent examples, however, like the RJR-Nabisco case, in which an opportunistic CEO has announced a management-sponsored buyout, thus putting the company on the block, usually with the result that another company or a more experienced LBO group has won the prize.

"But do these restructurings really work?" Ruth still wants to know. "Do they do any good?"

Well, the $400 billion in restored value to the shareholders from restructuring companies that management had run down (according to Professor Jensen) counts for something. It means that restructuring has worked for the shareowners of those companies. The money they received has been reinvested; that is, $400 billion of capital that wasn't being used at all before the restructuring has been put to work. And 40 or 50 percent of the $400 billion has been "earned" by institutional investors, many of which are pension funds or insurance companies or other such institutions whose success with their investments means a lower charge to the public for their services and greater returns for their investors.

For the restructuring to work it has to, as a minimum, avoid failure or bankruptcy and at least give the restructurers their money back. To do this, as a minimum, the business and assets of the company have to be operated or redeployed so as to cause the market values of the company to increase above the value that they paid for the company before the restructuring occurred. The additional value they hope to create is to come from (1) changes on the asset side of the balance sheet, which usually means selling off assets (or even as Jim Ling did, selling some shares in these assets directly to the public) at prices that at least reflect the prices paid for them; (2) changes in the operations of the business to maximize cash generation, which usually means drastically cutting all unnecessary expenses and slimming the company down to a fighting-fit machine; and (3) management of the liability side of the balance sheet so as to minimize the taxes to be paid (mainly by interest deductions), to refinance high-cost debt as soon as possible, and to apply all of the company's cash not urgently needed in the business to the repayment of as much debt as possible.

The sale of assets and the consequent use of proceeds to pay down debt reduce the size of the company quickly. These together with harsh expense controls reduce overhead sharply, thus increasing the company's productivity. Managers are often paid nominal salaries, with sizable bonuses available for meeting operating goals, which usually send a welcome surge of infectious invigoration through the place. Not paying taxes also helps considerably. Some examples of how productivity has been increased through buyouts are offered in Chapters 6 and 8.

Even the businesses being sold become more efficient. They will also have to work harder if they are going to service the debt that was borrowed, or the financial opportunity cost that was incurred, for *their* acquisition. Most will be run with fewer managers, often owner-managers with great incentives to succeed. There is plenty of evidence to support the assertion that efficiencies are derived from sell-offs when the new owners know exactly what to do with the property being acquired. If all the companies that were sold off to recover Michael Jensen's estimate of $400 billion of value creation were run like this, there surely would be signs of increased efficiency and productivity throughout the country. There are.

Jensen told the House Ways and Means Committee that there were now "several credible studies that have examined the operating characteristics of large samples of LBOs after the buyout and have found real increases in productivity." He refers particularly to studies done by Steven Kaplan and Abbie Smith at the University of Chicago, but there are many such studies. Even Alan Greenspan, who is paid to be more cautious, noted that evidence so far suggests that the restructurings of the 1980s are "improving, on balance, the efficiency of the American economy," though the strain they imposed on the financial system was "worrisome."

"It sure is," Ruth points out. "In fact, it's a lot more worrisome than when Greenspan actually said that. Many companies have fallen apart, some into bankruptcy. Junk bonds have ruined not only the companies they fed but also the firm that fed them, Drexel Burnham.

"At some point, even you guys have got to get a little worried. In the end, who pays?"

Well, Ruth, when the damage is bad enough we all pay, through lower growth rates, higher interest rates or taxes, or whatever, just as we did, for example, in the 1930s.

But, we also pay when our companies fall asleep, when they are not challenged, and when their market valuations are well below what they could be. As many more companies appeared to be asleep, as we entered into the 1980s, than were later driven, perhaps recklessly, into bankruptcy, the greater danger to our economy is from widespread underperformance than from more cases of insolvency than we would like.

In any event, when an LBO goes bust the equity is lost, along with some of the subordinated debt, in each case securities bought by sophisticated investors. The government doesn't guarantee anything, neither do banks holding the senior debt stand to lose much, if anything. Nobody rescued Campeau and everything went on as before. The market yawned.

Yet the risk to the entire financial system of large-scale restructuring is troublesome even to those who believe that restructuring is healthy and desirable for the United States. Whereas many experts in corporate finance such as Professor Merton Miller of the University of Chicago (co-author with Nobel laureate Professor Franco Modigliani in 1959 of the landmark Modigliani and Miller propositions on the cost of capital) believe that most American corporations have been underleveraged since the thirties and that the actual experience of financial accidents since the restructuring era began have been relatively limited, there are nonetheless those who are concerned by the rapid buildup of corporate debt. The issue of how much debt is too much is discussed further in Chapter 8, but at this stage one can say that the fears involve more what we think *might* happen than what has already happened. Anyway, the present boom is over, and though more defaults on junk bonds and takeover debt may arise, changed market conditions have abruptly ended the period of increasing debt buildup. The cycle has run its course and the system still stands.

Critics of restructuring also point out that in the quest for lean and mean operations, companies ruthlessly cut back their labor forces and slash research and development costs, thereby cutting well into the corporate bone, thus spoiling long-term prospects. There are not yet any good findings to affirm or deny this point, but it seems doubtful. Jensen cites some academic studies that indicate that neither severe job reductions nor research slashing has occurred. KKR denies that either of these cutbacks have occurred, on balance, in the various companies they have bought out and still control. On the contrary, they argue, these expenditures have increased.[9] Icahn says he has put fewer people out of work at TWA and ACF, two of his largest deals, than "have AT & T or GM, or for that matter other Fortune 500 companies in their [self-actuated] restructurings."

However, the main point ought to be that a company's value will be greatest if it is run at its maximum efficiency. Owner-managers have maximum incentives to achieve maximum efficiency. If workforce increases and further research and development are really necessary for this to be achieved, they will be provided. If decreases instead are called for, these too should be approved. The key words, I think, are *really necessary*. Many companies are overmanned, especially in the area of corporate overhead or in continuation of inefficient facilities. In such cases, cutbacks may be "really necessary," at least initially. Indeed, such cuts should have been made by the previous management. Also, some of a company's research and development expenditure may not be "really necessary" for current operations, or could at least be refocused onto more concrete objectives. Japanese companies for years focused their research on the production process and product development, not on new technologies. As their objectives were achieved, they broadened their horizons somewhat. Despite this practice, the Japanese have not been known for missing out on new technologies when they became important to their businesses. In the end what is "really necessary" or not can be judged only by those with a vested interest in seeing the company run at maximum efficiency.

"OK, but all this conflict and nastiness can't be helping," Ruth adds, "is it 'really necessary'?"

Merger Warfare

The first reality of restructuring is that one has to have control of a company to do it. And obtaining control these days involves a great struggle. Public attention tends to be focused on the struggle, which is colorful and newsworthy, rather than on the issue of realignment of values, which is theoretical and abstract.

Accordingly, the negative effects of the struggle may be somewhat exaggerated in the public's eye. Certainly a company that is the target of someone else's restructuring ambitions has to spend a lot of money and use a lot of management time in defending itself. If the defense is successful and the attack is repelled, then the old shareholders will have to foot the bill, a large one. They must also watch their stock decline to preraid levels. Few companies having fought off such an attack, however, can revert to the status quo ante—they are changed by the experience. They have been made aware of their vulnerability, of the fickle nature of institutional support; that not all of their shareholders were happy to see them "win" and that many will expect management to do something to get the stock's value back up to what a restructurer would pay for it. These are beneficial lessons if the company heeds them and endeavors to rectify its misalignment of values; indeed the high cost of a successful defense may be a small price for the stockholders to pay for such realignment.

For those companies who fail in their defense, the cost is paid by the attacker. Shareholders, especially if their management has put up a good fight and attracted more than one bidder, should be indifferent to whether or not the company is sold as long as the price they receive corresponds with the company's maximum restructuring value. Shareholders either way shouldn't find the cost of defense a problem.

For those employees and suppliers of the company who are not part of corporate overhead, that is, those who actually produce the company's goods and services, acquisition usually does not mean being terminated. Indeed, for many such people it is an opportunity. One friend of mine, a senior sales executive for a large sugar refiner, has been taken over or restructured three times in the last ten years or so, and each time he has benefited from it. Other friends, however, have not.

Only a few people really are in danger of losing their jobs: the top two or three corporate management people and those who service them on the corporate staff. These people almost always have share-holdings and stock options in the company that they can cash in for a substantial sum, and many have generous severance pay and pension arrangements in addition. Of course, if a company has been run with excess overhead in the past, the early round of pink slips may penetrate further into the company, though presumably these jobs should have been eliminated by prior management in its own quest for lowering operating costs.

Naturally, the chief executive is not eager to be ousted from his job. It's a good job, being the boss of bosses, the sole authority for whatever happens in the company. It's the job of a lifetime. It was hard enough getting it to let it go without a fight.

The larger the corporation the more resources and friends it has for putting up a fight. "Those little nobodys coming after us are going to see just how good a fight we can put up" would be a comment (with expletives deleted) typical of most CEOs under attack.

There is every reason, too, to fight as hard as possible to frustrate the attacker into settling things once and for all with a higher bid. The higher the bid the better. So although there may be entrenchment involved along with pride, ego, notions of manliness, anger, and everything else, it is also economic (and therefore in the shareholder's interest) for management to fight as hard as possible in order to be sure of the best price. If management "wins," however, it may have to actually do some of the things it was fighting to oppose in order to address the issue of postdefense alignment of values.

The best defenses are the most credible ones: the ones in which the defender convinces the attacker that he really means it and intends to fight to the finish. No attacker is going to raise his bid (especially if he is the only one bidding) if he isn't convinced he absolutely has to. Convincing is part of the game. Convincing is noisy and nasty and occasionally involves a low blow or two.

All through the merger wave of the sixties, hostile deals were strictly the preserve of New Men and their bankers. The blue chips didn't do such things: it was sordid, encouraged bad behavior in corporate

America generally, and was beneath them. The old-line investment banks did not represent raiders. Therefore, the population of takeover players narrowed down to raiders, targets, and "white knights," usually large blue-chip corporations who were prepared to rush in to rescue a target under fire but not to fire the first shot.

This changed in 1974 when the Canadian blue-chip International Nickel, represented by Morgan Stanley & Co., launched an unwanted $157 million tender offer for Electric Storage Battery. The offer, which was ultimately successful, attracted a lot of press attention and comment. Within months, other blue-chip companies were justifying unfriendly offers to shareholders of companies they wanted to acquire. They were no longer waiting for a white knight opportunity to arise (though they still responded when one did); they were becoming more aggressive, seeking out the companies they wanted to buy, making an initial approach to suggest "discussions leading to a merger," then, when this was rejected, going ahead with an offer direct to shareholders.

Over the years these struggles have led to a large body of tactics, countertactics, case law, changes in state and federal laws, financing techniques, and changes in securities and related matters affecting the control of corporations. These have tended to change how corporations must go about obtaining control of others, not whether they are able to do so. If anything, the efficiency of the market for corporate control, the "merger market," and the degree of "fairness" with which owner-manager conflicts are resolved have been the real beneficiaries of these struggles. These things affect friendly deals as well as unfriendly ones. Unless the maximum value is obtained for the stockholders, even in a friendly deal, then other, unwanted suitors will appear on the scene, forcing the friendly party to raise its bid or to withdraw. This is what happened to Ross Johnson, who launched what he must have hoped would be regarded as a "friendly" (if low-priced) deal at $75 per share for RJR only to attract other players to the game. Time Inc. also discovered this when its friendly "merger of equals" with Warner Communications was challenged by Paramount Communications (previously Gulf + Western), making a bid for Time. The distinctions between friendly and unfriendly deals have faded to the point that they are mainly made now by the Business Roundtable (a group of large company CEOs), public relations agents, and journalists. And most takeovers today end up as friendly ones if the board of directors finally decides to accept a bid at a price that turns out to be too high to turn down.

Getting Back to Normal

"That may be all well and good," Ruth interjects, "but there's been over a trillion dollars of mergers during this particular wave; they can't all be needing to be realigned, or whatever.

"Aren't all you guys getting a little blinded by the money you're making and starting to talk yourselves into thinking that this boom can—and should—go on forever?

"And aren't we all getting a little carried away here, with deals getting done that shouldn't, at increasingly higher and uneconomic prices, with more and more room for mistakes? Does it all make sense at this stage of the game?"

Maybe, maybe not. Surely some deals will be regretted later, as in the conglomerate days. Some already have been. Robert Campeau's 1988 acquisition of Federated Department Stores for $6.7 billion has come apart and fallen into bankruptcy. Revco Drug Stores, Integrated Resources, Fruehauf, all large LBOs, have also already failed, and several others are in trouble. Many of the deals that were done when interest rates were dropping and stock prices were booming couldn't be done today, even at the prices paid back then, prices that were much lower than what they came to be after several years of bull market excitement. As it usually does, the market took care of the rising levels of excess that the boom brought with it.

The fever has passed now, and the boom is over. The junk-bond market, on which so many acquirers depended for financing, has been wasted. Drexel Burnham is gone. So are "merchant banking," "bridge loans," and LBO funds, all of which played important if unpopular roles in the takeover boom of the eighties.

"Thank God," Ruth added. "Now things can get back to normal again."

Well, we have to explain to her that "normal" is not a time when nothing is happening, when all the animals of the financial forest share the same water hole in peace and doze passively in the sun. Such times, if they have ever occurred, would be highly abnormal. Normal means business as usual, with only average amounts of overpriced and overleveraged transactions.

Normal times have prevailed for most of the past year, while markets have adjusted. During this period Georgia Pacific launched a $3.5 billion unfriendly takeover bid for Great Northern Nekoosa, and won. Entrepreneurial raiders also continued to function: Harold Simmons became involved in efforts to control Lockheed and Georgia Gulf Corporation at the same time through separate appeals to shareholders to elect a slate of directors proposed by him at the companies' annual meetings. Shorn of junk, the proxy fight became the preferred method of attack for the New Men. Avon Products, United Airlines, and USX (formerly U.S. Steel) were among the many companies having to face proxy challenges at their 1990 shareholder meetings.

Though the junk-bond market lost almost 30 percent of its value in the first quarter of 1990, and many dealers discontinued market-making in the bonds, the market began to mend itself after a while. Research reports recommending RJR, Kroger, Beatrice, and various other individual securities as extremely good value at present prices began to appear on the Street. Tentatively, the market continued to function. New issues were rare in the first half of the year, and a defensive restructuring issue for Georgia Gulf was brought to market by its lead manager, Goldman Sachs, on a "best efforts" basis, meaning that the firm would not guarantee to purchase unsold bonds from the company to ensure the issues' success.

The LBO operators like KKR and Forstmann Little went off to tend to storm damage in their own portfolios or to look for new ways to make money with the funds they were entrusted with, such as bankruptcy workouts, or all-equity LBOs, or whatever came along next.

The stock market ended the decade near its all-time high. New issues, such as a $550 million initial public offering of the Readers Digest Association, were still being brought to the market and sold successfully. KKR surprised some of its investors by acquiring 40 percent of a new issue of shares for First Interstate Bank, an issue that had been hung up for a while. The Puerto Rican telephone company was put up for sale. So were hundreds of little oilfields owned by one of the majors. Life went on.

But the volume of business wasn't the same and many of the big investment banks saw their profits start to fall away. Shearson Lehman Hutton and First Boston, both suffering from large merchant-banking losses, had to run to their respective parents (American Express and Credit Suisse, respectively) for help. Merrill Lynch had to lay off another 4,000 people. Salomon Brothers praised its Phibro commodities division's contribution to profits. Morgan Stanley pointed to profits from earlier LBO deals it had invested in itself. It was the end of another Wall Street era. As before, the survivors would adjust and repair themselves and soon appear ready for whatever the next era offered.

The end of this era coincided with the production of a popular off-Broadway play, a comedy titled *Other People's Money*, by Jerry Sterner. The story involved a notorious Wall Street raider's effort to takeover an old-line, sleepy Rhode Island wire and cable company in order to restructure it. The raider, whose nickname was "Larry the Liquidator," had spotted the company as undervalued. He drove to Rhode Island in his stretch limo and announced his intentions to "Jorgey," the company's aging chairman who had been chief executive for thirty-eight years. The company's stock was at $14 a share; Larry wanted to buy it for $20; it was worth $25 after restructuring, he told Jorgey openly.

"Over the years you have diversified into other businesses, and these are doing well," he said. But the wire and cable business "is a dinosaur; it's dead, and it's killing the stock price. Get rid of it, sell off the machinery, land, and real estate, liquidate the pension fund and recover its surplus and you've got a company worth $25," said Larry.

"Impossible," said Jorgey. "We've always been in the wire business, it's our core. We can't sell it. Besides, what would I tell the men?" Jorgey was a sympathetic figure, an honest businessman looking out for his company and his men. He wanted nothing to do with the Sodom and Gomorrah that Wall Street represented. He owned 25 percent of the stock and wasn't worried. The first act ends with the audience nodding its approval of noble and resolute Jorgey and hissing under its breath at sleazy, overweight Larry.

During the second act we learn there are more shareholders, and shareholder dependents than there are workers left in the wire and cable factory, that Jorgey has done nothing to look after management, and that even "Ozzie, down at the bank," votes his clients' shares for Larry. Jorgey has been running his own little fiefdom for thirty-eight years, a fiefdom that has been 75 percent financed with other people's money who never challenged any of his decisions. Jorgey meant well when he decided to oppose Larry's liquidation plan, but he offered no alternative to it but to continue on as before.

Thanks to Larry the Liquidator, the shareholders got a choice. They would rather have $20 a share than continue to own unpromising shares worth $14. Under Jorgey, the shares will remain at $14, but under Larry, who will restructure the company, they will ultimately be worth $25. Their decision is strictly financial, just as was their reason for investing in the company in the first place. The shareholders realize that Jorgey's proposal is uneconomic, not rational in the context of a business decision.

Larry wins, packs up, and goes on to the next deal. The curtain drops. The audience realizes Jorgey was a fool who should have retired ten years ago. He made arbitrary decisions that adversely, not positively, affected shareholder value. The shareholders had hired him to look after their money and he was using it to protect a business long in decline. He was a nice man, with very decent instincts, and Larry was a schmuck. But either Jorgey didn't know what he was doing, or he was knowingly doing the wrong thing—in either case the audience sadly knew that Larry was right. Restructuring was what the company needed and, once the shareholders had a clear choice, what it got.

Maybe now this attitude will be normal. Before the decade began, it wasn't. So even as the waves of activity recede, something is left behind—a different perception of takeover activity, one that will be carried into the future.

It makes sense.

5

BATTLEFIELD
TACTICS

Martin Lipton is senior partner of the New York law firm Wachtell, Lipton, Rosen & Katz. Called "Marty" by just about everyone, including many people who have never met him, he is today the best-known merger lawyer in the United States. Ten years ago both he and his firm were virtually unknown; when the merger boom broke out, he and a few fast-moving partners set themselves up as specialists in the practice of merger law. Previously, the more established "white shoe" firms had not felt it necessary to create a specialization in mergers, which were, after all, just one part of their general practice of corporate law. Another firm, Skadden, Arps, Slate, Meager & Flom, equally obscure at the beginning, followed the same path and emerged as the "other" top merger firm. Before long these two firms found themselves opposing each other in a very large percentage of the deals being done. The white shoe firms, until they developed the specialization in mergers necessary to keep up, sat on the sidelines—another victory for the New Men.

Lipton is partial to the defense. He has been innovative in defending clients against raiders and has been given credit for devising the "poison pill" in 1984 and the "just say no" defense in 1988. The former involves the authorization by a board of directors of "share-holders' rights" to purchase additional securities of the company at absurdly low prices if any shareholder accumulates a threshold position of, say, 30 percent. If the threshold is crossed, all shareholders except the crosser are entitled to purchase the new bargain-price shares, thus diluting the threshold crosser's position and so increasing the cost of the acquisition, that he stays away. The poison pill does not prevent takeovers, but it does slow them down and forces the raider to negotiate with the target company (to withdraw the poison pill)—both of which assist the target company in preventing many takeover abuses while still maintaining a level playing field on which to evaluate and act on the acquirer's proposal. At first the poison pill was seen by many companies as a kind of last-ditch scorched earth defensive effort to entrench management, but no longer. The poison pill has become such a widely employed takeover defense that its absence is far rarer today than its presence. Nearly one thousand public companies now have poison pills of one form or another in place.

The "just say no" defense (named obviously after Nancy Reagan's simplistic anti–drug use slogan) is a newer, less widely applied though less successful stratagem in which the company makes no effort to come up with an alternative restructuring when confronted by a bidder seeking to have a poison pill removed—it simply calls for the company to do nothing beyond announcing that it is not for sale and intends to stick to its long-term plans, and therefore the pill will not be removed.

As well known as Lipton is for his legal advice, he is also known as a public opponent of hostile takeovers, mainly because of the injury to the financial system that he believes such takeovers cause. He is a frequent commentator on the evils of the merger scene and a contributor of proposals for how the system might work better. Since his substantial income is heavily dependent on takeovers, his comments are often criticized as hypocritical and somewhat pious for someone benefiting so extensively from the very evils he decries. He is overly abused for this, I believe, as his real objective is to preserve the free-market system within a regulated framework that is fair to all concerned and to protect the marketplace against excesses and misbehavior that could ruin it.

Lipton believes that the federal government has failed the system by refusing to establish a set of national merger-and-acquisition regulations. The merger marketplace, swollen by nearly a decade of freewheeling activity and abundant liquidity, has become a serious threat to good and sensible companies seeking to preserve their independence, notwithstanding Lipton's own innovations. "In recent years," he noted, "not one major company that became the target of a cash tender offer for all of its shares has remained independent or unrestructured."

This situation, he adds, is part of the price we pay for making takeover money easily available. Another part of the price is the financial risk that such easy money creates. And yet another part is the cost of having every takeover-related dispute, of which there are many, be resolved expensively and unpredictably in a court of law: "Failure to develop a national policy for takeovers has left the problem in the hands of legal and financial advisers, and moved the field of battle from the marketplace to the courthouse."[1]

Shifting Sands of Defense

During the merger boom of the sixties the courthouse was not much involved. Until the Williams Act was passed by Congress in 1968, there were very few restrictions on merger-and-acquisition procedures: federal and state securities laws still applied, of course, as did the rules of stock exchanges, but these had not been set up in contemplation of the wave of Saturday night specials and other types of cash tender offers that subsequently took place. The Williams Act required acquirers to announce their holdings and their intentions within ten days from the time their accumulations reached a threshold of 5 percent of a company's outstanding stock, and a minimum twenty-business-day period during which a tender offer would be open for tendering on a pro rata basis by shareholders.

As in many such situations, the rule did not accomplish exactly what it intended to; instead, many acquirers preferred to buy stock in great quantity as soon as the 5 percent mark was reached so that by the time disclosure was necessary as much as 10 or 20 percent of the shares might have been purchased. This particular feature of the regulation is now known as the "ten-day window."

There is an additional requirement for would-be acquirers: they must identify themselves as such under the Hart-Scott-Rodino Antitrust Improvements Act of 1976. This act was designed to speed up, or at least call attention to, a possible antitrust violation resulting from a possible acquisition. Under its terms an acquirer must notify the Federal Trade Commission (and the target) of its intentions before acquiring more than $15 million of the target's stock; or if its initial investment is for "investment purposes" only, it may acquire up to 10 percent of the target company's shares. Naturally, the latter limitation is the one that everyone routinely uses, even those who later change their minds and decide to make an attempt at acquiring control of the target.

The principal defensive tactics employed until the poison pill was invented were to combine a ferocity of lawsuits, regulatory actions, and political activity with a rigorous effort to justify a valuation for the company in excess of the bid price. The legal counterattack was to make the prospective acquirer look as self-serving, incompetent, and devious as possible—all supposedly contrary to the public image the company otherwise sought to maintain—and to find or create a regulatory loophole that would block the deal. The financial activity was directed at locating, quickly, a respectable corporation to act as a "white knight" who would rescue the besieged damsel from a grim fate by marrying her instead. Few such marriages proved to be happy ones for the brides, however, so this defense came to be regarded as a last resort.

As liquidity built up during the eighties, however, more and more players who had little or nothing to lose entered the game. They had no antitrust exposure, no public image or reputation to defend, and very thick skins. Large amounts of financing could be obtained easily through bank loans or from syndications of standby junk-bond facilities to enable these new players to challenge large companies. One ploy was to buy up some shares, arrange financing sufficient to acquire a control position, talk to the press a lot, and wait for the representatives of the beleaguered company to offer to buy back the position at a substantial premium over the market price, a premium that only the challenger would enjoy. This was called "greenmail." Even such large, presumably impregnable companies as Texaco and Walt Disney were subjected to greenmail. Sometimes, when a greenmailer was successful in selling shares back to the target, and subsequently the share price would drop and a second greenmailer would appear on the scene. Such repeat appearances at the same trough were called "double dipping."

In time, pressure from nonparticipating institutional investors, a ruling by the accounting standards board that treated any premium paid in greenmail buybacks as a current nondeductible operating expense, and the security of their poison pills encouraged companies to resist outright greenmail attempts. The 1987 Tax Reform Act also imposed a nondeductible excise tax on greenmail profits, which effectively put the final nail in its coffin.

Emboldened by their successes, however, the New Men went after whole companies. Again they had little to lose. Once a credible amount of financing was arranged and a sizable minority stake had been purchased, the company was "in play," meaning that it was fair game for any other company or group of investors to come around wearing their white armor. All the bidder had to do was wait for a company in play to react to the pressure. Usually something would happen—the company would restructure or sell out to someone else—and the profits earned on the minority stake would be considerable. The original bidder didn't actually have to win to make money. It was easy.

Up until this point, the legal principle involved in takeover defenses had been largely confined to the "business-judgment doctrine." This maintained that as long as members of a board of directors acted in good faith, were not negligent, and did nothing to enrich themselves at the shareholders' expense, then their decisions concerning all aspects of the company's affairs would be given the benefit of the doubt and not interfered with by the courts. For years this doctrine had applied to all decisions of boards of directors that could be attributed to a rational business purpose, that is, whether to close a plant or invest in a new technology—*enterprise matters*— or decisions related to corporate control or shareholder entitlements—*ownership matters*. The burden of proof that an offense infringing on the business-judgment doctrine had occurred was on the plaintiff. If a board acted in an informed and disinterested way, its decisions were very difficult to challenge. The business-judgment doctrine upheld a number of sophisticated and controversial defensive techniques employed by many boards to fight off unwanted bidders, including the poison pill, the "crown jewel lockup" (selling a principal asset to a preferred bidder to put it out of reach), and the "Pac Man defense" (tendering for the one who tenders for you).

Directors, however, do not have only the duty to remain pure and uncorrupted by self-interest in these situations. They also have a *duty of care*, that is, a duty not to be negligent in doing their jobs. In an important addition to the case law of the business-judgment doctrine, the Delaware Supreme Court held against the directors of Trans Union Corporation in 1985 for having agreed to a sale of the company to the Marmon Group without having exercised due care.

In this case Marmon had presented an *exploding offer* to Trans Union: an unexpected offer made at noon on a Saturday at about a 50 percent premium over the market that would expire on the coming Monday. The reason for the early expiration was to compel the directors to decide yes or no immediately. If they declined to accept the offer, Marmon would not be obligated to stick to it and a $55 per share offering price might go out the window. On the other hand, the directors argued, if they accepted the offer the company would be put in play and someone else might make a higher offer. In the end, no one did and the company was sold to Marmon and a shareholder sued the directors for breach of fiduciary duty. Damages were requested in an amount by which a supposed intrinsic value of the company exceeded $55 per share.

The directors, of course, were outraged when the court ruled against them. So were some legal observers, one of whom called the decision "surely one of the worst decisions in the history of corporate law." The company had done its best to retain an attractive bid that expired within an unreasonably short period of time. It had used a clever tactic to ensure that its shareholders would receive the better of either the Marmon or a higher offer.[2] The court did not buy the argument, however. Despite the explosive provisions of the offer, it said, the directors had been grossly negligent in, among other things, acting hastily on the basis of incomplete information, acting without any professional financial advice, and making no effort to ascertain the adequacy of the price offered, despite its being made at a premium to the market. The court ruled that the directors had not informed themselves as they should have and, therefore, were liable personally for the damages. The directors settled out of court for an undisclosed amount. Officers' and directors' liability insurance rates immediately shot up.[3]

The application of the business-judgment rule to ownership matters continued to be treated differently from enterprise matters by the courts, especially after the landmark *Unocal Corp.* v. *Mesa Petroleum Co.* decision in 1985.

In this case, T. Boone Pickens astride Mesa Petroleum attempted a takeover of Unocal, formerly the Union Oil Co., through a two-tiered, front-end loaded offer. The first tier involved a cash offer for a controlling position. The second tier, the offer for the rest of the company, would involve the issuance of junk securities to shareholders in a forced exchange for their shares. The first, or "front," tier was to be in cash and was thus preferable, or "loaded," in order to coerce shareholders to accept it instead of the back tier. Unocal did not want to be sold to a white knight, but it found few legal loopholes in which to snare ol' Boone. So it tried something radical: a self-tender for a sizable portion of its own stock at a higher price than Pickens's offer but with explicit provisions that Mesa's shares would not be accepted. Mesa immediately sued in Delaware (where Unocal was incorporated) to enjoin the transaction. The court upheld Unocal (though the SEC would subsequently disallow selective self-tenders) but did so in a way that had a dramatic impact.

The Unocal decision changed the rules for the application of the business-judgment doctrine to ownership matters. According to Stuart Shapiro, a merger–trial law specialist at Skadden Arps, *"Unocal* imposed a two-part threshold requirement which must be satisfied by a board of directors before the board is entitled to the evidentiary presumptions of the business judgment rule. That is, the burden of proof is shifted, as an initial matter, from the plaintiff to the board. This shifting of burdens has significant practical consequences."[4]

The first part of the *Unocal* requirement is to meet the ordinary standards of the business-judgment doctrine as these have been applied in ownership issues in the past: here the board must, through good faith and reasonable investigation, establish that a bid poses a danger or threat to corporate policy, effectiveness, and ownership interests. If such a threat does exist, for example, from an exceptionally low-priced bid, then the duty of the board is to oppose it. The second part, however, is new:

> A further aspect is the element of balance. If a defense measure
> is to come within the ambit of the business judgment rule, it
> must be reasonable in relation to the threat posed. This entails
> an analysis by the directors of the nature of the takeover bid
> and its effect on the corporate enterprise.[5]

This part of the standard results in an "enhanced" business judgment rule in which the court exacts an enhanced judicial scrutiny at the "threshold" in ownership issues. Under this further test of proportionality the board must show (with the burden of proof on it) not only that its actions are reasonable but that *they are reasonable in the circumstances of the threat*, or danger, that is posed. Because it is left to the court to be convinced of the standards of reasonableness, the court necessarily must impose its own judgments on the facts in each case. Indeed, now the court was required to substitute its own business (or financial) judgment for that of the board's, something courts in the past were reluctant to do.[6]

The consequences of the imposition of the enhanced business-judgment standards have been several. First, it has resulted in virtually automatic litigation in every bidding case by the acquirer to seek the court's intervention to remove a defender's poison pill and other defenses. The burden of proof that the defenses employed are reasonable—relative to the threat—now falls immediately on the defender, who must respond to the bid within ten days. Such a burden heightens the dependence of a defender on the advice received from legal and financial advisers, and his own role in deciding his own destiny shrinks in comparison.

All other factors being equal, the greatest pressure falls on the "adequacy" of the bid price. The magnitude of the threat tends to be determined mainly by the difference between the bid price and the price that the board and its advisers think is adequate. The latter is not easy to assess in a short period of time: adequacy tends to be determined by estimates of the highest price that might be bid in an auction, whereas "fairness" involves an appreciation of intrinsic value, long-term prospects, and other intangibles. It is perfectly possible for an adequate price to be greater than a fair price. These things are determined by investment bankers in the process of serving a client in an advocacy role for a large fee. Needless to say, investment bankers' opinions about adequacy or fairness in takeover cases are sometimes controversial, but most companies feel unable to prove that they have met an enhanced business-judgment standard without experienced professional help in assessing the adequacy or inadequacy of the price bid for the company.

Once opinions about the bid price and the auction value of the company are established, it then becomes necessary to devise a series of defensive measures that will not be deemed excessive relative to the threat. Some defenders feel they are being made to fight with one hand tied behind their back because of this restriction. Such defenders prefer instead to spend their time restructuring the company to give the shareholders an alternative to the bid rather than fight to keep the poison pill in place indefinitely (though in the "just say no" defense, that is what they have to do).

Once headed down the path of restructuring, particularly a restructuring in which management participates in an LBO, complications can quickly arise over self-dealing and conflicts of interest. At this point, the board must turn over virtually all of the decision-making powers to a special committee of nonexecutive directors who are required to show no favoritism between a management-led restructuring and a bid from any other party. The special committee hires its own investment bankers and legal advisers so as to retain its independence and to avoid the booby traps.

The issue of independence was brought to a head in another landmark case, which involved defensive measures taken by Revlon to escape the grasp of Ronald Perelman in 1985. Perelman's flagship corporation, McAndrews & Forbes, had made an aggressive bid for Revlon; the Revlon board (advised by Marty Lipton) decided to play hardball. It invited the LBO specialists Forstmann Little to organize a management-led buyout with some new features. First, Revlon would agree to deal with Forstmann Little exclusively; second, it would agree to sell Forstmann Little certain key assets of the company if any other bidder succeeded in acquiring 40 percent of the company's shares, a kind of "poison lockup." Perelman was represented by Skadden Arps, which immediately claimed in a lawsuit that by providing Forstmann Little with a lockup and a no-shop clause it had in effect ended the auction process that Revlon itself had begun by seeking Forstmann Little as a white knight. The board had shown favoritism, they claimed, which would prevent shareholders from maximizing their value or from making a choice.

The case, *Revlon* v. *McAndrews & Forbes*, was decided by the Delaware Chancery Court in favor of Perelman, and the Delaware Supreme Court upheld the decision, noting that once Revlon "put a 'For Sale' sign on the firm" by deciding to take it private through an LBO, then the role of the directors changed from that of corporate defenders to that of auctioneers, in which the main goal was to secure the highest possible price for the shareholders, not to tilt in favor of a deal in which management had an interest.

Companies are not required by any legal consideration to be sold, but the shifting legal complexities clearly reduce some of the defenders' advantages derived from poison pills and "cram-down" restructurings, that is, a restructuring that occurs through a large special dividend that the board can declare without shareholder approval, one that is supposedly crammed down their throats.

With the battlefield now in the courthouse, every bid is accompanied by a lawsuit citing *Unocal* and many of the other cases that have shed bits of light on one complex aspect or another of the many issues that pertain to ownership. As each case is unique factually, each one invites a different shading in the all-important decision of the judge hearing the case, which will determine whether the defender's defenses may stand or fall. All of this is in the interest of establishing that ever-elusive level playing field that free-market economists and regulators alike believe is the best means to resolve conflicts between owners and managers of corporations.

Some deals stand out more than others. Some companies seemingly deserve to be taken over as a reward for poor performance and tired managerial blood. Others have exceeded all standards of performance in their industries, seen their stock prices soar to levels that appear to reflect all the necessary aligning that needs to be done, and have carefully planned for their own defense in the event of a takeover bid. Even so, results are not always what might be expected.

The Siege of Macmillan

On October 22, 1987, three days after the great stock market crash of that year, Robert M. Bass announced in an SEC filing that he and a group of investors had acquired a 7.5 percent stake in Macmillan Inc., a large U.S. publishing and information services company, and that they expected to purchase additional shares. The shares had been acquired from August 21 to October 21 for $47.10 to $74.65 per share. Bass, a Texas billionaire who is active in acquiring and selling companies in the United States, had recruited Equitable Life Assurance Corp., the third-largest such company, in the United States, and other investors to join him in an effort to take control of Macmillan. The Bass group was advised by Morgan Stanley & Co.[7]

Though the announcement was unexpected and unwelcome and

certainly came at an awkward time (after Macmillan's shares had dropped about 36 percent in value as a result of the crash), it was not a surprise. Management was aware that the publishing industry was undergoing a worldwide consolidation and therefore companies like Macmillan, despite superior performance in their own right, were likely to find themselves under attack. The preceding May when a competitor, Harcourt Brace Jovanovich, was forced into an internal restructuring to escape the grasp of the British press lord Robert Maxwell, Edward P. Evans, Macmillan's forty-six-year-old chairman and chief executive, decided to tighten the company's defenses against a takeover and to prepare a restructuring plan of its own— just in case. Evans had been Macmillan's CEO for the past eight years. From the end of 1982 through the end of 1987, the company's stock price nearly quintupled; per-share earnings nearly tripled and sales more than doubled, all representing the greatest increases in the publishing industry over that period.

The Macmillan defenses, adopted between June and September, were fourfold: a shareholder's rights plan (poison pill) that would be triggered at a 30 percent accumulation; acquisition of shares by the company's Employee Stock Ownership Plan (ESOP), the trustees of which would be members of management; a series of special severance arrangements for top management in the event of a change of control of the company (called "golden parachutes") worth $60 million; and a tentative restructuring plan for the company that would enable management to roll up their present shareholdings and re- stricted shares and stock options granted to them by the board into a controlling interest in the company.

The ESOP purchase of about 2 million shares (about 7 percent of all shares outstanding) would be funded by a $60 million loan from the company. The golden parachutes were common though controversial device approved by many boards of directors to com- pensate management for loss of status as a result of a change in control of the company. By making it quite expensive for new owners to reduce the standing of senior executives, these executives sup- posedly were to be more objective when faced by the prospect of a takeover and thus would not act as entrenched management only trying to protect their jobs and future incomes. In the Macmillan case the parachutes came into effect automatically upon the change of control (the loss of status was assumed to be inevitable), and the $60 million that was to be paid out was backed by a letter of credit from a major bank.

The management-led restructuring plan was not fully worked out by the time of the Bass announcement, but the board had authorized the granting of 300,000 shares of restricted stock to Evans and William Reilly, Macmillan's president, in June and granted a further 200,000 shares under a stock option plan in September (these were canceled and replaced after the October crash).

On October 29, Macmillan announced that its board of directors had amended its poison pill to provide that on the acquisition of 15 percent or more of the company's shares by a person or group, the rights automatically would become activated, or "flip-in," and holders of the rights (other than the person or group holding the 15 percent or greater position) would be entitled to purchase new Macmillan stock at half market value. The company said that the modification represented a safeguard of shareholders' interests in the face of extraordinary market conditions.

On November 11, 1987, the "Heard on the Street" column of *The Wall Street Journal* noted that Bell & Howell Co., which had spent a decade battling a stodgy image as a movie camera maker, was attracting a lot of interest. Two major publishing companies, Macmillan and Maxwell Communication Corp. of Britain, recently bought stakes in the company (of 8 percent and 2 percent, respectively) and were seeking to acquire control through friendly means. The part of greatest interest to Macmillan and Maxwell was the Merrill book division of the Bell & Howell publishing unit. A group including Robert M. Bass had meanwhile become Bell & Howell's largest shareholder with a 16 percent interest.

A few days later Maxwell filed for permission from the Federal Trade Commission under Hait-Scott-Rodino to acquire control of Bell & Howell. Shortly afterward Macmillan did the same. Bell & Howell then retained Salomon Brothers to invite proposals for the acquisition of Bell & Howell from other possible suitors.

On November 25, 1987, Bell & Howell received an offer from the Bass group to acquire the company through a leveraged buyout in which management would participate. Two weeks later, Bell & Howell announced an agreement with the Bass group for the company to be sold to Bass for $678 million. The company expected to be divided into two: a publishing company and a movie camera business.

On December 1, 1987, the Bass group announced that it had increased its holdings in Macmillan to 8.8 percent.

The easy pickings of Bell & Howell made Macmillan nervous. At its March 1988 board meeting, a "blank check" preferred stock with uneven voting rights was authorized, though not issued, as a further takeover deterrent. An additional 130,000 shares was awarded to the company's four top managers, director's fees were increased, and a nonexecutive director's retirement plan was adopted that awarded to all nonemployee board members over the age of sixty (as most were) their current level of directors' fees for life.

On May 17, 1988, the Bass group announced an unsolicited tender offer for the 90.9 percent of Macmillan that it did not own at $64 per share, or about $1.5 billion. The letter transmitting the offer stated that the Bass group's actions were intended as friendly and that it hoped that Macmillan's management would participate in the transaction. The Macmillan stock had closed the previous day at $51.75.

The following day, May 18, Macmillan's annual meeting was held. Evans stated that the company was not for sale. The meeting was ended as quickly as possible, and no questions were taken, because of the Bass offer. The annual meeting was followed by a board meeting at which a special committee of nonexecutive members of the board was appointed to study management's restructuring proposal (it held its first meeting on May 24), the terms of the golden parachutes were amended to cause them to apply if any shareholder acquired 20 percent or more of the company's stock (even if such a holding were approved by the board and/or shareholders), and the nonexecutive directors' retirement plan was amended to include benefits for the spouses of directors.

On May 19, Standard & Poor's placed Macmillan's senior debt rating of A — on its credit review list, with negative implications, because of the Bass offer. Moody's Investors Services did the same thing with respect to its rating of Macmillan debt of A-3.

Macmillan responded with a lawsuit against Bass, Equitable, and Morgan Stanley & Co. charging that these firms had entered into a conspiracy to "put the company into play" so as to cause it to be sold. The suit was not intended to be won: its purpose was to harass and embarrass the defendants into backing away from Bass. It was not successful.

On May 31, Evans announced that the Macmillan board had approved a management-led restructuring of the corporation that it valued at more than $64. The restructuring would consist of a special dividend of $52.35 in cash, a half share of Macmillan Information Co. common stock (an information services subsidiary that would be separately constituted as a public company as a result of the distribution of its shares), and $4.50 principal amount of Macmillan Information subordinated debentures. Shareholders would continue to own their original shares in Macmillan Inc., which would be re-named Macmillan Publishing Co. Evans and his management group then owned 1.6 million shares of Macmillan restricted stock and stock options (about 6 percent of the company), which would be swapped for a 39.3 percent ownership of the Macmillan Information company. Securities analysts initially valued the offer at $65 to $70. Later, Macmillan asserted that the offer was worth $64.15 per share. The restructuring dividend would not be subject to shareholder approval, and it would be paid out to shareholders of record on June 10— only ten days after Evans's announcement of the plan.

A few days after this announcement, on June 6, Bass increased its bid to $73. It also filed a lawsuit in the Delaware Chancery Court (Macmillan being a Delaware corporation) to block the restructuring move on the grounds that, as a defensive measure, it was unreasonable and disproportionate in relation to any threat to corporate policy and effectiveness posed by Bass and that management had violated its fiduciary duties to shareholders by conspiring to appropriate Macmillan's attractive information services business for itself, without a shareholder vote.[8] Bass's suit was clearly aimed at applying the enhanced business judgment standards established in the *Unocal* case, and the standards of fiduciary conduct established in *Revlon*.

Macmillan formally rejected Bass's offer. On June 29, it also announced that it was considering litigation against Security Pacific Bank, which Macmillan had approached in connection with its effort to finance its restructuring plan. Macmillan was "surprised and outraged" to learn that Security Pacific had decided to provide a $500 million credit facility to the Bass group, despite having received confidential materials from Macmillan and committed $200 million to the Macmillan restructuring plan.

On July 14, the Delaware Chancery Court issued a preliminary injunction against the Macmillan restructuring plan, finding that it did violate the *Unocal* precepts against unreasonable and disproportionate responses to takeover bids in that "not only does it offer inferior value to the shareholders, it also forces them to accept it. No shareholder vote is afforded; no choice is given."[9] Macmillan said it would appeal to the Delaware Supreme Court. The Delaware Supreme Court ordered the case to be heard before all five of its judges; hearings would commence on September 20. Meanwhile the injunction against the restructuring plan would stand, and other events would unfold.

On July 18, the Bass group increased its offer to $75. The Macmillan stock closed at $78.125 on the day, as arbitrageurs speculated on a higher final outcome.

On July 21, Robert Maxwell, chairman of Maxwell Communication, announced an $80 cash offer for Macmillan. Maxwell Communication is 52 percent owned by Mr. Maxwell and a Liechtenstein-based foundation renamed the Maxwell Foundation earlier in the year. The foundation controls Maxwell's other assets, which include Britain's Mirror Group Newspapers Ltd., a national newspaper publisher, and investments in cable television and broadcasting. Maxwell, a large, exuberant, highly energetic self-made entrepreneur had fled to Britain from Czechoslovakia at the outbreak of World War II, joined the British army, and won a Military Cross. He made his pile after the war by borrowing large amounts and risking such sums boldly. Always a controversial man, he became known in the British press as "the bouncing Czech." He frequently boasted of his plans for a global communications network and of his own ambitions one day to become England's prime minister.

Maxwell had tried to acquire a U.S. publisher before: his unsuccessful $1.7 billion bid for Harcourt Brace Jovanovich fifteen months earlier had started Macmillan down the road to its management restructuring. Maxwell was advised by Rothschild, Inc., the U.S. arm of the U.K. merchant bank whose American head was Robert Pirie, a former merger law specialist at Skadden Arps.

Macmillan rejected both offers as "inadequate," although both offers were substantially higher than its own offer of $64.15, which its own investment bankers had described as "fair." The others were held to be inadequate because they did not provide as much of a premium for the sale of control of the company as Macmillan and its advisers thought they should. Their own restructuring, on the other hand, did not involve the sale of control of the company; therefore, a price without a control premium could be considered fair. Institutional investors pondered the logic of adequacy and inadequacy on their own, many resolving the dilemma by selling their stock to arbitrageurs to lock in the current market price and be done with it.

In early September, reports were circulating that Macmillan had requested KKR to explore a leveraged buyout proposal with it. It was also reported that Maxwell, in a letter to Evans, had proposed raising his bid to $84. The higher offer, said Maxwell, would be conditional on his "receiving a clear understanding of which members of senior management will be staying and which will be leaving" if the Maxwell bid succeeds. Maxwell said he was "surprised and dismayed" at an apparent threat by Macmillan that senior management would leave the company in the event of its purchase by Maxwell. Macmillan management was thought to be fiercely opposed to Maxwell's efforts to acquire the company. They were said to regard Maxwell as "an unpredictable and capricious businessman who knew nothing about the U.S. publishing business."

Maxwell added that he would withdraw if Macmillan had a "financed, binding alternative proposal" that would be worth more to Macmillan's shareholders than his offer.

He added that he was prepared to buy all or part of Macmillan; specifically he offered to pay "at least" $1.4 billion for eleven specific information service divisions. These included Standard Rate and Data Service, an advertising rate and circulation subscription service, and Michie Co., a legal publisher. Apparently Evans had previously indicated to Maxwell that Macmillan was only willing to sell between $400 and $750 million of information services assets to Maxwell as a means of financing its proposed restructuring plan. On September 11 the stock closed at $83.875, up $3.625.

On September 12, Macmillan announced that it had abandoned its restructuring proposal and instead agreed to a leveraged buyout by KKR valued at $85 per share, or $2.36 billion. Its poison pill would be withdrawn for this transaction only, which both Macmillan's management and board of directors supported.

This transaction would consist of a public tender offer for 94 percent of the 27.8 million Macmillan shares outstanding. Each shareholder would receive $80 in cash and $2.50 principal amount of subordinated debentures and a warrant that, under certain circumstances, could be exchanged for an additional $2.50 principal amount of debentures. The offer would be conditional on KKR's receiving at least 51 percent of the outstanding stock through the tender offer and on KKR's ability to arrange financing for the transaction. Those not tendering their shares to KKR would expect to be offered $85 also, but only in debentures and warrants—no cash—in the contemplated event of a forced merger following the tender offer.

The debentures would have a 15 percent coupon for the first two years, which would then decline to 14.5 percent. These were "pay-in-kind" (PIK) securities: KKR's affiliate making the offer could pay interest on the debentures in cash or in additional subordinated debentures for the first five years.

The KKR proposal would honor the golden parachutes of Macmillan's five seniormost officers to receive their $60 million payment. Management's shares, valued at the buyout price, were worth $141 million; Evans's own shares were valued at $67 million.

Management would be entitled to purchase or otherwise accumulate 20 percent of the new ownership company controlled by KKR. Initially they would be permitted to purchase $23 million of shares in this company. Any additional shareownership would be acquired through stock grants or options.

KKR's financing for the transaction would be provided by Bankers Trust, which committed itself to lend KKR $500 million and to use its best efforts to arrange an additional $1.48 billion, for which commitment fees of $7 million and drawdown fees of $32 million would be paid. KKR had pledged $250 million in equity and $230 million in a subordinated bridge loan, both from limited partnerships controlled by KKR.

In addition, Drexel Burnham Lambert stated that it was "highly confident" that it could privately place or underwrite a public offering of $960 million of high-yield debt securities. Of these proceeds, $230 million would be used to repay the KKR bridge loan and the rest would go to reduce bank debt. Banks, accordingly, were very interested to know just how confident Drexel would be of arranging the financing that would reduce their exposure to the LBO. Drexel received a fee of $1 million for its advice and would manage the issue of junk bonds for fees expected to exceed $33 million.

If KKR's offer was topped by another party, Macmillan agreed to pay a "breakup fee" of about $29 million to KKR to pay all of the nonrefundable fees of its bankers and advisers.

Late in the day on Thursday, September 15, Maxwell Communication increased its offer to $86.80, plus the $0.20 per share dividend payment payable to shareholders of record on October 4. The offer was subject to Macmillan's withdrawing its poison pill so shareholders could decide for themselves which offer they preferred. His offer would be financed by a $1.1 billion tender offer facility provided by a syndicate of European banks led by Midland Bank of the United Kingdom and a $1.32 billion credit facility extended to Maxwell Communication by a group of banks led by Crédit Lyonnais. Maxwell would also provide about $400 million of equity. Maxwell said that as an alternative to his new offer, he remained willing to purchase for $1.4 billion the information services businesses he had written to Evans about before.

The next day Bass withdrew its offer, noting that its "willingness to initiate a lawsuit against the management's proposed restructuring and to begin a tender offer led to a full and fair price." Bass's profits were around $15 to $20 per share on nearly 8 million shares, less legal and financing expenses, a substantial reward for putting the company in play.

On September 22, the Macmillan board withdrew its approval of the $85 offer from KKR. It then undertook to request each of the bidders to submit their best and final offers by 5:30 P.M. on Monday, September 26. That evening Maxwell offered to raise his bid to $89; a revised KKR bid then stood at $89.50: $82 in cash and the rest in subordinated debentures and warrants. The KKR bid, obviously favored by management, also contained conditions: Macmillan must give it a "lockup option" to acquire eight of Macmillan's businesses for a total of $950 million; a definitive sale agreement must be executed by noon the next day; and KKR's bid must be kept entirely confidential or else it would expire automatically. A few hours later (after an unauthorized phone call from Evans and Reilly to KKR that communicated the amount of the Maxwell bid) KKR bid $90.05, in a new package consisting of $82.50 in cash, $3.00 in subordinated debentures, and $5.00 in warrants to purchase additional subordinated debt. Macmillan's advisers discounted the KKR package to $89.70 to $89.80, and the board announced that it had accepted KKR's revised offer and recommended that its shareholders likewise accept it. Again, the poison pill would be lifted for this transaction only.

Maxwell was unhappy with this result, believing he had not been given time to react to the most recent KKR offer before it had been accepted. In a prepared statement, Maxwell said he was "shocked that the Macmillan board would enter into this hasty, ill-conceived, front-end loaded, two-tier, junk bond financed offer . . . without even contacting me." Maxwell added that he was "reviewing his options."

On September 29, Maxwell bid $90.25 in cash, subject to the removal by the board of the poison pill, the cancellation of the option given by the board to KKR to purchase the publishing businesses, and a limit of $70 million to be placed on breakup fees paid by

Macmillan to KKR. Maxwell also offered to purchase instead four of the publishing businesses covered by the KKR option for $900 million.

Macmillan subsequently announced that it would not accept Maxwell's higher bid as it had already accepted KKR's bid after a request for final bids from each side and because it was obligated by the lockup agreement to sell the publishing companies to KKR.

Maxwell then sued to have the poison pill and the lockup agreement rescinded on the basis of the argument that, in the first case, the two bids now on the table were substantially similar in value and shareholders should not be precluded from a choice because management had a preference for one of the bids. In the other case, Maxwell argued that the auction process had been so flawed and corrupted as to be invalid and, because it was invalid, its product— the lockup agreement—should be thrown out.

On October 17, the Delaware Chancery Court announced that it had disallowed Macmillan's poison pill, on the basis of the Maxwell reasoning, but would allow the lockup agreement to stand. The auction process had been flawed, the court allowed, but Maxwell had an opportunity to bid higher, which he, a competent, well-advised player in this highly sophisticated game, passed up. Maxwell said he would appeal this decision to the Delaware Supreme Court. Both sides were enjoined from purchasing additional shares until the Supreme Court acted.

On October 22, KKR announced it had been tendered two-thirds of all the Macmillan stock outstanding. On October 22, the Macmillan stock price closed at $87⅞.

On November 2, 1988, a three-judge panel of the five-member Delaware Supreme Court overturned the Chancery Court's ruling and disallowed the Macmillan-KKR lockup agreement. The court unanimously agreed that the auction was "neither evenhanded nor neutral," adding, "There must be the most scrupulous adherence to ordinary principles of fairness in the conduct of an auction"; the Macmillan actions had been a "departure" from these principles.

Maxwell then announced that he would complete his tender offer by 12:01 A.M. the next day, November 3. Owners of shares already tendered to KKR who preferred an all-cash payment, as almost all did, withdrew their shares and retendered them to Maxwell. He also announced that he had met with Evans and other members of senior management and that he was "pleased by their willingness to cooperate in an orderly transaction." Maxwell also noted that his son Kevin would be joining the senior management group.

Maxwell added that his effort to acquire Macmillan had been long, expensive, and arduous and his patience had been tried on many occasions, but in the end, the process had resulted in a fair and just conclusion.

The Macmillan defense was as good a game for spectators as any Superbowl playoff. All of the players were supremely competent, tough as could be, and played to win. The outcome was a cliffhanger, decided only at the last minute. Macmillan lost in the end because it incurred too many penalties.

The Macmillan case demonstrates all of the principles, activities, and stratagems of the time. A raider started it off and went home rich. Though well prepared to resist an offer from Bass, Macmillan blundered badly with its management-led restructuring plan. Evans and Reilly were clearly using the opportunity provided by the offer to enrich themselves right under the eyes of its board and advisers. The board, passive and lulled to sleep by a combination of well-deserved confidence in Evans and a surfeit of amenities, neither restrained Evans nor took control of the auction process. The advisers, not paid to judge management's morality, didn't. In the end the only players who could claim influence over Evans, the advisers, did not succeed in doing so, thus deciding the outcome.

The outcome, however, was entirely determined by the court, applying case law that prescribed new rules and procedures that did not exist a few years before. Management's cram-down restructuring at $64.15 would probably have succeeded and ended the matter if it had occurred before *Unocal*. However much the transaction seemed to favor the management group, the unenhanced business-judgment rule would likely have been applied and the restructuring plan allowed.

The true and perhaps only winners in the Macmillan deal were the Macmillan shareholders and the IRS. Maxwell had been forced into competition with KKR to bid an "adequate" price that may have exceeded the "fair" price for the company; only time will tell. Evans and his management colleagues left Macmillan, losers in the contest, but still needing a Brinks truck to carry their capital-gains and golden parachute payments to the bank. KKR, which had devised a finely engineered plan for acquiring Macmillan, walked away unvictorious but undamaged, its expenses covered by the breakup fee. The lawyers and bankers, of course, were well paid for their expertise, just as brain surgeons are, regardless of the outcome. Certainly their efforts resulted in a gloriously high price for the Macmillan shareholders, one that might not have been attained if the auction had not continued or had not been so dependent on sophisticated financial techniques to keep KKR in the game: Bass's highest bid was $75, and Maxwell offered only $80 to top it. The extra $10 per share that KKR was able to draw out of Maxwell was worth $273 million to Macmillan shareholders.

Finally it is clear that savage, hardball defenses must now be measured against a standard of fairness that did not apply before. As Marty Lipton says, the securities laws don't require fairness and there is no government policy on what should and should not be allowed. Thanks to the poison pill, state courts in deciding issues related to their removal through corporate law now apply the missing standard of fairness. This has changed the game, improved the marketplace, and removed abuses: all things that Lipton, author of the poison pill, has argued and fought for.

Successes of companies that become subject to raids are relatively rare, success being defined as retaining independence without undergoing a restructuring that is almost as painful as losing the battle. In 1989 there was one that will be remembered, and emulated, for quite a long time.

New Developments at Polaroid

On July 13, 1988, I. MacAllister Booth, president and chief executive officer of Polaroid, announced that the company was planning a major Employee Stock Ownership Plan–based restructuring to protect itself against hostile suitors. The company would guarantee a loan by its ESOP to purchase approximately 14 percent of Polaroid's common stock.

Polaroid is a Delaware corporation. Under a 1988 amendment to Delaware corporation law a prospective acquirer is prevented from consummating a business combination with a Delaware corporation for a period of three years after it becomes a 15 percent stockholder— unless it obtains board approval before becoming a 15 percent holder or it acquires 85 percent of the company's stock in the transaction that caused it to become a 15 percent holder. In other words, the ESOP's 14 percent of the company (a very large amount for such plans) together with family and other friendly shareholdings would be sufficient to invoke this provision of Delaware law. A raider would have to want to own Polaroid pretty badly to be willing to shell out all the money for it and then have to wait three years before controlling the company, eliminate its troublesome minority interests, sell off its assets, or consolidate it with its financing vehicle for tax purposes. The only question was, Would the Delaware courts allow such an ESOP arrangement, which had the effect of precluding a takeover under Delaware law? Would it pass the scrutiny of the Chancery Court's enhanced business-judgment review?

There had been many rumors of potential takeover attempts of Polaroid. The company was experiencing operating difficulties and expected that its second-quarter earnings would be well behind those of the preceding year. Camera sales had been down for two years in a row. Management had been working for some time on various cost-cutting and profit improvement programs that Booth believed would bear fruit in due course but to date had not.

Polaroid was also engaged in a lengthy treble-damages lawsuit with Kodak, in which it was charging patent infringement: the suit was begun in 1976 and had been decided in Polaroid's favor in 1985, though damages that Polaroid estimated at $2.5 billion had not been assessed and Kodak was still hoping to appeal the suit to the Supreme Court. The outcome was still unknown, though Booth believed it was promising.

Polaroid's stock, which had reached a high of $41 during 1987, had traded in the low $20s to high $30s range during 1988 (it was now about $30), reflecting the aftermath of the crash in October 1987 and the operating problems the company had, but also, since March, a speculative optimism that either the Kodak settlement would pay off big or someone would take the company over at a premium price.

Booth knew the company was vulnerable, which is why he announced that it was planning to restructure itself, but he also felt that the invigoration the restructuring and substantial employee ownership would offer would be an important element in Polaroid's profit recovery efforts.

A week later, on July 21, the uncertainty was over and Polaroid was in action. Shamrock Holdings, a family investment company controlled by Roy E. Disney, the son of Walt Disney's brother and lifetime business partner, announced a hostile bid for Polaroid at $40 per share, a price that valued the company at $2.3 billion. Polaroid's stock jumped $6 to close at $40.

Shamrock had been stalking Polaroid since late 1987, when it had received a takeover plan from Wertheim Schroder (an investment bank in which the British merchant bankers J. Henry Schroder hold a 50 percent interest) for breaking up the company to fund a leveraged buyout. Neither Shamrock nor Wertheim Schroder had ever played major roles in deals of this size before, but in the current environment that fact was not inhibiting. The Wertheim plan involved selling Polaroid's plants to Kodak for $1.2 billion, firing half of its marketing and administrative staff, cutting back on its $150 million R & D expenditures, and shelving Polaroid's plans for entering the 35-millimeter film market. The plan also called for settling the Kodak suit quickly for cash, possibly for $600 million or so as opposed to the $1 to $2 billion Polaroid was hoping for. The Wertheim plan became part of the public record in due course.

Aware of its exposure, the Polaroid board had considered additional takeover defenses late in 1987. Though it already had a poison pill, it had studied the formation of an ESOP that would own 4 or 5 percent of the company's stock along with other possibilities. There were a number of tax and other advantages associated with ESOPs that could be advantageous to the company. It had consulted Shearson Lehman Hutton and the corporate lawyers Cravath, Swain & Moore on its alternatives in the event of a takeover. Management was instructed to stiff-arm any requests for meetings or telephone conversations with senior officers of other companies that might try to spring an unwelcome proposal on them.

Early in June 1988, Shamrock decided to move. It began to accumulate Polaroid stock. On June 16 Roy Disney attempted to telephone Booth to request a meeting. He could not get through, so he wrote Booth a letter that was received on June 22 announcing that Shamrock had acquired 5 percent of Polaroid's stock and requesting that a meeting be arranged. Booth delayed the meeting until July 13, immediately called in his advisers, and began to review Polaroid's options.

Though Booth certainly wanted to repel Shamrock (which was yet to make an offer), he did not want to find himself forced to merge with someone else as a consequence. Nor, as an alternative, did he want to undertake such a severe restructuring of the company as to be left with an amount of debt that he and his board would consider insupportable. The board assumed that it had less than a month, until July 13, to work something out before Shamrock pulled the trigger.[10]

The ESOP idea appealed to Booth and the others. If they could make it a big one, involving, say, about $300 million, they might be able to acquire as much as 14 percent of Polaroid's outstanding stock, thereby bringing the Delaware merger statute into play. The employees, however, would have to band together to support such an effort and be prepared to borrow the money through the ESOP (from Polaroid) to make the purchase. If so, there would be a number of substantial tax and financing advantages available to Polaroid and the ESOP. All payments into the ESOP by Polaroid (of interest *and* principal *and* of dividends on ESOP-owned Polaroid shares) would be deductible against Polaroid's federal income taxes. Also, Polaroid as a lender to the ESOP could exclude from its taxable income 50 percent of the interest income earned on the loan, thus permitting it to offer interest rates about 20 percent below market rates to the ESOP.

To repay Polaroid, employees would have to accept a 5 percent pay cut and agree to forgo some portion of their future pay increases. Polaroid's employees responded quickly and enthusiastically. They feared the possibility of a takeover, no doubt, but also liked the idea of becoming substantial shareholders in the company. This was something Booth hoped would raise company morale and productivity as reportedly it had in a number of companies with substantial ESOPs that were analyzed in a September 1987 article by Corey Rosen and Michael Quarrey in the *Harvard Business Review*.

For management not to be deemed to be in control of the ESOP shares, each employee must have the right to vote and tender his own stock as he sees fit. Otherwise, such shares would be excluded from the 85 percent Delaware requirement. Employees, however, could be expected to support management in takeover situations, at least up to a point where either the price becomes irresistible or management has let the employees down in some way.

Remarkably, by July 12, Polaroid had its $300 million ESOP in place, which it announced the next day along with an outline of a plan to repurchase Polaroid shares in the market or through a tender offer. The meeting with Disney was canceled. Shamrock then launched its $40 offer and sued Polaroid in the Delaware Chancery Court to rescind its poison pill and the ESOP that Shamrock claimed had been knocked together quickly as an unreasonable and disproportionate response to an offer that had not even been made. Hearings, however, would not begin until October 19. Polaroid stock traded at a high during the month of July of $43.75.

In August Shamrock raised its offer to $42 and announced that Drexel Burnham was willing to provide financing for it. This offer, too, was rejected, as was a friendly approach to Polaroid by the LBO operators Forstmann Little.

Meanwhile, Polaroid was working on four fronts simultaneously:

the stock repurchase program, the Kodak suit (which had progressed favorably), an internal profit improvement program that involved work-force reductions, and an effort to put together an investor group friendly to management that would purchase a substantial minority interest. Such individuals or groups, not quite having the impact of a knight, are called "white squires." White squires are often in demand by companies under attack that do not want to give up control, but not many squires come forward who are willing to enter into the necessary long-term "standstill agreement" (preventing further accumulations of the company's stock without permission) that turns them into passive investors.

Polaroid was also defending itself against numerous lawsuits filed by Shamrock. All were proceeding slowly. In order to influence the court, a group of employees independent of management organized a petition in opposition to Shamrock's efforts, which was signed by fifty-eight hundred of Polaroid's eighty-five hundred employees. By this time, of course, the employees were familiar with the Wertheim Schroder plan.

On January 6, 1989, the Chancery Court upheld the ESOP. The court was influenced particularly by the fact that Polaroid had been considering the plan before an offer was made, that the plan made business sense for the company, and that it was not coercive of employees, who voluntarily had agreed to pay cuts to finance it. Shamrock, naturally, appealed to the Delaware Supreme Court.

On January 19 Shamrock raised its offer again, to $45. Polaroid rejected it too.

Then on January 31 Polaroid announced the details of its restructuring plan. It would consist of a repurchase of approximately 24.5 million of Polaroid shares through an $800 million tender offer for 16 million shares at $50 per share, and open-market purchases of another 8.5 million shares for approximately $350 million. The repurchases would be financed by a Morgan Guaranty Bank–led $950 million loan syndication and by a $300 million purchase of new voting convertible preferred stock by an investment partnership, Corporate Partners L.P. The plan's aim, according to Booth, was "to deliver to shareholders directly a portion of the company's current value while enhancing the company's prospects for future growth in share-holder value." It would also protect shareholders' interests in a possible distribution of some of the proceeds from the Kodak lawsuit.

The effect of the plan was to create a pool of shareholders that were friendly to management (the ESOP and Corporate Partners), which would own about 16.6 million shares, and to reduce the total number of shares outstanding by the 24.5 million shares to be repurchased. Thus the friendly shareholders would own about 26 percent of all Polaroid shares when these exercises were complete: enough to block all but the most determined, and patient, of bidders. If and when any Kodak money came along it could be used to buy in more shares or to repay debt, which at its peak would push Polaroid's debt-to-capitalization ratio to only 35 percent. This was a much more modest debt level than most companies undergoing radical restructuring experienced, though it would not prevent Polaroid from seeing its bond ratings collapse below (but just below) investment-grade levels.

Corporate Partners, organized from among the partners and clients of the investment bankers Lazard Frères, played an important but not essential role in the restructuring. The ESOP position by itself would serve as a substantial takeover defense in the future, and Polaroid could have increased its borrowings further to repurchase shares or stretched out the repurchase program over a longer time. However, with Corporate Partners the maximum impact could be achieved when Polaroid needed it most. The terms of the preferred shares bought by Corporate Partners were tailored to suit its investors, a limited partnership that passed all tax benefits directly back to its partners. The preferred stock paid dividends of 11 to 11.5 percent, but only 3 percent of these were to be paid in cash. The rest was paid in more shares of convertible preferred, and the conversion into common stock would occur at $50 per share, a price 16 percent above the market for Polaroid at the time of the announcement. However, Corporate Partners would receive warrants to purchase additional common stock, would be invited to designate two representatives to be elected to the Polaroid board of directors, would have 6 million common voting rights even before the preferred was converted into common stock, and would have special rights to sell their shares back to Polaroid by 1993 for a price set to guarantee the investors an all-in minimum return on investment for the period of 30 percent per annum. Counted against this return would be market appreciation on the common stock and warrants, dividends, and any distributions of Kodak damages. On balance most observers believed the securities were fairly priced for both sides.

The struggle ended when the Delaware Supreme Court upheld Polaroid on both the ESOP and its other antitakeover measures on March 20, 1989, and Shamrock withdrew. Polaroid shares closed on March 31 at $37.125.

Management had been successful in establishing that the best interests of the company were served by declining an offer of $45 now, in order to retain ownership of shares worth at least $37 now *plus* the opportunity for appreciation in the near future from improved earnings, fewer shares outstanding, a more leveraged capital structure, a motivated work force, and the future possibility of a windfall from Kodak.

The backing of the courts was crucial, of course. In the Polaroid case the judge was impressed by the timing of the ESOP—it had been seriously considered before the threat of a takeover appeared. If it had come afterward, the result may not have been the same.

One result of the Polaroid case has been the widespread rush to set up large ESOPs, usually with company loans or loan guarantees, by companies not currently under attack. In August 1988 J.C. Penney arranged a $700 million ESOP financing, and in January 1989 (just after the favorable Polaroid Chancery Court decision) Procter & Gamble announced that it would add $1 billion of borrowed money to its ESOP, upping its ownership in the company to 20 percent. Since then dozens of other companies have followed suit. No doubt many present or future takeover attempts that might have occurred will not because of Polaroid's developments.

There were some signs in early 1989 that the tide was beginning to turn away from the large LBO back toward the more familiar shores of industrial mergers arranged through the friendly exchange of shares. The $10 billion merger of SmithKline Beckman Corporation with the U.K. firm Beecham Group plc was one; the $12 billion merger of Squibb and Bristol-Myers was another. The market was not especially surprised when on March 3, 1989, Time Inc. announced its planned merger with Warner Communications in a transaction in which each share of Warner common stock would be exchanged for 0.465 shares of newly issued Time stock. The closing price of Warner on the day before the announcement was $45⅞; the offer valued each of these shares at $50¾, a modest 10.6 percent premium, suitable for a "merger of equals" situation in which neither side would gain control of the other. Warner's chairman, Steven Ross, commented, "Time and Warner have complementary business and artistic resources," adding, "Together the combined company will be well positioned for the future and able to compete effectively throughout the world."

Buying Time

The market reacted immediately, and in complete defiance of financial laws of gravity drove Time's stock up, not down, and more so than Warner's: Time's shares went to the $122 area (up 12 percent) while Warner's rose to a level just below the original offering value, around $50. With Time at $122, the Warner shares were trading at a 12 percent discount from the value of 0.465 for Time shares. It should have been the other way around, with Time's shares falling some and Warner's rising. Time's offer valued Warner at more than $9 billion; Time itself was trading at a market capitalization of $6.9 billion at $122. The Time-Warner deal would also involve an interim cross-purchase of shares and some other provisions to deter alternative offers.

The reason for the apparently peculiar market reaction to the deal was that although Time, the better-known company, appeared to be the stronger party in the transaction, the reality was otherwise.

Both companies were about the same size (revenues of $4.5 billion), but Warner shareholders, who would receive a modest premium for their shares, would end up owning more of the combined company than Time shareholders. Thus, of the two companies, Time was the one thought to be more vulnerable to an offer from some other party. Its stock moved up further, to a high of $135. The arbitrageurs were backing Time this time.

They were right.

On June 7, 1989, Paramount Communications (the new name of Gulf + Western, a born-again 1960s conglomerate) announced a $175 per share cash tender offer for Time, valuing it at $10.7 billion, a 60 percent premium over its price before the Warner announcement. "Time and Paramount are a superb business fit," said Martin Davis, chairman of Paramount. "Together we will be the foremost American communications company, capable of competing on a global scale against foreign media giants."

Davis added that Paramount was also commencing litigation in Delaware Chancery Court seeking to enjoin the Time-Warner deal on the grounds that Time had actually put itself up for sale to Warner by virtue of the share-exchange ratio in which 61 percent of the voting power of the combined company would be vested in former Warner shareholders. If the court agreed, Paramount noted, then Time's directors, according to *Revlon*, could not arbitrarily block through its poison pill a higher offer from Paramount.

There it lay. If Time were ruled to be selling itself, then it was likely that the court would force the directors to allow its shareholders to choose for themselves which offer they preferred. If not, then the struggle could go on, the next events in which were the shareholders meetings that had been called for June 23 for both companies to vote on the Time-Warner merger proposal. If Time allowed its meeting to take place on schedule then there was a good chance that the shareholders (increasingly consisting of arbitrageurs despite the size of the deal) might vote against the merger.

So Time and Warner regrouped and adopted a different approach instead. The merger proposal was withdrawn and replaced by a plan in which Time would offer to purchase about half of Warner's shares for $70 per share in cash, then merge Warner into Time by acquiring the rest of the Warner shares through an exchange of new securities (or cash) worth not less than $70 per share. This plan would not require a Warner shareholder's vote and was supported by Warner's management and protected by Time's poison pill, which would block a hostile bid from Paramount. Thus, although the deal would require that Time pay out between $7 and $14 billion in cash, most of which it would have to borrow, thereby leveraging itself almost to LBO levels, if it could win in court on the "For Sale sign" issue, then it would be home free.

The deal had some sensitive aspects, however. There was the fact that Time's directors were acting on a de facto merger proposal of vital interest to shareholders in such a way that shareholders would be confronted with a fait accompli. Time would be very highly leveraged after the merger (its senior debt would be downgraded to BB by Standard & Poor's—a junk bond rating) and had agreed to very attractive compensation arrangements for Warner (and their own) executives. An unhappy Time shareholder would be unable to vote for the Paramount offer, which was subsequently raised to $200 per share. Analysts were saying that the intrinsic value of a well-managed Time was about $240. If the court ruled in Time's favor, the Paramount offer would be rejected and Time's stock price, which reached a high of 160 on June 30, would plummet. Many shareholders (certainly including those who had only just become shareholders) supported the higher priced Paramount bid and were outraged that Time directors could get away with suppressing it.

The Chancery Court heard both sides in July and rendered its decision in late August in favor of Time. The court ruled that Time's board had a long-term strategy for the company, to which it had adhered over the years, calling for a combination with a communications company in the best interest of the enterprise. In such a case the ownership issue was not paramount. Time, it held, had not made itself available for sale; on the contrary, it had pursued long-established enterprise objectives. Therefore Time's actions were consistent with enhanced business-judgment standards and the court could not force it onto the auction block. The board was held to be within its rights in acquiring Warner without a shareholder vote while the Paramount offer was on the table, even though it knew, in doing so, that its share price would decline for the short run (as it did, to below $100 by March 1990).

The court noted that (as in all enterprise matters)

> the financial vitality of the corporation and the value of the company's shares is in the hands of the directors and managers of the firm. The law does not operate on the theory that directors, in exercising their powers to manage the firm, are obligated to follow the wishes of a majority of shares.

The opinion, though reviled in some quarters as having denied Time shareholders an opportunity to sell for a 100 percent profit, was welcome in others. Having seen the poison pill overturned, leading to an immediate change of control in Revlon, Macmillan, and Pillsbury (which was taken over by Grand Metropolitan plc in 1988), corporate defenders were beginning to lose heart. The *Polaroid* and *Time* decisions demonstrated that all was not lost and that there were reasonable escapes from the unwelcome embraces of others through intelligent restructuring and long-range planning. After the Time decision Marty Lipton sent his clients memoranda urging them to consider and document the long-term requirements for the firm for possible use in courtrooms of the future. Under such circumstances, "just say no" is eminently more defensible.

Lipton believes that the takeover battlefield has moved from the marketplace to the courthouse, as indeed it has thanks to a significant innovation of his own design, the poison pill. Now, perhaps, with a growing body of case law setting forth new rules by which the battles are to be waged, the battlefield will shift again, perhaps to the Labor Department, which administers ESOPs, or to the Department of Transportation, which had a great deal of influence on airline acquisitions in 1989, or the Federal Communications Commission, which can affect the outcome of media industry mergers, or the

Federal Reserve Board or even the FTC, which periodically threatens to bear once again the fangs of antitrust action. In time, the battlefield may drift back to the marketplace again where a substantial body of new practices will have accumulated. Certainly the tactics do change, again and again as the battles continue. And the tactics have been refined by competent and considered intervention by the courts. Takeovers are no longer ruled only by laws of the marketplace (a jungle to some); now consideration must be given to issues of fairness, balance, and rights of enterprise preservation.

The courts have indeed checked the savage arm of the raider, but equally they have forced management and boards of directors out into the open, making it difficult for them to manipulate affairs to their advantage. As evidenced by the *Time-Warner* decision, the courts currently appear to favor rewarding evidence of long-range plans to maximize values, whether or not there is conclusive evidence that such plans can do so, even to the extent of allowing ultimate ownership issues to be concluded without a shareholder vote.

No doubt there is much controversy yet to be resolved in these issues. But for the time being, Polaroid's "victory" in beating off an aggressive junk-financed, bust-up leveraged buyout offer without having to undergo a crippling inversion of its own capital structure to do so, and Time's success in demonstrating that sensible long-term plans were worth having, have been cheered all across the land—at least in those homes in which Time shareholders did not dwell.

6

THE AMAZING LBO
MACHINE

"They made $250 million! On an investment of only a million—in eighteen months. That's incredible!"

So said countless readers of the *Wall Street Journal* on the morning of May 19, 1983, when they had finished the article describing the successful sale of 3.5 million shares of Gibson Greeting Inc. in an initial public offering of 30 percent of the company's stock. The sellers of the shares were the company itself (selling new shares to repay debt) and Wesray Corp., an investment partnership owned by William E. Simon, former Salomon Brothers bond salesman and U.S. Secretary of the Treasury until 1977, and Ray Chambers, a professional money manager with whom Simon had teamed up after returning to the private sector. Wesray had bought Gibson Greeting Cards from RCA in 1982 for $80 million. RCA had been slimming down and was happy to get rid of Gibson, which fit into none of its businesses.

Both Simon and Chambers had invested only about $330,000 of their own money in the transaction. They had borrowed the rest from banks and two sophisticated finance companies, General Electric Credit Corp. and Barclays Business Credit. They didn't change much in the company during the year they owned it—the same management was there, though it now owned about 20 percent of the stock in the company and therefore had an extra incentive to work hard to increase earnings. In 1983, Gibson's earnings before interest and taxes increased 49 percent over 1982 results.

The financial markets, however, did much better in 1983 than they had in the preceding year. The Reagan bull market was in full surge; interest rates on long-term government bonds had fallen, and the stock market flourished, rising from a low point Dow Jones average of about 800 in mid-1982 to close out the year at about 1200. Early in 1983 Wesray realized that it might be able to refinance some of the debt undertaken to acquire Gibson Greetings at substantially lower interest rates and sell off some of the stock in the company into the strong market that was then developing for initial public offerings, or IPOs. Such steps would enable Simon and Chambers to "cash out" of the deal, or to retrieve all or part of their investment, much sooner than they had expected. Markets had moved in their favor, increasing the value of the company they had bought, at least on paper. To realize these gains, they would have to be opportunistic.

By the time they were ready to bring the IPO to market, conditions had improved further. They decided to sell more stock, finally agreeing to offer about 30 percent of their holdings. At the offering price of $27.50 per share, which valued the company at $330 million, Wesray had earned a $250 million profit, before taxes, in just over a year, and about $70 million each for Simon and Chambers.

Commentators at the time claimed that Wesray had bought Gibson cheaply from RCA, which having become overweight and inefficient didn't know the value of what it was selling, and that Wesray had caught the markets just right. Shrewd, said some. Lucky, said others.

In any event, their timing was right. After the public offering, the stock hung in the range of $18 to $26 per share until July 27, 1984, when Wesray announced that Gibson would be merged into Walt Disney for stock or cash worth about $30 per share. Within two and a half years after the LBO, Simon and Chambers had gotten all of their money out.

The Gibson Greetings deal attracted enormous attention, partly because of the extraordinary and quick returns and partly because of the involvement of Bill Simon, a colorful, outspoken, strongly conservative individual who seemed to attract success no matter what he did: as a Salomon partner, as a young appointee in the Nixon administration who ended up there as Treasury Secretary, as an author—his philosophical defense of free-market capitalism published after leaving office was a best-seller—and now as an investor. But mostly, attention was attracted to *leveraged buyouts*, or *LBOs*—a special financing technique that seemed close to alchemy in its ability to produce great and sudden riches for those savvy enough to become involved with them.

The basic concept of the LBO was to find a company that was seemingly undervalued by the stock market if already a public company, or otherwise by its corporate owners; to purchase the company for the purpose of rejuvenating it by strong incentives to operating management; and then to resell it either in the public market through an IPO or in the merger market. The business to be acquired did not have to be an especially successful one. Preferably it would be a mundane, underappreciated non-cyclical enterprise with a reliable cash flow and comparatively small requirements for expensive capital investments. On such a base the new owner could borrow a considerable amount against the purchase price. He could borrow even more if he was willing to pay exceptionally high interest rates on a tranche of junior debt that would share in some of the future financial values of the company. Thus the new owner, not having any real interest in the business beyond its ability to act as a vehicle for investment profits, could minimize the amount of his investment, and thus his risk, and with the advantage of all the borrowing be able to maximize his returns.

All the borrowing, of course, enabled the LBO owner to recapture the money that the company had previously paid out in taxes, a substantial advantage that would help it repay debt quickly. The borrowing also forced the company to cut out all non-essential expenditures and to work hard lest everyone's investment be lost. After a few years of running the company for cash and to repay debt, its earnings would recover and it could be sold, or refinanced, earning large profits for its equity investors.

The structure of these deals was not greatly different from the commercial real estate deals that had made so many billionaires during the past decade. Nor were they much different from the railroad recapitalizations done by J. P. Morgan in the late nineteenth century. A hundred years later, however, the LBO would have enormous impact on American corporate finance; it would increase by nearly a third the volume of transactions occurring in the great merger boom of the 1980s in the United States.

In 1980, LBOs aggregating about $2 billion in capitalized value were completed. By 1984, the year in which Gibson Greetings cashed out, the volume had swollen to 76 LBOs totalling $11.8 billion. LBOs became very hot.[1] Some of the more experienced operators sold funds to institutional investors through which they could participate in the equity investments of LBOs. KKR sold its first such fund— for $30 million—in 1978; in 1984 it completed its fourth fund, this one for $1 billion. Banks, having learned much about how to structure their participations in LBOs, increased them. And, perhaps most important in the explosion of LBO deals that followed after 1986, junk bonds became the principal source of subordinated, or junior, debt financing. Anyone who could raise the junior financing could get the rest easily, so access to junk financing, which was then controlled by Michael Milken of Drexel Burnham, was crucial to those who wanted to master the great, infallible money-making machine of the eighties.

Milken and Drexel contributed a number of players to the game, mainly highly ambitious, aggressive financial entrepreneurs. Most lacked polish and experience, and all lacked money. In 1984, Milken decided that he would arrange table stakes for these deserving New Men of American finance, and by propelling them into the heart of the lucrative merger-and-acquisition business, he would get Drexel in there too. According to Milken's painstaking biographer, Connie Bruck, Milken arranged small war chests—of $50, $60, $100 million—for a handful of individuals who were willing and, in his view, able corporate raiders. From these individuals he extracted high fees and, generally, substantial equity stakes in whatever companies he enabled them to acquire. The equity stakes were a means for Milken not only to amass wealth but also to maintain a measure of control over his chosen acquirers. By early 1985, Milken and Drexel had provided many millions of ready cash, or "hunting capital," to Carl Icahn (who with Drexel financing acquired TWA in 1985), Ronald Perelman (who similarly acquired Revlon in 1987), Nelson Peltz (who similarly acquired National Can in 1985), and Bill Farley (who armed with Drexel financing acquired Northwest Industries for $1.4 billion in 1985 and West Point Pepperell for $3 billion in 1989).[2]

In 1986, 212 LBOs aggregating $37.6 billion were completed; in 1988, 239 were completed worth $81.2 billion, approximately 40 percent of all merger-and-acquisition transactions (by value) in that year.

There were a number of variations that the LBOs could take. They could involve a company's management or principal owners, who, desirous of avoiding the disadvantages of public ownership or unsatisfactory partners, would "take the company private" through a management-led LBO. Henry Ford I did this in 1919. More recently the Thompson family, which owned the 7-11 convenience store chain, and Edward Finklestein and his management colleagues at Macy's did it too. Ross Johnson and Edward Evans tried to, but did not succeed. Overall, about 18 percent of all LBOs from 1983–88 were going-private transactions. Mainly, however—to the extent of about 68 percent in the 1983–88 period—the LBOs simply involved the sale of divisions of companies that no longer fit in, as in the Gibson Greetings case. About 16 percent of transactions involved family-owned companies, or companies that had previously arranged LBOs in order to sell out to others later on.[3]

The father of the modern LBO is generally reckoned to be Jerome Kohlberg, Jr., the founder of KKR, who began working on what were then called "bootstrap acquisitions" in the middle sixties, when he was co-head of the corporate finance department of Bear, Stearns & Co., a small investment bank mainly known for its brokerage and trading activities. One of the earliest deals that Kohlberg did at Bear Stearns was for Stern Metals (later called Sterndent), a dental supply and precious metals business owned by a seventy-two-year-old patriarch. The business was purchased for $9.5 million in 1965. Most of the financing for the transaction was borrowed, with a small amount provided by Bear Stearns and its clients. The Sterns, who had retained an ownership interest in the company, continued to run it. The company went public and later began to acquire other companies. After a few years the original investors sold off their $500,000 investment for $4 million. The deal caused Kohlberg to think more about the kind of engineering it involved.[4]

"It wasn't like inventing the wheel because other people were doing bootstrap deals," Kohlberg said. "I refined it by adding the role for management as owners."[5]

Other deals followed, and greater efforts were made to drum up financing for them, especially for the crucial subordinated tranche, called the *mezzanine* financing—positioned where it was between the first floor (the senior bank debt) and the bottom floor (the equity). As more of these deals came to be worked on, Kohlberg needed to increase his team. Henry Kravis and George Roberts, two young Bear Stearns associates who were first cousins, joined him in the early seventies. In 1976 they left to form their own firm, Kohlberg Kravis Roberts & Co., with capital of $120,000. In April 1977, using mostly borrowed money, KKR bought a small truck suspension maker, A.J. Industries, for $25.6 million. They sold this company in 1985 for $75 million.

There were a few other pioneers doing LBOs in the early 1970s. Gibbons, Green and van Amerongen was formed to do bootstrap deals in 1969. Edward Gibbons had been at Laird & Co. early in his career and learned some of the techniques early. Laird specialized in finding promising, ambitious young managers who were eager to become CEOs, giving them an office while they looked for a company to bootstrap and then, once one was found, they worked with Laird to finance it. Forstmann Little, the first LBO firm to specialize in raising money from pension funds, was formed in 1978. Its principal founder, Ted Forstmann, had knocked around on his own for a few years doing a deal here, and a deal there—it didn't take much to get into the business then. Another early player was Martin Dubilier, co-founder and CEO of Clayton and Dubilier, which started as a "crisis management team" for distressed companies and moved into the LBO field in 1978. Dubilier, an operating-management expert, had once been chairman of Sterndent.

The original LBOs depended on close relationships between the investors and management. Deals were not only friendly, the friends got to know each other pretty well before they joined forces. Management had to deliver for the investors—they could not be at odds with them; at the same time, the investors made management commit themselves to a large stake in the company, often by undertaking large personal loans to do so. The investors offered management a chance to become rich that they would not have had without them. Of course, sometimes individual managers had to be replaced, but even then the successor managers had to get along well with the investors. Kohlberg believed that the only way the LBOs could be expected to overcome the heavy burdens and risks that the large amounts of leverage put on them was to have a closely knit association between the financial and operating sides of the business.

Once motivated by both a juicy carrot and a sharp stick, management could be expected to perform to its utmost ability, which in fact was often exceeded when competent, inspired individuals stepped out of the bureaucratic harnesses they had worn before as large-company employees, and began to perform instead as a small task-oriented team with an urgent objective. Not only did they cut out the obviously unnecessary expenditures, they also found ingenious ways to perform their functions differently—usually in ways that used less cash, moved it more quickly, or passed burdens the company had traditionally carried to suppliers or customers. Concentration of focus paid off, as did common ownership. The management group believed they were working for themselves.

In 1979 KKR surprised all of Wall Street with its announcement of a $355 million buyout of Houdaille Industries, a maker of pumps, machine tools, and automotive parts. This was by far the largest transaction of its type ever done, and it caused "the public documents to be grabbed up by every firm on Wall Street," said Frank Richardson of Wesray. "That showed everybody what really could be done. We all said, 'Holy mackerel, look at this.' "[6]

There was a kind of formula for measuring how much an investor group could pay for a particular company. The key to the formula was the company's prospective earnings before interest and taxes, or EBIT, a measure of the company's cash flow available for debt service and profits. The EBIT divided by the annual percentage of debt service to be paid would indicate how much could be borrowed to acquire the company. If EBIT were $1 million, for example, and all of it were to be used to service debt in the early years after the purchase, then $6 or $7 million of borrowings might be undertaken, depending on the interest rate and the repayment schedule in the early years. Perhaps an insurance company, or a knowledgeable industrial-credit company like General Electric Credit Co., could be persuaded to invest an additional $1 or $2 million in a preferred stock or a subordinated debenture that didn't pay out much for a while; maybe the seller would take part of his payment in such a security. Other factors had to be taken into account too, such as the ability to generate cash through the sale and leaseback of assets, sale of underutilized or non-essential assets, changes in working-capital management practices, cancellations or deferrals of capital expenditures, revising pension and benefit programs, and similar efforts. Cash liberated by such activities can be used to repay acquisition debt, reducing it to a residual amount to be repaid further out of cash flow from operations. Perhaps $1 or $2 million of such surplus cash could be found for the example above which a bank would provide bridge financing for, bringing to approximately $9 million that which might be financed for the purchase of the company entirely against its own assets. On the other hand, the equity investor wants to limit his exposure to the transaction to no more than about 5 or 10 percent of the purchase price.

The formula can be juggled about quite a bit depending on the circumstances, but two inviolable principles had to be met: the investor group would not guarantee or collateralize any of the debt with assets outside the company, and it would control all of the equity. The investment would have to stand on its own, and "pull itself up by its own bootstraps."

By the late 1980s, LBOs had become sufficiently active and intriguing to academic observers that a number of scholarly research papers on the subject were published. Whereas some studies claim that the good results for investors are produced mainly by laying off workers, reducing wages, or by possession of insider information on the part of manager-buyers, most focused instead on tax savings, improved market conditions, and various incentives that have increased efficiency and value. One such study, by Steven Kaplan of the University of Chicago, concludes that a review of 76 large management buyouts of public companies completed between 1980 and 1986 showed that the companies experienced post-buyout increases in operating income and net cash flow, and a median increase in market value to the LBO investors of 77 percent. These results were due to improved incentives, Kaplan says, not to layoffs or management exploitation of pre-buyout shareholders through inside information.[7]

Reseeding O.M. Scott & Sons

One recent LBO that reflects the classic features of the LBO deals of the 1970s was the acquisition of O.M. Scott, a lawn fertilizer and grass seed company, by Clayton & Dubilier in December 1986. The business had been bought from ITT, where it had been ignored for years, for $211 million. Banks lent $121 million; other lenders provided $70 million. The equity investors providing $20 million were Clayton & Dubilier and the top ten or so managers of the company, each of whom was offered 60,000 shares at $1 a share, a cheap price.[8]

Martin Dubilier put the deal together, but before he did so he got to know Tadd Seitz, President of the Marysville, Ohio, company. Dubilier believed that Scott had long lacked inspiration. A subsidiary of a subsidiary of a subsidiary of a giant conglomerate, Scott's management was largely ignored at headquarters, paid modest bonuses that were dependent on how ITT did, and generally given little incentive to excel. They didn't work much harder than they had to and had lots of time for Little League.

The business, however, was a healthy one with a good market share and brand recognition. Its plants were all built and operating and needed little additional investment. Research-and-development outlays were modest. Its cash flow was steady and reliable. Still, Dubilier told Seitz over dinner, overhead costs were too high, inventories too big, and management too relaxed to win over new customers. To make the buyout a success, Dubilier added, "your standards are going to have to increase drastically.

"If you don't think you're the guy to solve these problems, let me know, and we'll get someone else," he added.

Seitz and the others in management decided to give it a try. They were scared of their exposure (few had $60,000 they could afford to lose) and the prospects of giving up their nice, safe situations, but they liked Dubilier and saw how the deal could work.

Scott began by selling off a large division, Burpee Seeds, in March 1987. ITT had bought Burpee thinking it would be a good fit for Scott, but Scott decided it would prefer the cash. It unloaded inventories of finished goods. It closed or rearranged certain high-cost summertime production lines, replacing workers with unemployed wintertime farm workers. It negotiated better financing terms from major suppliers. It replaced some senior people and laid off a few workers, asking everyone who remained to increase their productivity. And it arranged a $25 million tax break by writing down some of the assets it had written up on acquisition.

After its first nine months as an LBO, Scott had increased its EBIT by 30 percent. Working capital had been reduced by $15 million, and $40 million of bank debt had been repaid. Such a performance resulted in large cash bonuses for management—Seitz earned $378,000 for the year, well over his $220,000 base salary. Other managers received 20 to 50 percent bonuses.

Dubilier noted, "We could have sold the company after the first year and made ten times our money, but I think in another two years Scott will really reach its potential."

The Runaway Train

It all seemed pretty easy. Huge amounts of money to be made on greeting card and grass seed deals just by applying a new financing technique. For those investors unable to arrange LBOs themselves but large enough to invest in the funds—investors such as state and municipal pension funds, university endowments, insurance companies, and many different banks—they seemed ideal. By investing in a fund which would be invested in many different transactions, an investor's company-specific risk could be diversified away. There was some systemic, or market, risk in such a portfolio, but this could be limited by restricting all such investments to a modest amount of total assets. The high rate of return that the funds promised was hard to resist, especially for performance-oriented investors. The early funds, those organized between 1978 and 1984, did well, some boasting of total returns of more than 50 percent per annum. KKR's first four funds each produced total annualized returns between 30 and 44 percent after carry.

The KKR results, which through its first four funds involved investments in only about thirty deals, were not thought to be appreciably different from those of other funds. In the eight-year period from 1978 to 1986, however, over a thousand LBOs of all types were completed, many of them quite small. Whereas it may be statistically unsound to extrapolate the results of a small sample of the larger, better deals and apply them to the entire population of LBOs, a presumption ought to be justifiable that the superior performance of these sampled funds was shared in to some degree by the rest. The LBO technique appears during this period to have produced results substantially superior to those of acquiring firm returns in general, which Professor Michael Jensen summarizes as being about 4 percent in hostile takeovers and roughly zero in mergers.[9]

Though the LBOs during this period had the special benefit of tax savings from high interest charges (most non-LBO acquirers increased debt substantially to make their acquisitions), their main advantage relative to the others appears to be that due to exceptionally favorable market conditions they were able to cash out fairly quickly at high realized returns, while the stock market did not reflect the comparable unrealized returns in the share prices of the normal, non-LBO corporate acquirers. Whether the LBO was a truly superior acquisition vehicle or not, it was probably too early in the mid 1980s to tell—how LBOs would fare in a serious recession, for example, would make a big difference in longer-term performance assessments—but a lot of people thought they were.

The early LBO operators generally made their money by investing as a principal in a deal. If it worked they could make a large return on their investment; sometimes they would pull some cash out of the company to pay their expenses as they went along, but mostly their profits came from capital gains. KKR, however, was quick to discover a better way to make money from LBOs, with much less risk—by operating as fund manager, not as a principal investor. They would originate, engineer, and execute transactions for a disparate group of investors seeking a participation in the LBO deal flow. They would charge their investors 1.5 percent of the principal amount for managing the fund (somewhat less once it was fully invested), and in addition they would retain a *carried interest*, or *carry*, of 20 percent of the realized profits on the funds' investments after cashing out of particular deals. Further, they were permitted to charge the company in which the investment was made regular investment-banking transaction fees when the company was originally acquired by the LBO group and upon the sale of any divisions or subsidiaries. For each deal, always arranged on a stand-alone basis so liabilities could never wash over to other deals, a special limited partnership would be formed by KKR, which would serve as the required general partner and would make an investment (of its own money) of 1 or 2 percent of the *equity* to be raised for the deal. The rest of the money for the equity (and sometimes for some of the subordinated debt or bridge financing) would come from the funds.

If the investment worked out, KKR would have income from four sources: the management fee, the transaction fees (almost always larger than the amount they invested in the equity), the carry, and capital gains from their small investment.

They would, in short, invest virtually none of their capital and stand to make a fortune on practically every deal for using their know-how, their contacts, and their managerial ability to make money for their clients. The fortune was then divided among only a few partners and less than a dozen professional employees. It is doubtful whether anything J. P. Morgan ever did resulted in such extraordinary leverage of his talent and resources without risking any of his capital.

KKR's total return on its 1984 acquisition of Amstar, a sugar refiner, shows how the system worked: The acquisition price was $465 million, of which $52 million was to be in equity—of this only 1.6 percent ($830,000) was put up by KKR itself. The rest of the equity was provided from the KKR funds. Three years later, Amstar was sold to a Merrill Lynch LBO partnership for a profit of $232 million, a compound rate of return (before the carry) of over 80 percent. Of the profit, KKR received its 20 percent override, $46 million, plus a capital gain of 1.6 percent of the profit, another $3.7 million. The transaction fee for the acquisition of Amstar was probably about 1 percent ($4.65 million), and KKR probably charged another transaction fee on its sale, or 1 percent of $697 million, another $7 million or so. Finally, there was the 1.5 percent that it earned for managing the $51 million that the funds invested in the Amstar equity. Altogether, KKR earned about $62 million—on an investment of less than $1 million. (These figures are not from KKR, but are estimated based on their usual compensation arrangements.) And this deal was only one-fiftieth the size of the RJR-Nabisco transaction.[9]

This kind of profit potential quickly attracted the attention of others. Several traditional investment banks, such as Merrill Lynch, First Boston, Shearson Lehman Hutton, and Morgan Stanley became aggressive investors in LBOs with their own money and with funds they had sold to clients. Most of them took a couple of years to get cranked up and to learn the business. When they did, they became quite aggressive. Goldman Sachs and Salomon Brothers also participated in deals, but were more cautious about getting in the way of their clients. They preferred to act as advisers and to take part of their fee in the form of equity shares in the new firm. Goldman Sachs devised a variation of the LBO in 1984, called a *leveraged partial distribution*, in which a corporation could sell off an uninteresting, low-growth subsidiary to an LBO group in which the seller would be one of the equity investors hoping to realize significantly enhanced returns. Thus a corporation could get the benefit of selling the business and of keeping at least part of it in a highly leveraged, off-balance sheet corporation that might produce far superior results. Several of these deals were done.

By now, investors, intermediaries, and those seeking to sell companies were turning to LBOs. But a bigger change was about to happen, according to Fred Eckert, head of leveraged buyouts at Goldman Sachs in 1985:

> The concept of LBOs was gaining social acceptability in the board rooms of America. The Macy's transaction was probably the one that people will look to as the breakthrough. There is probably no bigger household name than Macy's and the Chairman, basically frustrated by the prospects for future stock market-related incentives for key executives, said, "I want to buy the company for $4.5 billion." It wasn't smooth, but it got done. Suddenly, every CEO looked at what Ed Finklestein stood to make on the transaction and what it had done to his organization to spread stock around to 300 executives, and all those CEOs said, "I want to get in on this." Then we had the start of a runaway train.[10]

By 1986, however, the LBO scene was beginning to change. More and more funds were being raised, and all of this money was in competition with itself for deals to invest in. The big investment banks had begun to power into the market in competition with the fund managers. The size of the average deal increased several fold.

Merrill Lynch (which had been active LBO investors in smaller deals since 1981) bought Jack Eckerd Corp. for $1.5 billion and together with management bought Fruehauf for $1.1 billion in 1986. In 1987, it bought out Borg Warner for $4.7 billion and Supermarkets General for $2 billion. Shearson Lehman joined with Cadbury Schweppes to acquire an interest in Dr. Pepper/Seven Up and with another British company, Beazer plc, to make a $1.6 billion hostile takeover of Koppers, a fiercely resisted transaction that attracted a lot of controversy for Shearson and its parent, American Express, in 1988. Morgan Stanley led groups that purchased Container Corporation of America for $1.2 billion in 1986, Burlington Industries for $2.6 billion in 1987, and Cain Chemical in which a 1987 equity investment of $25 million was cashed out of very successfully in 1988. Morgan Stanley was generally thought to have been the most successful with its LBO portfolio, which consisted of forty deals that accounted for about a third of its total 1988 profits.[11] The firm periodically was rumored to be considering splitting itself into two parts, one the traditional investment bank, which would be sold off, and the other an LBO investor and fund manager that would be retained by current management.

Before long, a manager like KKR trying to invest a $1 billion fund in new deals had to wonder where the deal flow was going to come from to use up all of his own and everyone else's money. By the end of 1988, approximately two hundred LBO funds of one sort or another were competing for deals. Those with large amounts to invest had to go out and hustle deals up and compete hard in public auctions with industrial companies seeking to acquire businesses in their own industry, where substantial synergies were possible.

Soon the market for LBOs became quite crowded. Every acquisition situation generated at least two or three proposals for an LBO. A raided company had to look at his alternatives—perhaps a management buyout would be best. The raider thought about ways to make the most money from the takeover attempt—certain properties might have to be sold, perhaps to other LBO buyers. Meanwhile white knight LBO proposals were drawn up all over town once a target company was put into play. A situation like the Robert Bass offer for Macmillan, Inc. in 1988 resulted in LBO plans being drawn up not only by Bass and KKR, but also by Forstmann Little, which did not bid, by the board of Macmillan, to see what else might be possible, and by Robert Maxwell (the ultimate winner), who wanted to understand better what he was competing against. Several of these deals would have involved discussions with lawyers and commercial banks, which in turn would try to do analyses of their own.

The market had become fully priced after four years of rising stock markets and increasing competition for deals. It was much more difficult than it had been at the beginning of the LBO era to find undervalued companies. Nor could friendly deals be worked out quietly without the seller company's board feeling it had to look for the highest bidder through an auction. It was increasingly difficult to find sizable investments without having to bid top dollar for the companies against a bunch of other LBO types or Johnny-come-lately entrepreneurs who were desperate to get into the business and had the financing in hand. Such shoot-out victories were often difficult or impossible to turn into money-makers. In addition, it was difficult in the time frame permitted by public takeovers to really get to know the management group of a company, to feel as comfortable with them as Martin Dubilier had with Tadd Seitz.

Finally, it was difficult to treat the heads of large public companies, one's new management partners, like the heads of one-product subsidiaries in Marysville, Ohio. They were much more sophisticated, tougher, well advised, and capable of playing one LBO group off against another (with neither of them knowing it) in search of the best possible deal for themselves and their management team.

In 1986 William Simon, who had made several successful LBO investments since Gibson Greetings, announced that Wesray was cancelling a $300 million LBO fund then being organized because the prices of LBOs were now too high and he was going to invest in other things, such as bargain-priced savings and loan associations in California. Though Simon was leaving the scene, Wesray would continue to make investments in LBOs—though cautiously, he said.

And early in 1987, after three large, highly visible, and controversial deals in which KKR had been required to bid top dollar for publicly held corporations in competition with other bidders, Jerry Kohlberg left the company because of "philosophical differences." He had been reluctant to become involved in high-priced, contested situations and was especially reluctant to precipitate them through hostile activity. Such behavior risked the close, trusting relationship between management and investors that he believed was necessary in order to make LBOs work. If the firm found itself on the outs with management, it might have to replace it with new people who would be strangers to the business and the ways to run it most effectively for cash, or worse, it would start having to make management decisions itself, something KKR, at least, was not qualified to do.

Kohlberg, now in his sixties, was ready to consider other aspects of life. He had had a serious illness in 1984—a brain tumor that proved not to be malignant but required complicated surgery and a long convalescence—during which time his two partners ran things. By all accounts they ran things well; in 1984, while Kohlberg was recuperating, KKR did both the first $1 billion LBO, for Wometco, and the first large LBO done by public tender offer, for Malone & Hyde.

They also increased the pressure on themselves in 1985 by launching a fifth KKR fund for $1.8 billion. Then they waded into the Beatrice situation.

The Bust-Up of Beatrice[12]

Long before Beatrice, there was Esmark, and before Esmark there was Norton Simon, Inc. The latter was a 1960s food conglomerate based on the Hunt Foods group that was controlled by Norton Simon, an eccentric, elusive art collector and businessman who had long since left the running of his company to tough, capable, self-made professionals like David Mahoney. In 1983, Mahoney, like many others, thought his company's stock price was too low and offered a management buyout to the board. Instead they sold the company for $945 million (considerably more than Mahoney was offering) to Esmark, formerly Swift & Co., the famous Chicago meat packers. Esmark was headed by another tough, competent, self-made professional, Donald P. Kelly from the South Side of Chicago. Kelly was smart enough to see what was going on around him. Companies were being sold for extraordinary prices, making their stockholders happy. Then the buyers broke up the companies into pieces which they in turn sold in order to get back more in the end than they had paid in the beginning. Out of all this buying and selling there were surely good opportunities for those looking for them.

Kelly decided that the best opportunities came from being an owner of one of the LBO operations, not just one of its workaholic employees. He went to see KKR in 1984, and he worked out a deal for an LBO of Esmark at $55 per share that would leave him in charge and a substantial stockholder. However, he did not reckon on James L. Dutt, Chairman of Beatrice Cos., entering the fray. Dutt badly wanted Beatrice to become the world's leading consumer-products company. When he heard Esmark might be for sale, he paid close attention. He topped the Kelly/KKR bid immediately, and then topped it again, to $60 a share, or $2.7 billion, without any other suitor appearing on the scene. But he got what he had come for. Kelly shrugged, pocketed his $18 million golden parachute payment, and went off to play golf.

Actually Kelly was quite disappointed, and resented being out-maneuvered by Dutt, a strong, difficult man who had offended several Beatrice directors in the manner in which he had gone about acquiring Esmark. Things did not get any better for Dutt with his board after the Esmark acquisition. A number of executives complained that he was acting irrationally and threatened to quit if Dutt continued as chairman and chief executive. Finally, in the latter part of 1985, the board removed him, but had no immediate replacement in mind. A retired vice-chairman, William W. Granger, Jr., was called in as interim chief executive.

KKR immediately took notice. So did Kelly. So did everyone else on Wall Street who was looking for the next mega-deal. Though no offers were made or in discussion, the arbitrageurs were acting as if Beatrice had been put into play. The stock price jumped. KKR and Kelly met, engaged lawyers, hired Drexel Burnham to raise several billion in junk bonds, and retained Martin A. Siegel, Kidder Peabody's merger head, to advise them on the deal. On October 16, 1985, Siegel made an offer of $4.9 billion for Beatrice on behalf of the group. The board was in disarray—it didn't want to sell, but was unable to get the idea across. It was also greatly troubled by its lack of leadership. The KKR offer was polite but very firm and official. It was what the Street calls a "bear hug," not an outright mugging but a fully priced embrace that can be hard to escape.

The company certainly was in play now. Its board had to do something. Arbitrageurs were buying up the stock and urging the company to sell out (one of these arbitrageurs was Ivan Boesky, who was being fed information illegally by Martin Siegel). Without strong management the company seemed weak. "Why fight," many shareholders asked, "when we haven't got the management on board to realize our full potential?"

Two Beatrice executive vice presidents, however, thought a competing LBO proposal might work. They asked Goldman Sachs to explore the possibilities with KKR. Their proposal would exclude Kelly, and therefore, according to Kravis, could not succeed. The banks were nervous about lending so much to an LBO not headed by competent management; they would back a group led by Kelly but not any other. The bear's grip tightened. The price was nudged upward. Beatrice was unprepared to adopt a scorched earth defense or a drastic self-restructuring.

On November 14, KKR and Kelly decided to try to end the matter by raising their price one last time, stretching themselves out as far as they could in order to secure board approval for a "friendly" deal. This time they succeeded and an agreement was reached, modified in January and finalized in February 1986, for Beatrice to be sold to an acquisition vehicle called BCI Holdings Inc. for $40 per share in cash and $10 worth of securities, or $6.7 billion for the equity, $8.2 billion including the Beatrice debt to be assumed. Kravis is reported to have commented at this point that "we were sort of crawling when we crossed the goal line."

The deal was the biggest LBO ever. The amount of leverage was prodigious—the KKR group would put in only $417 million in equity (about 6 percent of total capitalization), of which KKR's funds would own 63.5 percent, Drexel Burnham 22.5 percent, and management 14 percent (of which Kelly would own or have options to own 7.5 percent personally). Drexel would sell about $2.5 billion of junk bonds for BCI Holdings, and banks led by Bankers Trust would lend over $4 billion.

Drexel's role in the transaction was vital. Without the huge amount of junk bonds being sold, the KKR group would never have been able to put together enough money to finance their offer. The banks had gone as far as they could, and the Beatrice board would not accept any less than $40 per share in cash. The bidders had to fly out to meet with Michael Milken in Beverly Hills to be sure his mind was really focused on the task and that Drexel's commitment to sell the bonds was firm and confident. Drexel's 22.5 percent interest in BCI Holdings is attributable to the importance of its role in the financing.

The fees that were paid in the Beatrice deal were beyond anything seen before. Drexel earned $86 million, or 3.5 percent of the principal amount, for selling the junk bonds. KKR charged an advisory fee of $45 million, 0.6 percent of the transaction value, and Kelly received an advisory fee of $6.7 million (plus a bonus of an additional $13 million after his first year as chief executive of BCI, in addition to his salary of $1.3 million). Kidder Peabody, soon to lose Siegel to Drexel Burnham, where he would remain until his arrest a year later on insider trading charges, earned a fee of $15 million, or 0.2 percent of the total transaction value. As percentages these fees were about normal for large transactions, but when multiplied by the tremendous amounts involved, they became mindblowing. Kelly was right—there was a better way to make money than slaving away as a workaholic in a meat-packing company.

Once the deal had been closed and the fees paid, it was time to make the investment pay off. On the positive side, Beatrice had a strong cash flow and a stable of very attractive brand-name businesses it could sell. The market for selling assets had probably never been better and interest rates had been declining, thereby giving some breathing room. On the other hand, Beatrice was now overwhelmed with debt, and the interest bill of more than $2 million a day exceeded Beatrice's earnings for all of 1985. The banks had insisted on debt reduction and this could only come from selling off businesses.

But which businesses? Kelly said he intended to be choosy about what was sold and when. "If you have five wonderful companies, five medium companies, and five dogs," he said in an interview in *Fortune* in June 1986, "the real trick is to avoid ending up with five mediums and five dogs." Kelly's job was to decide which was which, what groupings to make for the Beatrice companies to maximize both their sales and their retention potentials, and, while doing this, to move quickly to dispose of some of the properties both to make the banks happy and to take advantage of the excellent market conditions for disposals that then existed.

Kelly divided the company into ten business segments: Avis, soft drink bottling, intimate apparel and cosmetics, dairy products, printing, warehouses, non-food consumer products, bottled water, international food products, and U.S. foods. He sold the first six of these business groups off during 1986.

The non-food consumer-products business, rechristened E-II Holdings (presumably meaning the second coming of Esmark), was spun off in July 1987 to BCI shareholders and was followed by a public offering. E-II, run by Kelly, next tweaked the nose of mighty American Brands by suggesting it might bid for it, thereby stimulating a Pac Man "defense" by American Brands that resulted in its acquiring E-II—no doubt a satisfactory outcome from Kelly's point of view.

Also in July, Kelly sold off the bottled water brands to Perrier, and arranged a management buyout of the international foods businesses.

Whew! Nine out of ten business lines sold within a year and a half. Proceeds were $6.4 billion, with $1 billion in debt assumed by acquirers. And the major part of the business, the U.S. food lines worth between $2 and $4 billion, were still in hand. If these businesses could be sold for what they seemed to be worth, and the $2 billion of debt associated with them assumed by the buyers and the final LBO debt repaid from the proceeds, then the liquidation of Beatrice would have been completed with a profit of $3.5 billion or so for its investors, a seven-fold return on equity invested in less than two years. One newspaper estimated that the deal would produce profits of $2.4 billion for KKR, $810 million for Drexel, and $277 million for Kelly. The Beatrice bonanza was seen by everyone toward the end of 1987 as a sure thing, a coup de main for KKR and especially for Henry Kravis, who had been the most visible KKR partner involved, whose deal it appeared to be. Beatrice popped the KKR partners up to celebrity status, something they could never have believed was possible for people in their obscure, specialized line of work.

The Beatrice transaction, however, was a deal of an entirely different color from the original Kohlberg bootstraps. Here the plan seemed to be to bust up the company and sell off all of the parts as quickly as possible, before market conditions changed. It was a bet on negative synergy, that the company was worth more broken up than together, more dead than alive.

Whereas the notoriety of the Beatrice deal has remained, the prospects for the liquidation have subsequently tumbled. The final food businesses have not been sold, their estimated market value after the October 1987 crash has declined (despite a gradually recovering stock market), interest rates have risen, and some of the businesses Kelly stuck with may indeed have turned out to be either mediums or dogs.

The Beatrice game, of course, is not yet over—things might get better, but in any case, as investors seeking to cash out, KKR must look at its portfolio of food businesses as being highly exposed to market risk.

In the aftermath of the Beatrice deal, financial entrepreneurs appeared from all over, frequently buoyed by promises of junk financing to stake them. Five of the businesses being sold by Beatrice were bought by LBO investors; Wesray bought Avis (and resold it to an ESOP), Riordan Freeman & Spogli bought Webcraft, a printing company, a Drexel-sponsored group bought International Foods, Kelso bought Americold, a cold-storage warehouse company, and a management group bought Playtex.

The Many Lives of Playtex

Playtex was the leading American brassiere and intimate-apparel company, but its business was sagging in December 1986 when it was sold by BCI Holdings, the KKR affiliate that was the successor to Beatrice, to a group consisting of management (28 percent), BCI Holdings (20 percent), Drexel Burnham (19 percent), and a group of institutional investors (33 percent). Playtex had been acquired by Esmark in 1975, where it was run by Joel Smilow until Beatrice acquired Esmark in 1984. Under Beatrice management Playtex began to lose market share and profits. Smilow thought he could fix things at Beatrice, and talked KKR and Drexel into letting him try. He offered $900 million, and it was accepted.

The transaction was financed by borrowing $310 million from banks, $430 million in junk bonds sold by Drexel, $150 million in preferred stock, and $10 million in common stock.

In 1986 Playtex consisted of the apparel company, a Playtex family products company, and Max Factor, Almay, and Halston cosmetics businesses. The cosmetics companies were sold off immediately to Revlon for about $345 million. The proceeds were used to repay the bank loans. The company now had total assets of about $625 million, 69 percent financed by junk bonds, 24 percent by preferred stock, and only 7 percent with common stock.

Smilow immediately set out to improve earnings and Playtex's cash flow. He slashed inventories to only one week's worth of sales, reduced new product introductions, switched his advertising to promote fashion over function, and boosted margins for retailers. The steps were successful. Operating profits rose from about $100 million in 1986, to $155 million in 1987, to what looked like would be $200 million in 1988.

In September 1988, Smilow announced that Playtex would be sold again, for $680 million, mostly in cash, to a new investor group that included several of the original investors. The original investors had made a profit of $520 million in two years on an investment of $160 million, a more than threefold return.

The new capitalization was a reflection of both how the stock market might value the new, rejuvenated Playtex versus the old one, and how much new debt the company could put out for the purpose of recapitalizing the business. There were no actual market prices involved since both the equity and the debt were privately owned, but both sides used 1988 market approximations in negotiating the deal. Whereas operating income had doubled, the total assets involved had tripled. After the debt was paid off, the difference went to the stockholders, i.e., to management, KKR, Drexel, and some institutional investors. They had releveraged the company, based on its stronger cash flow and competitive position, and used the opportunity to reshuffle the ownership of Playtex, with the financial people getting out and the management people, together with a firm specializing in apparel industry buyouts, going in deeper. Smilow would announce a further reshuffling six months later, when Playtex would sell the apparel business to himself and the company's managers.

The long odyssey of Playtex had seen it travel from being a specialized apparel company to being sold several times, being combined with cosmetics companies, losing market share through unfocused and merger-distracted management, then dropping again into capable hands and effecting several refinancings that have further simplified the company's business and returned its ownership to those who manage it.

One important lesson that was being learned in the late 1980s was that one financial restructuring is often not enough. When markets are good, take advantage of them by cashing out some of your holdings and revaluing what you own of the rest. Several LBOs during the period were releveraged and reconstituted many times.

Frequently the recapitalizing of the business was to create cash or paper that could be paid out to shareholders as dividends, to insure adequate returns on investments by the funds. Operating managers like Kelly and Smilow had learned that to make real money in the 1980s you had to get yourself a vehicle that could be run well, yes, but also manipulated financially to provide the really big returns.

The Beatrice deal had made Jerry Kohlberg very uncomfortable. It certainly had not been a friendly deal dependent upon a close working relationship with management. Kelly was often described as a crude, devious, ruthless man who had a strong need to get even with the Beatrice management, even though his archenemy, Jim Dutt, had been bested. The size of the deal too had been worrisome: Such a large amount of debt could only have been undertaken with a plan for an immediate, almost total bust-up of the company, something KKR had never done. It also meant that KKR would have become dependent upon Michael Milken and Drexel Burnham to sell $2.5 billion of junk bonds; otherwise the deal could not have been done. Though this was not the first time a public LBO had been completed with junk, it had probably attracted the most negative publicity. The danger to the public image of LBOs was potentially great; they might quickly come to be seen as greedy, junk-backed bust-ups of respected, long-established companies fighting for their lives. Up until now LBOs had not attracted very much public attention, and what there had been tended to regard LBOs as a special technique for producing positive results that were good for the American economy through effective financial and managerial restructurings. If the image of LBOs were changed rapidly from good to evil, then they would lose public support, be seen as a threat to American industry, and be subject to intense regulatory interference. If so, then the nice, simple, profitable, and beneficial business that KKR had conducted for the past decade would be annihilated.

The internal debate at KKR was launched with the Beatrice transaction. Kohlberg's dominating influence was no more, his two protégés had grown into highly competent deal-makers in their own right, and his long absence from the firm had increased their confidence and independence and apparently their ability to earn huge amounts of money for the firm. They did not see things the way Kohlberg did; things were different now, for access to junk financing meant that the sky was the limit—any size deal could get done—and the money to be made was enormous.

"Why turn your back on it?" Kravis and Roberts must have asked, astonished by their mentor's concerns. There was no real distinction anymore between friendly and unfriendly deals, the courts had seen to that. KKR was still determined to behave as gentlemen and never to initiate a hostile offer, but you had to move fast these days to bring home the bacon, and sometimes that meant a little nudge, or bear hug, from time to time. And management of these big companies had to be handled differently from those of the smaller companies in the old days. First of all, they weren't so important to the deal—many of them were sort of bureaucrats anyway, or financial men, or whatever. They weren't operating experts upon whom KKR had to depend. Also, their egos were incredible and had to be fed some kind of raw meat every day, which was a real bore. With large-deal strategies calling for selling off different businesses, reducing overhead, and running a much smaller business, KKR might actually be better off selling the assets themselves and maybe bringing in somebody new to lay off the overhead and reconstitute the company on a smaller basis, like they had done at Beatrice.

"Anyway it's all different now. Who can tell how it will all come out in the future? Maybe the government will interfere—so far it has been the least interfering government of the twentieth century—or maybe a recession will come and blow the whistle on all the merger activity and easy financing, after which we will just regroup and do whatever it makes sense for us to do then. But we can't turn our backs on all this action, Jer, we just can't."

The debate went on throughout the year, since it was too important to them all to be resolved quickly. They were also distracted by an enormous deal flow in 1986 and 1987. Late in 1986 KKR stepped in as a white knight working with management and acquired Safeway, which had become subject to a hostile bid by the Haft family, for $5.7 billion. Management came up with an aggressive restructuring plan, and the deal was as close to a classical Kohlberg-style deal as anything costing nearly $6 billion could be. (Two years later the Safeway LBO would be seen as KKR's most successful large-scale deal.)

The darker side of the debate, however, was also stimulated by unfolding events. Late in 1986, Owens-Illinois, the glass bottle maker, was rumored to be the target of a raid, though none appeared. KKR went to visit management and found them interested in a buyout. Several powerful outside directors, however, had other ideas and preferred to keep the company independent. They fought KKR's efforts bitterly. In the end, KKR raised its bid and offered an all-cash deal and won. It wasn't exactly hostile, but it wasn't friendly either, and to overcome the last bit of opposition, KKR had to stretch its bid price to a point that may have exceeded reason.

Six weeks after the Owens-Illinois deal Kohlberg left. He re-signed as a general partner of KKR and announced he was going to set up a new firm, Kohlberg & Co. The parting must have been very emotional and difficult, but it was done in a dignified, gentlemanly way. Kohlberg's name would continue to be used in the KKR firm, he would continue as a limited partner in the firm (i.e., some of his money would continue to be invested, passively, in KKR), and nei-ther side would bad-mouth each other then or later. Kohlberg's comments were restricted to noting for the *New York Times*, "I guess you could say I'm too old not to do things my way." His new firm, he said, would not be restricted to small deals, but "I'll stick with deals where reason prevails."

Kohlberg announced his withdrawal to investors in the firm in a talk in which he addressed the decline of ethics in financial life and what he called "the overpowering greed that pervades our business life." There must be a return to higher standards, he said, or "we will kill the golden goose" of opportunity in the United States. "One of Jerry's great strengths," said George Roberts on the occasion, "was his consistency over the years and his value systems."[13]

Kohlberg & Co. has since set up offices in Mt. Kisco, near Kohlberg's home, and in New York City, has raised about $300 million for a new fund which unlike most other funds shares its transaction fees fifty-fifty with investors, has brought a bright and eager Kohlberg son into the business, and in June 1988 announced its first deal—a $330 million buyout of Alco Health Services, a totally friendly, classic Jerry Kohlberg deal.

Kravis and Roberts continued on in their own way, doing large deals at competitively determined prices, finding themselves always at the center of controversial deals like Macmillan and RJR-Nabisco, but never really being tarnished by them. In 1987, KKR offered its largest fund ever, a $5.6 billion colossus that will take years to fully invest, but gives the firm awesome financial credibility that is far beyond that of any other player in the game. It will also generate management fees for KKR of $84 million per year until 1992 or whenever the full amount of the fund is invested, whichever comes first.

Though departing, Kohlberg retained a substantial financial interest in KKR; he retained a partnership interest in the firm, interests in all the companies KKR acquired before 1987, and the right to buy specified stakes in future KKR deals through 1995. The arrangement, however, was fated to be difficult: The three had elegant disagreements over policy matters and crude ones over money. Under their arrangement, KKR could unilaterally reduce Kohlberg's ownership in specific deals when the companies involved were substantially recapitalized. Kohlberg felt that the others were reducing his interests when only superficial recapitalizations occurred, and after a lengthy effort to resolve the matter amicably failed, he brought a lawsuit in August 1989 against his partners seeking restitution of his earlier ownership interests.[14] The suit was settled quietly six months later.

The 1987 KKR fund, in a departure from past practices, provides for "toehold" investments of the sort that old-style raiders make before springing their bids. Toeholds, it said, would be used selectively to "lower the cost of potential management buyouts." In March 1988 KKR announced that it had acquired a 4.9 percent toehold in Texaco, then struggling with Carl Icahn over a restructuring plan. KKR has also backed further away from its prohibition against hostile behavior, and in 1988 it moved in the direction of a fully hostile takeover of Kroger Co., though it subsequently withdrew.

At the end of 1989, KKR remained well out in front of the parade of LBO operators, though their ranks are diminishing. Kravis and Roberts, both in their mid-forties, are listed fairly high on the *Forbes* list of the richest men and women in America. There is now a Henry Kravis Wing at the Metropolitan Museum of Art in New York, and no doubt something comparable in San Francisco, where a somewhat lower-profile George Roberts lives. The firm has funds under management sufficient to generate bids totaling $40 or $50 billion, which requires all but a handful of companies to pay attention. The combined revenues of the thirty or so companies they control (the number is constantly changing) total somewhere around $40 billion, about the size of General Electric. Their operations now scan opportunities in Britain as well as the United States. Large deals of any kind are brought to their attention. They have the power to generate fees and commissions to other investment bankers and to brokers in the hundreds of millions. They are the nine-hundred-pound gorillas of their day—they can sit where they want to.

Distant Rumblings

Kohlberg was right about one thing—after 1986 the LBO business changed fundamentally. First, the deal flow exploded, especially for deals valued at over $100 million, nowadays something of a "round lot." In the period from 1980 through 1985, 92 such transactions with a deal value of $47 billion were completed ($36 billion of which occurred in 1984 and 1985). In the period from 1986 through 1988, 232 deals over $100 million in value totaling $150 billion were completed (25 percent of all completed domestic mergers and acquisitions in the United States)—the $25 billion RJR-Nabisco deal, which didn't close until 1989, was included in these figures announced in 1988. In the 1986–88 period, 84 additional deals totaling $120 billion were offered but not completed.[15] Altogether, $240 billion of large LBOs were attempted in the three-year period beginning in 1986.

This extraordinary volume is partly explained by the exuberance of the times, a merger boom in progress, bull markets, and a deal-making frenzy. It is also explained by the enormous amount of financial resources that were thrown up by the markets to support LBOs, which most investors then thought were one-way tickets to wealth and prosperity. By the end of 1988, the $30 or $40 billion committed to all LBO equity funds, leveraged ten to one, would yield $300 to $400 billion of potential investing power. And the availability of seemingly unlimited amounts of bank and junk bond financing meant that this potential was achievable. The stock market crash in October 1987 seemed to have very little effect on the dynamics of the LBO market; nor did the indictment of Michael Milken and the related problems of Drexel Burnham seem to impede the junk bond market much until later in 1989.

On the other hand, the market could not run on as it had without making some pretty serious mistakes. Investing conditions, already made difficult by the intense competition for deals, were worsened by rising interest rates, a skittish stock market, and, perhaps most important, a junk bond market that finally began to sag under its own weight.

KKR continued to do big deals after Beatrice. The pressure for investment performance was on them as much as it was on any other investment manager. After Beatrice came Safeway, Owens-Illinois, Jim Walter, the home building company, and Duracell, a battery company purchased in 1988 from Kraft after an auction for $1.8 billion. The prospectus issued in conjunction with the financing for the Duracell deal stated that "the cash flow [of Duracell] must be substantially increased" from its historical levels or otherwise the company might not be "able to make required interest and principal payments on its bonds." It was one thing to go into deals with only a small cash flow cushion against known debt service obligations, it was quite another to go into deals with a known deficit in debt service coverage.

There was virtually no margin for error in the more recent KKR deals. If management miracles couldn't be performed, then the companies involved would inevitably slide into default, in which case some kind of refinancing would have to be tried. Increasingly, the best strategy from the outset of a deal was to reduce the risk as quickly as possible by busting up the company and liquidating it in pieces. The problem was, the more you paid in competition with others for the whole, the more you ate into whatever differential there was between the whole and the sum of its parts. Also, the value of the sum of the parts was, first, an estimated value (usually expressed in a wide range), and second, a value subject to considerable market risk for periods of at least two to three years. If the stock market, interest rates, the merger market, the junk bond market, or the LBO market changed, then the estimated value of the sum of the parts had to change too. After 1986 most observers felt the various financial markets affecting LBOs had all been at historical highs, and the next move might be down.

The basic ideas supporting LBOs had changed radically since their early days. Rather than seeking durable companies with non-cyclical cash flows capable of repaying substantial amounts of debt, the game had changed to a competitive battle to capture from others large break-upable companies that would need to be financed only until they could be liquidated. It was a big change.

One close observer of the LBO scene, Leon Cooperman, then director of research at Goldman Sachs, noted in 1987 that by simply leveraging purchases of the S&P 400 stocks at the same ten-to-one ratio used by LBO operators, an investor could have earned an annualized rate of return of 75 percent from June 1982 to September 1987 (from the market low to just before the crash)—nearly 20 percent more than KKR had earned for its investors over a ten-year period. Doing it yourself with publicly tradable stocks would not have saddled investors with the extraordinary fees that were paid out along the way, nor exposed them to the market risks of having to sell off illiquid assets over a period of years to pay off the debt. Cooperman's picture was perhaps a bit overdrawn, but it served to make the point that the extraordinary economics inherent in LBOs were perhaps not quite what they had been seen to be.[16]

Many of the older, more traditional LBO firms didn't do much business at all during 1987 and 1988, thinking that the deals they saw were overpriced and too risky. Even some of the earliest of the enthusiastic LBO investors were beginning to ask if the LBO market too had peaked.

There were some reasons to think so. One investment consultant to pension funds advised in September 1988 that "the ideal time for investing in LBOs was five years ago." Future returns, he said, are likely to be "at best in the 20–40 percent range, and the risks will be significantly greater." He had described earlier returns as being in the 50–100 percent returns.[17]

Although RJR-Nabisco seemed to be in good shape, announcing favorable refinancing news at the end of 1989, some of KKR's other "sure-fire winners" like Beatrice, and Owens-Illinois and Jim Walter, both acquired in 1987, began to look in mid-1989 like the only folks who would make any money on them were KKR. In August 1989, two other KKR companies, Seaman Furniture (acquired in 1988) and SCI Television (a leveraged spin-off from the Storer Broadcasting deal) announced that they were unable to meet interest and principal payments and would have to restructure their outstanding debts to avoid bankruptcy, not a promising outlook for their equity or junk bond investors.

In September 1989, Beatrice announced that it was planning to borrow again in order to help pay investors a special dividend of about $1 billion in preferred stock and debt securities. Without the dividend it was becoming doubtful that the investors would make anything on the Beatrice deal at all. Moody's Investor Services immediately criticized the plan, saying it threatened Beatrice's ability to service existing debt, which it threatened to downgrade. Beatrice also filed $350 million of new junk securities with the SEC, which had to be scaled back to $250 million in November, when the issue was ready to be priced, due to lack of investor response. "I don't want to see money being upstreamed away from the operating company," said one large junk bond portfolio manager. The market had turned skeptical.

On December 28, 1989, KKR announced that it had been unable to restructure $624 million of junk bond debt of Hillsborough Holdings and therefore commenced Chapter 11 bankruptcy proceedings, the largest ever for an LBO. Hillsborough had been the corporation set up by KKR to acquire the assets of Jim Walter Corp., purchased in 1987 for $2.4 billion. Hillsborough said at the time that its operating businesses were sound, but the company had become ensnared in asbestos-related litigation against a former Hillsborough unit, and this had "severely handicapped" the company's ability to repay or restructure its debt.

The expectation for returns on the 1986 and 1987 KKR funds began to drop fast; one investor which had invested with KKR since 1982 said in mid-1989 that he thought "it is too early to say whether they can generate 20 percent returns," the minimum he thought acceptable for such investments. By year end this investor was probably expecting the returns to come in well under his minimum. Other KKR investors expressed doubt that if the actual returns declined to that level that they would invest in future funds. Some investors also expressed concerns that KKR was charging too much in fees. These were not the sounds of happy investors purring themselves to sleep.[18] Instead they resembled the deeper rumblings of a mutiny in the making.

KKR deals were not the only ones feeling the pinch as 1989 came to a close. Revco D.S., a large drug chain, had collapsed into bankruptcy in mid-1988, eighteen months after its $1.3 billion LBO had been arranged by management and Salomon Brothers. Merrill Lynch's Fruehauf deal was also on the ropes and in the process of being restructured. A $4.6 billion 1987 LBO of Southland Corp. by its founders, the Thompson family, was in serious trouble. A smaller deal involving a $118 million acquisition of Simplicity Pattern Company by a Wesray group defaulted on $61 million of junk bonds issued to finance the deal within months of its closing. Though no one expected LBOs to escape their share of difficulties, these deals, all apparently going wrong very soon after having been completed, cast large, ominous shadows over the LBO marketplace and the chief operators.

One of these, Gibbons, Green and van Amerongen, perhaps the oldest of the LBO firms with more than thirty deals under its belt, announced in the space of only a few months that Leonard Green, a founder, was quitting the firm because of a "pattern of philosophical differences"; it had lost a substantial sum on the sale of a 46 percent interest in Sheller Globe Corp., which it had bought from Knoll International; and, perhaps most serious, its efforts to refinance a $450 million bridge loan for its $980 million buyout of Ohio Mattress had failed. The Ohio Mattress deal had been described as overpriced since it was announced, and take-out of the bridge loan through an offer of junk bonds had always been thought to be difficult.[19] Ohio Mattress came to be called the "burning bed" by Wall Street traders.

The Ohio Mattress deal was caught up in another LBO crisis when Robert Campeau was unable to completely refinance the bridge loan undertaken in the 1988 $6.7 billion buyout of Federated Department Stores, and subsequent weak operating results threatened both Federated and Allied Stores, another Campeau LBO, with bankruptcy. Late in 1989, Campeau announced that to save his company, he would give up control to other investors, the Reichmann family, and offer Federated's flagship store, Bloomingdale's, for sale. His efforts failed and his company slid into bankruptcy in early 1990.

There were also problems in the junk bond market unrelated to LBOs, as mutual funds specializing in junk began a stumbling retreat from the market. Drexel, as part of its reorganization following its December 1988 settlement with the SEC in the Milken scandals, decided it no longer wished to be in the retail business and unilaterally commenced liquidation of the junk bond funds which it managed. There was no liquidity for the bonds being sold, and as a result the investors were charged with large losses. The fear spread to other retail funds and the market sank into disorder. These funds had been large buyers of new issues of junk bonds, accounting for approximately 25 percent of all outstanding junk bonds as of the end of 1988.

These difficulties intensified in late 1989, when the banks, also concerned about the declining strength in the junk bond market and the increasing number of deals in trouble, began to pull back from LBOs. And the pull-back was dramatic indeed in the case of UAL Corp., the operator of United Air Lines.

With United We Fall

In September, UAL announced a complex $300 per share, $6.75 billion buyout led by the company's employees, mainly its pilots union, management, and British Airways, which would make a $750 million equity investment for a 15 percent stake. Employees, who would put up about $250 million in the form of wage concessions, would own 75 percent of the company and management 10 percent. There were many problems with the deal, including the U.S. government's reluctance to see a major U.S. airline substantially owned by a foreign carrier, and the fact that not all of the unions were going along. One problem that did not exist, however, was the exposure of the deal to the problems of the junk bond market. No junk bonds would be issued in connection with the deal; UAL's banks, Citicorp and Chase Manhattan, had offered $3 billion of financing themselves and had issued "highly confident" letters (borrowed from Drexel's practice of indicating that a junk bond could be raised for a particular acquisition) for the remaining $4.2 billion of a $7.2 billion credit facility. The UAL stock price optimistically climbed to $280 per share on strong activity by Wall Street arbitrageurs.

On Friday, October 13, 1989, however, the banks announced that they had been unable to syndicate the $4.2 billion piece—mainly because the Japanese banks on which the managers had expected to rely were unwilling to participate—and the deal collapsed in chaos. The stock market, supposedly panicked by the prospects of LBOs coming unstuck all over and the junk bond market sinking further, fell 200 points, the largest drop since black Monday two years earlier. The market had been driven too by program trading abnormalities at the end of the trading day in New York. UAL's stock fell over $100 per share within the next few days, devastating risk arbitrageurs with losses aggregating more than $1 billion.

The banks had finally balked, though on careful analysis many observers believed that Citicorp and Chase had bungled the deal, which had had too much senior debt in its capital structure and fees that were too low. Management's position too was considered exceptionally "rich" (i.e., greedy) for the kind of deal that was being arranged. After UAL there were no more public LBOs attempted during the year, and many signs pointed to the likely possibility that the period of buyout speculation had finally come to an end because of deteriorating markets and overpricing.

There was also trouble blowing up in Washington, where LBOs had developed a very bad name. In the quiet days before 1986, no one in Washington paid too much attention to LBOs, which were then regarded as being only a special financing technique. However, once LBOs were married to junk bonds (which had never been well regarded in Washington) and started to be used for takeovers of well-known, establishment companies by greedy corporate managers, pirates, and pug-uglies of all types, the picture began rapidly to change.

After the 1988 presidential election, many senior government officials like Secretary of the Treasury Nicholas Brady (a former chairman of investment bankers Dillon, Read & Co.) and Senate Finance Committee Chairman Lloyd Bentsen, among many others, began to denounce LBOs along with junk bonds as a national menace that had to be substantially restrained. Others, like Alan Greenspan, chairman of the Federal Reserve, regarded the present phenomenon strictly as a market aberration—probably only short-lived in nature—which should not be interfered with directly. But the huge amounts of risky debt that were accumulating and could, as a result of an accident, a recession, or a sudden burst in interest rates, put the entire U.S. financial system at risk, were worrisome. Most economists, especially the free-market fellows still basking in the late afternoon sunshine of the Reagan administration, didn't fear LBOs so much as they did the difficulties that might come from widespread defaults. There was growing, if typically disorganized, support for something to be done.

One thing that was done as a direct result of this Washington concern was the publication by KKR of a document it had prepared with the assistance of Deliotte Haskins & Sells, a major accounting firm, which attempted to explain that, contrary to what was being said about them, LBOs were "an effective technique for acquiring a company and result in more efficient and more profitable operations which:

- increase employment
- increase research and development
- yield higher taxes to the federal government
- keep capital spending strong
- are able adequately to handle negative events such as economic downturns
- are not run with a view to quarter-to-quarter earnings
- and yield high returns to investors."[20]

KKR's findings were based on a tabulation of data from the seventeen companies acquired through LBOs in which KKR still had an ownership interest. The report calmly gave statistical evidence to support its conclusions. Carefully prepared by an independent accounting firm, the report was persuasive, if not entirely dismissed as an advocacy piece.

The report was not out long before it came under fire from the academic community. William Long, a Brookings Institution scholar, and David Ravenscraft, a University of North Carolina associate professor, claimed that the KKR findings were suspect because they were inconsistent with other research findings and because they contained methodological problems, namely, its sample of seventeen companies was too small to permit generalizations (and raise questions about what happened to all the other companies KKR was credited with having helped through LBOs), and that too much post-1985 data was based on projections, not actual results.

Academics in general believe that all studies aimed at verifying or disproving the claims made by KKR are deficient, and a lot more work will have to be done before the final result can be known. It is also true that too little time has passed since the majority of the deals (particularly the large, fully priced deals) were done for anything solid to be known yet, including the positive results claimed by KKR.

While Washington ponders what, if anything, to do, matters discussed further in Chapter 10, investors are going through their usual cold-hearted review of where they stand. The money committed to funds is committed, if called upon, to be invested—it can't easily be recalled. Such commitments are in the past. In the future will lie the decision as to whether or not to roll over these investments, increase them, or not invest in subsequent funds.

There is bound to be a runoff in money committed to LBO investments, since most of the investors are well-informed institutions that know that all good things, like LBO funds, sooner or later wind down or come to an end. Certainly many investors will withhold subscribing for more until they see what sort of actual returns come in on the post-1986, second-phase-of-the-market, funds. Most know that there are serious risks in being the last fellows in to a receding market, such as some of them experienced with real estate investment trusts in the 1970s, and with collateralized mortgage securities and even junk bonds in the 1980s.

Many will be looking at the next game, which some suggest will be funds that will invest in bankruptcies, in order to back someone skilled at recovering assets from chaotic situations. At a conference at the Stern School of Business at New York University in the spring of 1988, more than four hundred people turned up to hear how this was done, several times more than were expected.

Then maybe the market will turn next to junk equities.

7

TREASURES IN
THE JUNKYARD

"Really, Mr. Milken," said the senior insurance executive, "I can understand why somebody might own one of these below-investment-grade bonds—most of them are the remains of once fine companies that got into trouble, our 'fallen angels' we call them—but for the life of me I cannot understand why anyone would *buy* one."

This was a sales call typical of many that Michael Milken, then a twenty-six-year-old bond trader employed at Drexel Firestone, Inc., would have in 1972. He was trying to generate greater interest in high-yield bonds, his specialty.

"Let me explain why someone would," replied Milken, by now quite familiar with this disdainful attitude. "First, these bonds are very cheap. Second, your downside risk is only moderate. And third, the upside potential is considerable." Milken was using the jargon of the professional bond trader. He looked carefully into the executive's eyes for signs of glazing over: senior insurance executives often didn't know much about bonds, even when they were responsible for the firm's overall investment policy. He found what he was looking for and decided a simpler explanation would be better.

The language of the bond business can put people off. That's because it all seems backward. Economists and senior insurance executives tend to think in terms of interest rate *yields* when they consider fixed-income securities. More knowledgeable bond traders, however, think in terms of *price*. If a bond promises a 10 percent interest payment (its *coupon*) for ten years and is selling at 100 percent of its face value (*par*), then its investment yield is 10 percent. But if, because of a change in interest rates or the perceived quality of the bond issuer, the market might require a higher yield on the bond, say, 10.5 percent, then the offering price of the bond must change: it must go to a discount in order to provide the necessary increase in yield. In this case the discount would be reflected in a purchase price of 96.95 percent instead of 100 percent. The purchase price would be a little higher if the bond's life were shorter than ten years, a little lower if longer, because of the mathematical effects of compounding interest rates over the life of the bond. If the bond for some reason should be available to the investor at a price less than 96.95 percent, then a bond trader would say it was "cheap"; if the price were higher then he would call it "expensive." The terms are strictly relative to what the investment yield *ought to be* at the time.

Downside risk is the exposure the purchaser has to the bond prices' falling to lower levels, which would mean a loss to him, though as a result of the lower bond price the yield would rise. *Upside potential* is the probability of the bond price's rising, thus providing a profit. Bond traders like to find bonds that are slow to decline in price as a result of changes in interest rates and quick to rise.

"Sir, when I say that below-investment-grade, or 'high-yield,' bonds are cheap, what I mean is that by all statistical and economic measures their distress is exaggerated by the market. Currently, for example, you own some BBB-rated bonds that yield 11.5 percent. The next superior investment grade, those rated A, currently yield about 11.0 percent. U.S. Treasuries of comparable maturity yield about 10.1 percent. But a composite of a portfolio of two hundred to three hundred high-yield bonds yields 13.3 percent, 180 basis points more than your BBB-rated bonds and 320 basis points more than Treasuries [a *basis point* is 0.01 percent of interest]. These differentials, between the composite and either Treasuries or the

A-rated yields, are much greater than they ought to be, on the basis of substantial, academically recognized statistical evidence of default rates of below-investment-grade securities. The market, for whatever reason, doesn't understand the default history and therefore places too high a yield on these bonds. Too high a yield means that they are available at lower purchase prices than they should be. Therefore, they're cheap.

"Being cheap is part of the downside protection you get with high-yield bonds, a little cushion. But in addition a portfolio of these bonds provides better protection against the common dangers of the bond business: 'call risk,' 'event risk,' and 'volatility.' Because the bonds are weaker credits they tend to have less exposure to being called for redemption by the company if interest rates decline. Either the terms of the bonds don't provide call rights or the company's credit has deteriorated so that it cannot afford to call the bonds out of the proceeds of new financing.

"*Event risk*, or something bad happening to the individual company whose bonds you own, in the case of high-yield bonds is moderated by the fact that the market price already reflects the bad news [it doesn't for investment-grade bonds] and that the recommended way of investing in high-yield bonds is through a portfolio of ten or fifteen different bonds so as to dissipate the event risk over the whole portfolio.

"And studies show that the *volatility*, or the bond's price sensitivity to market interest rate changes, is actually less than for higher-grade bonds. This is because of their high yields, relative to the others. If interest rates change by 1 percent, for example, a ten-year 10 percent coupon Treasury [changing its yield from 10 to 11 percent] will experience a price decline of $5.98 per bond, whereas the price of a high-yield security of similar coupon and maturity [changing its yield from 13 to 14 percent] will only drop by $4.66, or 2 percent less. This condition is simply the effect of mathematics, however, and may not fully reflect the differences in liquidity and in investor biases that appear when interest rates change sharply; but on the whole the natural, mathematical advantage in volatility works to the advantage of the high-yield investor."

"Ah, Mr. Milken . . ."

"Sir, just a couple of additional points. Then I'll be finished. It's the upside potential that really makes these bonds interesting. As you know, investors can make money in bonds three ways: if interest rates drop and prices go up, if the market changes its view about the rate differentials that should apply to bonds of different ratings, and because of an upward rerating of a particular bond.

"The market is constantly changing the differences in yields between bonds of different ratings. Today the difference between Treasuries and high-yield bonds is about 320 basis points. This differential will narrow as more investors acknowledge that high-yield bonds are cheap and move in to buy them. In other words, a significant part of the upside is the ultimate repricing of high-yield bonds as a category.

"And finally, a carefully selected portfolio of high-yield bonds [one that eliminates industrial sectors that are suffering structural economic difficulties] will include a number of companies that will be perceived as returning to good health. These bonds will be either upgraded by the agencies or repriced by the market into the upper tier of the high-yield market. Either event will result in a substantial profit to investors. A yield reduction from 13.3 percent to 12 percent, for example [still substantially higher than today's yields on BBB-rated bonds], will raise the bond price from 82.03 to 88.53 percent, an improvement of 7.9 percent, which will provide the holder of the bond with a 21.2 percent total return (13.3 percent yield plus 7.9 percent capital gain) for the year.

"These upside features do not exist to nearly the same extent in investment-grade bonds. They provide an embedded 'kicker' to investing in high-yield bonds that is similar to investing in bonds with equity features."

"I'm sorry, Mr. Milken, but I have another meeting. I shall pass your materials along to our bond department for them to look over. I cannot promise that they will be enthusiastic. They may feel that the default rate data you have provided are not sufficiently compelling to project them into the future. If they have any questions, I'm sure they will call you.

"As for myself, considering the interests of our policyholders and working as I do with our trustees and regulators, I must confess some hesitation in having it appear that our longstanding reputation for prudence and conservatism has been disregarded just so we can go hunting for bargains in the junkyard. I'm not sure we're ready yet, Mr. Milken, to be known as investors in 'junk bonds.' "

Michael Milken had had this response to his sales pitch on junk bonds before, indeed many times before. It was extremely frustrating, but he was getting used to it. He knew his facts were right: he had studied fallen angels and their default rates while at Berkeley and Wharton and boned up very thoroughly on the considerable amount of academic work that had been done on the subject. He had prepared his own charts and diagrams to show the potential values in these bonds and had honed his presentation, he thought, to a sharp edge. But still he wasn't cutting it with these guys.

In the early 1970s, when Milken was making his rounds, investors in corporate bonds were largely confined to life insurance companies and some bank trust departments that managed money for wealthy families and some pension funds. These institutions bought corporate bonds in two forms, publicly tradable bonds bought at new issue or in the secondary market, and "private placements" of nontradable bonds purchased directly from corporations, generally at a higher yield than would be available in the market. Many of the private placements purchased were not rated by rating agencies—the insurance company relied on its own ability to assess credit capacity—and in many cases these had to be classified for regulatory purposes as "basket loans." Most state insurance commissions had rules that limited the quantity of unrated or noninvestment-grade securities that an insurer could own. Generally speaking, noninvestment-grade securities had to be lumped together into a common "basket," which could not exceed a specified percentage of a company's total assets, for example, 10 or 15 percent.

Life insurance companies invested in a mixture of long-term assets to back their long-term life insurance policies. If an insurance policy had an embedded yield of 8 percent, then the return on the assets invested would have to be at least 8 percent to cover it. As the policy might not be paid off for thirty years, the investment had to be good for that long; that is, it had to lock in the yield for as long as the company's actuaries thought the policy would be outstanding. Therefore, investment departments were looking for long-term, good quality, high-yielding assets in which to invest policy premiums. Generally these were made up from a mixture of government bonds, corporate bonds and common stocks, and real estate. Government securities and real estate together might represent 40 percent or so of an insurance company's assets, with the rest being divided between corporate bonds and stocks, of which the bonds (tradable and private placements) would comprise the greater part, maybe as much as 40 or 50 percent of the company's total assets. It was this segment of the market that Milken was hoping to convince of the merits of high-yield bonds (which were even then increasingly being referred to as "junk bonds"). Even if junk bonds had to be put into a company's noninvestment-grade basket, the insurance companies were still the largest market for them.

In the 1970s the economics of the life insurance business changed drastically. This was a consequence of high inflation, soaring interest rates, the obsolescence of many traditional life insurance products, and the appearance of many new interest-rate-sensitive policies that were sold in competition with financial instruments as well as in ferocious competition with other insurers trying to increase or protect their market shares during a time of dramatic industry upheaval. By the middle 1980s every insurance company would realize that the preceding decade had produced changes that threatened the existence of one of the country's oldest and most stable industries. It became much more difficult to match the new insurance liabilities with appropriate assets; the new policies they were issuing were of shorter maturities and needed high investment results to be successful.

To address these changes, insurance companies would have to rethink their business entirely in the 1980s and, above all, find ways to increase the yield on the investment portfolios they managed, without which their ability to repair some of the damages sustained to their investment "surplus" (or net worth) and to attract profitable new business would fade away. For this they would need to become active investors in permitted amounts of junk securities. But they didn't yet know it in 1972 when Michael Milken came calling.

One thing the large insurors had never done before was to risk their reputation for prudence and conservative financial management. Even if someone in the bond department had recognized the value in Milken's proposals (and many did), getting permission to invest in junk bonds was another matter. This could be authorized only by the investment committee, consisting of senior executives who were "concerned with policyholders' interests" and who "worked with our trustees and regulators," who were unlikely to grant the approval needed. Even if they had, the board of trustees and/or the regulators, all products of the traditional financial establishment, might have disliked it and overturned any such move.

The Father's Footsteps

Milken himself had few establishment characteristics. His father had been a tax accountant in Encino, California. He had had a good education at establishment schools, but there it seemed to end. He had no important friends and few social graces and was known to be somewhat arrogant and intolerant of the opinions of others.

He appears to have had a very focused notion of what he wanted: to learn what he needed in school so he could go into business and make money. He attended Berkeley at the time of the worst of the student uprisings, though these seemed to have had no impact on him. When everyone else was having a good time smoking pot, burning bras, and using foul language in public, Milken was engrossed in the works of W. Braddock Hickman, whose enormous multivolume *Corporate Bond Quality and Investor Experience* analyzed bond performance and default rates from 1900 to 1943. Milken was struck by the fact that throughout that long period, in which both a depression and a war had occurred, the prices of lower-grade bonds reflected a lot more defaulting than actually happened. Later he found a follow-up study by T. R. Atkinson covering bonds from 1944 to 1965 that reached the same conclusion.

He carried his enthusiasm for low-grade bonds with him to Wharton, where he finished in 1970: a straight-A student with a formidable reputation. One of his professors recommended him for a summer job at Drexel Harriman Ripley, then an old-line Philadelphia firm, which hired him after he left Wharton. By that time, however, the firm had to be rescued from collapse by a large infusion from the Firestone family, after which the firm was renamed Drexel Firestone.

Milken joined Drexel Firestone in its Wall Street office as head of fixed-income research and later migrated into trading. Immediately he set out to locate and trade high-yield bonds. He researched every available bond and learned all there was to know about them and the companies that had issued them. He was then, as ever, very thorough.

His trading was successful from the start, but Drexel, itself not much of a trading house and certainly not disposed to low-grade securities, was reluctant to grant him enough capital to trade at the level Milken aspired to. He was rescued from a fate in which undoubtedly he would have found himself at the wrong place at the right time by Drexel Firestone's further collapse. In 1973, Burnham & Co., a small brokerage house with a great thirst for a great name, acquired Drexel Firestone and renamed it Drexel Burnham. Soon afterward, I. W. "Tubby" Burnham, the firm's chief executive and an ace trader himself, spotted Milken and immediately agreed to increase the amount of capital he would be free to trade to $2 million. Milken never looked back.[1]

The regular bond markets in the late 1970s were characterized by relatively high volume and relatively low dealer *spreads*, or the differences between the *bid* and *ask* prices; that is, the price difference between what a trader could buy and sell a bond for. The U.S.

Treasury market was highly liquid, but dealer spreads were measured in "s'teenths," or in one-sixteenth of a percent. A trader in Treasury bonds, for example, might bid to buy bonds for 99$\frac{1}{16}$ to be sold to investors at 99$\frac{3}{16}$. The corporate bond market, much less liquid than the superabundant Treasury market, would permit larger spreads, perhaps as much as a $\frac{1}{4}$ or $\frac{3}{8}$ of a percent. A trader could make money by pushing as much volume through these spreads as possible, while hedging his inventories so as not to be blindsided by sudden market changes.

The market for junk bonds, however, was very different. Not many firms traded them at all. The liquidity in the bonds was limited: they were hard to find when you wanted to buy and hard to sell when you wanted to unload. The traders could make a market in these securities with a very large spread, perhaps as much as 2 or 3 percent (for example, 96 bid, 99 asked). This market was more like trading little-known over-the-counter stocks than it was like dealing in rated corporate bonds. And the dealer's role was similar to that of the equity trader's; he had to know where the securities that could be traded were, and he had to monitor the supply to the market as well as price it.

To expand the volume of trading in the junk market, Milken knew he could not rely on traditional bond investors. He had made too many unsuccessful calls on large insurance companies' executives. To develop that market would take forever and probably drive him crazy in the process. To expand, he would instead have to create the market for junk securities by himself. This meant that he would have to create investors who wanted junk bonds and who would come to Drexel to get them. These investors would not be traditional white-shoe types with old-fashioned trustees and regulators. They would be people who could see the merit in what he was talking about but, more important, see how it could help them solve their problems.

So, to start with, who had problems that high-yield investments could help solve?

The large, well-established insurance companies did, but they didn't know it yet and they were proving very difficult to persuade.

There were, however, some less-well-established insurance companies run by financial entrepreneurs who might be more interested. Saul Steinberg, who once attempted a raid on Chemical Bank, now owned Reliance Insurance, which served in part as a funding source for Steinberg's ventures. Meshulam Riklis also owned an insurance company. So did Larry Tisch. These companies lived or died on their investment income; surely a sound program for investing in high-yield bonds would appeal to these people, all of them smart as could be but certainly not (yet) establishment types. There was also a small insurance outfit in Beverly Hills, First Executive Corp., that had been bought by Fred Carr, one of the more notorious (though failed) gunslingers of the 1960s. Carr wanted to sell more interest-sensitive products in competition with the majors. To do this he would have to outperform the others in terms of investment yield; a portfolio of junk bonds would fit him nicely. Milken identified these prospects and persuaded them to invest in the securities he could find for them.

He found other customers among the high-performance mutual funds. The seventies had been difficult years for the stock market, and investment companies had suffered substantial withdrawals. Some, however, quick to read the changing times, saw opportunities in high-yield securities after Milken (who understood their needs) had cultivated them. Early investors included Massachusetts Mutual, Keystone, Lord Abbott, and the number-one performing bond fund in the United States in 1975 and 1976, First Investor's Fund for Income. These funds became, and remained, substantial investors in junk securities.

During the early 1980s it had already become evident that the financial sector with the most difficulty to face in the future would be the savings and loan institutions. These had existed for years as time-deposit-taking institutions that lent their funds to finance home mortgages. As the U.S. government had decided to sponsor home ownership after World War II, it encouraged these institutions by insuring their deposits up to what later became $100,000. Their deposit bases were very stable, and mortgages were always in demand, so these institutions prospered.

Until 1968—that was the year when a series of changes commenced by the Federal Reserve Board changed the industry for good. In the latter 1960s interest rates rose to levels reaching the ceiling on interest rates placed by the Fed on what banks could pay for deposits. This led to the growth of the commercial paper market and money-market securities in general. To allow banks to compete with the money market, which soon included money-market investment funds sold to individuals in competition with checking and savings deposits at banks, the Fed lifted its ceiling and allowed both banks and savings institutions to pay whatever the market demanded for deposits. The S & Ls, however, had a portfolio consisting almost entirely of long-term, fixed-rate home mortgages that had been funded in the past by stable time deposits. No more: all the deposits now would have to pay market rates, but the fixed-income mortgages made earlier were, in the late 1970s and early 1980s, paying interest well below the high deposit rates then demanded by the market. The S & Ls were doomed unless they could find much higher yielding assets to invest in. Some tried real estate, to their later distress; some sold mortgages as collateralized mortgage obligations; and some invested—heavily—in junk bonds. One of the first to do so was the Columbia Savings and Loan Co. of Beverly Hills, when its chairman Tom Spiegel, realizing he needed a way out, first met Michael Milken.

Columbia became one of Drexel's largest customers for junk securities. Milken personally administered a tutorial to Spiegel until he was convinced. Spiegel then opened the floodgates. Several years later, Columbia had about 35 percent of its assets in junk bonds: about $5 billion altogether. "I needed a way to diversify our portfolio," said Spiegel, "and Mike needed a broader market for high-yield bonds. Working together made perfect sense."

Milken carried the message to other S & Ls. He began persuading their worried operators that having a diversified portfolio of junk bonds that would yield 300 to 400 basis points over Treasuries would make much more sense than buying new mortgages for 150 basis points over Treasuries. The extra yield could be used to cover some of the losses on the rest of the portfolio. It was tempting and many S & Ls followed his advice.

Before he knew it, a surplus of demand had developed—a number of buyers of junk bonds had emerged, and demand began to exceed the supply of available bonds. Most of these bonds were fallen angels that Milken had accumulated over the years and kept close track of as they were bought and sold.

What was now needed was a new source of junk bonds, new issuers that would issue a supply of new bonds into the market to be fed into the surplus of demand. Milken looked around. Who needed money badly enough to pay outrageous rates for it?

Rated corporations didn't. There was no money in selling bonds of small unrated businesses, such as dry cleaning companies or service stations. Milken focused on a new category of borrower, the large company that was generally known to be in trouble.

In 1977, Lehman Brothers, in an effort to assist some of its troubled clients, arranged ingenious devices for several of them to float new issues of bonds at times when their creditworthiness was in doubt. Among these were debt issues for Pan American Airways, Zapata Oil (George Bush's old company), and LTV, then facing the aftermath of James Ling. These issues were not well received by the market to which they were offered, the traditional bond market, so Milken stepped in and bought them for redistribution to his growing stable of investors.[2]

Discovering that he could distribute the new issues of high-yield paper underwritten by others persuaded Milken and the then-head of Drexel's corporate finance department, Fred Joseph, to cut out the middlemen and go into the underwriting game themselves. Drexel had only a few underwriting clients, however. To challenge the white-shoe firms that dominated the underwriting business Milken and Joseph would have to attract new clients. These they found among the rogues and controversial characters of business and finance, the as-yet unappreciated entrepreneurs of the day. These people—the New Men of the 1980s—were often shunned by the traditional financial establishment (as Milken himself had been), but they always had ideas about what to do with money, if only they had some. Wildcat drilling companies, gambling casinos, and moviemaking and other entertainment industry ventures came to mind.

In April 1977, Drexel made its first new issue of junk bonds, an offering of $30 million of subordinated debentures for Texas International, a small oil exploration and equipment-making company. By the end of the year the firm had done six more deals, ending the year in second place behind Lehman. That was the last year Drexel would be even close to its competition in underwriting new issues of junk securities. By 1978 Drexel had underwritten fourteen issues for a total of $440 million, nearly three times that of its closest competitor.

After acquiring Drexel Firestone, the Burnham group found itself staring into the face of the worst market environment since the thirties. The oil crisis occurred in 1973, and rampant inflation, runaway interest rates, and a miserable stock market followed. Drexel Burnham's own business barely broke even in those years, but amazingly Milken's junk operation prospered. Milken's trading lines were increased. Being then responsible for most of the entire firm's profits, he was granted a 35 percent share of the earnings of his junk-bond operations, which he could distribute as he saw fit to worthy associates. By the end of 1976 both Milken and a close colleague at the time earned approximately $5 million under this arrangement: an undisclosed amount that, if known, would have shocked Wall Street, where no one (well, hardly anyone in 1976) made that much money.

In 1978 Milken, then thirty-one, demonstrated the power he had accumulated in the firm. He announced that he wanted to move his entire department—everybody—to Beverly Hills, of all places. He claimed that this would give him "three more hours each day to work," but everyone knew that, though he had personal reasons to want to return to California, he simply wanted to get away from New York and run his own shop. If Drexel wanted him, fine—if not, he would find a way to get by on his own. Drexel was horrified: nobody conducted serious trading operations outside the watchful and cautious eye of the head office, and certainly not in a flaky place like Beverly Hills. This was absolute heresy. But Drexel's management considered the other side of the issue.

"He does make a lot of money for the firm, you know," explained one of the considering managers, "and now that underwritings are starting to come along, maybe we ought not take such a 'traditional' view of the matter. In fact, maybe we oughta let the guy sit wherever he wants."

But Tubby Burnham thought a guy like Milken ought to have some of his own money in the firm, like most of the other executives. Sure he'd only been at Drexel since 1970, and he had no interest in management, but he still ought to be a "partner" along with the other key players in the firm. Milken was not all that interested, but he finally allowed himself to be persuaded to purchase subordinated debentures of the firm convertible into 6 percent of its shares, more than any other single individual. In retrospect it was clear that even before the heyday of the junk market, Milken had in effect "taken over" Drexel himself, letting those who wanted to run it while he continued to pocket an incredible proportion of the firm's earnings. By 1982, for example, Milken's share of Drexel's earnings exceeded $45 million. In 1983, it would total $120 million.[3]

Milken certainly didn't doze off in sunny California, out of sight of his nominal superiors. If anything his passion for work intensified. His working day began at 4.30 A.M. His constant trading and promoting of junk bonds as both exceptional high-performance investments and financing vehicles that could make the impossible come true caused him to be sought out by many who had heard of him and thought he could help them. By now many of his earlier clients had made a great deal of money by investing in securities he sold them. Milken had become the guru of the high-yield market.

Soon after arriving in California, Milken began meeting with some of the have-nots who would be corporate raiders. He was looking, like the Marines, for a few good men to back: a few really determined, clever, persistent men who would take big risks to win the success they wanted so much and share some of that success with him. For such new clients, Milken would arrange some seed money, money that could be used to refinance existing debts and provide enough for an initial stake in a raid. Then, if the raider locked on to something promising, Milken could arrange a standby facility providing sufficient credit for a takeover attempt (or for the portion of a takeover not otherwise available from banks) by syndicating subscriptions for the facility among his stable of junk bond buyers. With the syndication complete, Drexel could then announce that the money to back the raid, money that no one thought the raider had, was in fact fully committed.

Such an announcement made all the difference. Without it, the market would not take the raider's threat seriously and the stock price would never rise much above what it had been. But, with Drexel's confirmation that the funding was in place, the stock price would pop up to the level of the bid, the company would be in play and something was likely to happen, and the raider was bound to make money. Either the bid would succeed (in which case he should expect a profitable result), the company would buy back his shares in a greenmail transaction, or someone else would come in at a higher price and the raider would sell out to him.

Milken understood how much the initial stake meant to these people. He could charge them whatever he wanted (there was nowhere else to go at the time for this sort of money). Milken pointed out to each that it made sense for the raider to take some of the seed money Milken provided and use it to invest in standby facilities arranged for other raiders. These facilities were usually not drawn down (as the early raiders usually didn't succeed in taking over the targets), but they earned substantial standby fees for their providers. While raider A was waiting to launch his strike, he could invest in raider B's standby facility. In time a great many of Milken's issuing clients became investing clients too, even if only in the standby facilities. This was one of Milken's hallmarks: the best clients were those who had nowhere else to go for the money he could provide and who would serve as both issuers of and investors in junk bonds.

In 1980 the total par value of the forty-three new issues of high-yield junk bonds was $1.4 billion, an amount representing less than 4 percent of all straight-debt new issues by corporations. By 1982 the total par value had doubled, though the number of new issues was about the same. In 1983, the par value jumped to $7.3 billion on eighty-five issues representing almost 20 percent of the total corporate new issue market. The average high-yield new issue was for $86 million in 1983, as compared to $34 million in 1980. Drexel accounted for more than half of the total market for these issues in 1983, leading underwritings for $4.3 billion. These issues averaged underwriting commissions of about 3 percent, which meant that Drexel alone was generating more than $120 million in such commissions, most of which were retained by Drexel as Milken's group, having little need of an underwriting syndicate, could sell the bonds to its growing network of investors: high-yield mutual funds, S & Ls, smaller insurance companies, financial entrepreneurs, and raiders on the make. Drexel's success with junk bonds enabled it to leap ahead in the annual rankings of bond underwriters, achieving second place in 1984, just behind mighty Salomon Brothers.

By this time the junk market had captured wide attention. The rapidly increasing volume and the large underwriting commissions and dealer spreads meant substantial profit opportunities for those investment banks willing to become involved with the business. The market also became interesting to those companies that contemplated financing large, ambitious takeovers or restructurings. Not all the junk securities were broken-down wrecks teetering on the edge of default—many, indeed an increasing number, were healthy, ambitious companies that had just recently swallowed a large amount of debt for a specific purpose. Among the largest such issues in 1982 and 1983, for example, were offerings by Aristar, City Investing Corp., General Host, U.S. Home, and Jim Walter Corp. In 1984 the first wave of the large junk-backed takeover attempts occurred: Boone Pickens made a run at giant Gulf Oil, ultimately driving it into the arms of Standard Oil of California, and Saul Steinberg went for Walt Disney, and Carl Icahn for Phillips Petroleum in transactions ending in substantial greenmail payments to the raiders.

The public profile of the junk-bond market in the early 1980s, however, was still substantially negative. It was still seen as a market of uncreditworthy securities issued by inexperienced and unsavory characters to finance dubious corporate raids and other projects. The business establishment believed that the bonds were being flogged to investors who ought to know better by a second-rate investment bank trying to upgrade its status while pocketing obscene amounts of profit.

The leading investment banks were very skeptical of junk bonds in the beginning, expecting high default rates, legal entanglements, and customer disappointments that would ultimately cost more than the front-end profits might be worth. Although some firms such as Merrill Lynch, Prudential Bache, and Bear Stearns, attracted by Drexel's success, began soliciting junk bond business in 1983, others, including most of the leading houses, were more cautious. At Goldman Sachs, for example, the firm had virtually no contact with any of the New Men wanting to issue the securities, did not like representing raiders in takeovers, had few investor clients interested in purchasing junk bonds, and believed that the business could hardly tolerate the firm's high legal and corporate finance standards. Junk didn't make sense to Goldman Sachs; therefore, it couldn't last.

But it did. In 1984, new-issue volume doubled again to almost $15 billion, attracting issues in excess of $200 million in size by Occidental Petroleum, Rapid-American Corporation, Metromedia Broadcasting, Resorts International, and Chrysler Financial Corporation. Some of the early junk bond issues had performed very well, attracting some professional money-management institutions to set up high-yield bond funds. In 1982 there were twenty-four such funds in existence, and their average return in that year was over 30 percent. Old-line insurance companies too became active in the high-yield markets at last.

In 1985 a substantial amount of takeover and restructuring financing would occur in the junk bond market, including large issues for companies controlled by Boone Pickens, Ted Turner, Ronald Perelman, and KKR, whose Storer Broadcasting deal was the first junk-financed public takeover by an LBO firm. In 1986, the big year for takeover and LBO financing, the market would explode to a volume of $33.4 billion.

Beginning in 1979 Milken developed an effective, if unorthodox, approach to promoting the junk bond market by bringing issuers and investors together to meet each other and hear presentations on new aspects of the business, plus a stirring wrapup speech by the father of the market. An initial success, the meeting held in Beverly Hills for fifteen hundred to two thousand guests became an annual event, and invitations soon were greatly coveted. The affair involved hard work during the day and fancy dinners and Hollywood (and other) entertainment during the evenings. Mainly, however, it was a convention of men with enormous egos and ambitions who thought they were using Milken, not the other way around. The event became known as the "predators' ball" in honor of all of the financial pirates and swashbucklers who attended. As Connie Bruck described them:

> The honored guests of this conference were the takeover artists and their biggest backers—men like T. Boone Pickens, Carl Icahn, Irwin Jacobs, Sir James Goldsmith, Oscar Wyatt, Saul Steinberg, Ivan Boesky, Carl Lindner, the Belzbergs—and lesser lights about to shine, such as Nelson Peltz, Ronald Perelman, William Farley. The names tend to meld into a kind of raiders' litany, but they are not all the same. For Milken, they would have separate roles during the coming months, performing discrete functions in a vast interlocking machine of which he alone would know all the parts.[4]

The 1985 ball took place in April. Just before it Drexel had financed two large takeover attempts that had succeeded: Coastal Corporation had acquired American Natural Resources for $2.5 billion ($600 million in junk bonds), and a tiny company controlled by the then-unknown Nelson Peltz had made a successful offer for National Can Co. for $456 million, all of it financed with Drexel junk bonds. Within weeks after the 1985 ball, five more companies would launch giant takeover bids financed by Milken's machine: Pickens went for Unocal, Lorimar for Multimedia, James Goldsmith for Crown Zellerbach, Steve Wynn's Golden Nugget hotel group tried for Hilton Hotels and Farley went for Northwest Industries. The system worked; other bids would follow, and then the large LBOs.

Junk's Gentrification

Despite its extensive association with hostile takeovers, junk was nevertheless becoming better understood and somewhat more respectable by the end of 1985. Hostile deals continued to attract a great deal of negative attention, but in knowledgeable circles these were looked upon somewhat more dispassionately as part of the necessary industrial restructuring of the United States. There was growing sympathy for raiders, whose notions of liberating wealth properly owned by the stockholders from the self-perpetuating grip of entrenched management were frequently and eloquently aired. Junk itself finally had begun to make sense and to be accepted as a breakthrough in the understanding of securities markets. Certainly it was evident that investors were purchasing an enormous volume of high-yield securities, which seemed to have found a place of some sort in almost all types of fixed-income portfolios. Several factors shaped this changing picture.

First, during the early part of the 1980s the bond business, inflated by the federal deficit, deregulation, globalization, and substantially greater volatility, entered a period of very active hands-on portfolio management. This involved much greater amounts of trading of institutional holdings and a new reliance on quantitative analytical methods to locate new opportunities. Money managers, salesmen, and traders alike were all looking for ways to increase annual returns while minimizing risk. The huge volume of outstanding government, corporate, and international fixed-income paper provided a vast ocean in which to search for profitable opportunities.

The lingua franca of the bond business at that time was expressed in terms of *spreads over Treasuries*. These spreads (not the dealer spreads between bid and asked prices) were the measures of the yield difference between a particular security and a no-risk U.S. Treasury security of comparable maturity. As daily price fluctuations were considerable, it was easier to visualize the market for, say, A-rated bonds as being seventy-five basis points over Treasuries than it was to be constantly checking the absolute rates against each security and the clock.

During this period portfolio managers became very attuned to quantitative methods of money management. They became concerned about the match-up between the maturities of their assets and their liabilities, the sensitivity of each to yield changes in the market, and the need to hedge their risk exposures. Along this road the scientific method prevailed more than the gut feeling. Everything could be measured and compared, and the right selection was strictly based on the numbers. These portfolio managers were interested in a scientific approach to identifying risks and opportunities. Many academic studies were made of market phenomena, and actions were actually based on their results.

A second factor was that the high-yield bond market attracted a number of highly credible academic figures who backed up much of Milken's original sales pitch. The proliferation of junk bonds was fascinating to many financial scholars who had pondered the optimal capital structure of corporations since the 1950s. Because of the tax benefits of borrowing, highly regarded figures such as Franco Modigliani (a Nobel Prize winner) and Merton Miller had helped to establish the idea that leverage was desirable in the corporate capital structure, the more the better, up to a point where the benefits would be outweighed by the burdens and costs of too much debt. Others referred to these burdens and costs as "expected bankruptcy costs." Efforts to measure these costs and to explore defaults and the predictability of bankruptcy followed.

Edward Altman, a professor of finance at New York University, has studied corporate bankruptcies since the late 1960s. First in 1968 and again in 1977, he published papers describing statistical methods for identifying bankruptcy risk in corporations, the "Z-Score" and the "Zeta Analyses," that are widely in use today. Altman became interested in the high-yield bond market and undertook to measure the default experience of junk bonds over an extended period, from 1974 to 1985. What he found was that the default rates on high-yield bonds (measured as the par value of defaulting bonds as a percentage of the par value of all outstanding high-yield bonds) averaged 1.53 percent over the period, ranging from an annual high of 4.5 percent to a low of 0.16 percent. Investment-grade bonds, by comparison, averaged a default rate during this period of 0.10 percent.

What this meant was that when you subtracted the high-yield default rate from the spread over Treasuries of high-yield bonds, which averaged 3.60 percent between 1978 and 1985, the difference, 2.07 percent, was what you would have made *on a risk-free basis* by investing in a portfolio of junk bonds instead of Treasuries.

Altman went on to calculate the *actual* losses sustained from high-yield bonds. He pointed out that defaulted bonds did not become valueless; instead they traded, on average over the 1974–85 period, at 41 percent of par shortly after the default. Thus, "after accounting for the bonds' retained value and the loss of interest, the average reduction in returns to the investor would have been in the 96 to 101 basis point range annually (as compared to 153 basis points based on default rates), assuming purchase at par." In other words, somewhere around a third of the default risk was offset by the value of recoveries after bankruptcy.[5] Altman was not alone in researching default rates; at the same time as his work was being published, Professors Blume and Keim of Wharton offered similar conclusions, and numerous others have since joined the field.

These conclusions, though only a statistical study of past events that assumed a portfolio of bonds held continuously over a twelve-year period, had considerable impact. Junk was awarded a legitimacy that it had lacked before; it now had statistical justification, so that, however seamy some may think them, it made sense to own at least a modest amount of junk bonds. Where else could such a net high rate of return on a risk-free basis be obtained?

Altman's studies proved that Milken was right: that high-yield bonds were cheap; the market's disdain for them resulted in mispricing to the extent that a much higher risk-free return was available from investments in these bonds than the "perfect market" predicted. The word got around. Investing in junk bonds was intellectually sound, the latest thing. Prudent men could invest in them, to a reasonable extent. Little by little the more traditional institutional investors—insurance companies and pension funds—became investors too. And those investment bankers who had been hanging back from the junk-bond market reversed their positions and entered the field of competitors. All the players were now represented.

Also, the mergers-and-acquisition, LBO, and restructuring activity offered an Olympian role for junk bonds to play, not just in financing the raiders but also in restructuring important companies like Storer Broadcasting, Macy's, Southland, Kroger, Levi Strauss, and Beatrice Foods. Association with such venerable companies lifted the image of junk securities even as it increased the public controversy surrounding them.

There was still more to be done, however, to promote junk bonds among all the constituencies affected by them. Drexel had the greatest stake in the market and began a series of television advertisements aimed at showing how much good junk bonds did in making capital available to small and ordinary companies, to unions trying to prevent their businesses from being closed, and to all the little people everywhere. These ads were very professionally done and may have been influential among regulators, as well as among prospective new issuers. The increasing commitment to the junk market by Wall Street also meant that an ever-larger number of well-trained salesmen and corporate finance experts were promoting the securities among their issuing and investing clients.

The meteoric rise of junk bonds from 1978 to 1986 thrust both Milken and Drexel Burnham high into the heavens. Though the volume of new issues increased tenfold between 1978 and 1985 and doubled in the following year, the impact on Drexel's profits and Milken's own earnings was even greater. Not only did Drexel dominate the new-issue business, it dominated secondary market trading as well. There was approximately $100 billion of junk securities outstanding in 1986, and Drexel made markets in most of them, knowing better than anyone where the inventories were and who wanted to buy and sell at any given moment. Dealer spreads of 1 percent or so were not uncommon in this market. Drexel also used its retail brokerage network to distribute mutual funds of high-income securities called high-income trust securities (HITS), which it managed. By flexing its muscles in the junk arena, Drexel was able to increase its appeal to new corporate finance customers with whom the firm was hoping to increase its nonjunk business. Perhaps most important it learned how to turn the merger and LBO markets to its advantage.

Doing the Big Deals

In 1984, Milken proposed to his colleagues that they use their new-found skills to shoehorn their way into the merger advisory business, which would further increase the firm's visibility, respectability, and profits. There were to be three parts to such a program: first, financing the have-not raiders in return for a significant minority interest in their postacquisition corporations; second, financing the junk-bond component of large LBOs and restructurings; and third, earning high merger advisory fees as a result of a growing capability to compete with the major firms resulting from their junk-related relationships.

This plan made a lot of sense. It was a perfect way for Drexel to roll up industrywide benefits from its dominant expertise in a newly important segment of the business. Salomon Brothers had done much the same when it began to cross-sell its other corporate finance skills to its bond market new-issue clients. Merrill Lynch also had similarly exploited its retail stock distribution capabilities some years before. Further, the Drexel plan was clever in spotting all the areas where the value of its particular skills could be maximized.

Milken himself would be responsible for the first two legs of the program. He already knew the predators; they had nowhere else to go and indeed were grateful to and dependent on him for the capital they needed to pull off their schemes. Milken, on the other hand, could not waste his placing power on duds. If his hand-picked men failed, his credibility with the investors would slip. Milken was careful in selecting those he would sponsor and insisted on face-to-face meetings at his office in Beverly Hills, often at ungodly hours in the morning. Invariably, Milken would insist on a tranche of low-priced warrants exercisable into the common stock of the acquisition vehicle company being issued to Drexel Burnham, which would then distribute these goodies to investors as it saw fit. These warrants were not worth much when they were issued, but if the venture succeeded in surviving after a couple of years they could be worth a fortune. They were after all a kind of doubly leveraged investment: having an option on the stock of a company with 90 percent or so of its capital structure represented by debt. Ten times leverage might result in thirty times leverage if the original stake were in the form of a warrant. It became a standard Drexel-Milken practice to extract warrants for a 15 to 25 percent equity ownership position (after the warrants were exercised) as a part of the cost of getting the financing. This was an extraordinary price for Drexel's clients to pay for the financial assistance, but most had no choice: if they wanted the money they gave up the warrants. Once Drexel controlled the warrants it could distribute some, none, or all of them to investors as an inducement to purchase the junk bonds being issued. Those it didn't give up it kept for itself.

In the Beatrice LBO with KKR, Drexel agreed to underwrite $2.5 billion of junk bonds to provide the mezzanine financing for the deal, without which it is unlikely that KKR's offer could have met the price required by the Beatrice board for its approval. Drexel had the upper hand because it had the ability to do what no other firm then had. As a result Drexel insisted on warrants to be issued as part of the package and KKR, certainly no pushover, reluctantly agreed. Accordingly, Beatrice sold fifteen-year warrants exercisable into 33.4 million shares of its common stock, or 24 percent of the LBO, to Drexel nominees for 25 cents each. The warrants, exercisable at $5 per share, were to be used in conjunction with the offering of the debt securities Drexel was to underwrite. Two years later a filing with the SEC revealed that Drexel retained an interest in warrants exercisable into 22.5 percent of Beatrice, then estimated to be worth approximately $26 per share. In other words, Drexel had been issued warrants for 24 percent of Beatrice for which it paid $0.25 per share, which could be used two years later to purchase for $5 a share stock in Beatrice then valued at $26 a share. Drexel had retained approximately 94 percent of the warrants it had originally been issued, and thus could point to an unrealized profit of more than $650 million.[6]

Not all the deals (including Beatrice) would work out so well, but Drexel did more deals than anyone else and demanded warrants in most of them so that over time Drexel's earnings from the warrant component of its business would be enormous, explaining perhaps more than anything else the prodigious profits that the firm earned.

Milken, of course, was also responsible for selling the bonds that the firm committed to purchase in conjunction with an acquisition. This too was an extraordinarily profitable business for the firm: the Beatrice underwriting produced fees of $86 million, most of which was retained by Drexel (the rest was paid out to other underwriters). This business had three parts: the prefinancing commitment, the bridge financing, and the final sale of long-term securities.

Arranging standby commitments from his junk investors was something Milken had done for some time. More established clients such as KKR, however, thought it was too expensive and preferred instead to persuade banks to commit to credit facilities sufficient to see the deal through. The banks would do this, providing they could see their way clear to reducing their exposures to the company quickly through the issuance of permanent subordinated debt and the sale of assets, in each case with the proceeds going to reduce bank debt. Before committing themselves, the banks would insist on a commitment in turn from Drexel that the subordinated debt would be available to take them out. Usually a period of several months would have to intervene between the time of the offer, when the financing had to be in place, and the time when the junk bonds were to be sold. Milken proposed that the banks agree to bridge this gap if Drexel offered them a letter stating that the firm was "highly confident" that the bond issue could be sold. There were no interest rates in the letters; the companies had to proceed with the subordinated financing at whatever rates Drexel said it would take to get the issue sold. The banks went along with the plan, thereby virtually locking Drexel into the job of underwriting the large junk-bond issues for most takeovers and LBOs. Drexel would charge an advisory fee of $1 million or so for agreeing to give the highly confident letter, and if and when the time came to do the financing it would lead it.

By the time of the RJR-Nabisco deal in late 1988 and early 1989, several additional innovations had occurred in the deal-financing business. Many different types of subordinated debt (that is, junior in liquidation to the claims of the banks and any other senior creditors) were created. These provided a variety of layers from which the financial engineers could select to build the optimal capital structure. This would produce the highest bid by creating the maximum value of debt securities that could be sold against a company's existing cash flow–generating capabilities. The process led to some odd securities, including junior subordinated debt, high-yield zero-coupon notes, pay-in-kind securities, other deferred interest bonds, extendable reset notes, and different forms of preferred stock. Many of these securities were extremely difficult to value, as their claims were almost always pushed well out into the future. In almost every large deal one or more securities seemed to be individually tailored to fit the particular transaction. These securities would almost never trade at or near par when issued; estimating where they would trade became an important part of the investment banker's advisory job.

In the RJR deal, the banks, though providing credit facilities of $15 billion, could not provide all of the bridge financing necessary: the deal was just too big and made too many bank boards of directors nervous. In order to be able to finance the amount of cash needed at the first closing in February 1989—$18 billion for 74 percent of RJR-Nabisco's stock at $109 per share—KKR had to rely on bridge financing to supplement the bank loans. The bridge was to be from the first closing until the permanent financing (of permanent subordinated debt) could be arranged. KKR accepted an offer from Merrill Lynch and Drexel to supply $5 billion of such bridge financing, from their own funds (the largest such offer of bridge financing ever made by investment banks). Drexel, however, had another idea. It would offer to sell short-term junk notes to its clients, the interest rate on which would increase the longer the notes remained unrepaid, after a base period. To everyone's surprise, Drexel succeeded in placing the entire $5 billion of bridge financing in the form of "increasing rate notes" and then refunding them all with $5 billion of permanent subordinated debentures, leaving very little for Merrill Lynch to do. For Drexel this was yet another tour de force, another in a string of brilliant ideas backed by powerful execution capability that were designed to make Drexel the one indispensable party to any large takeover or LBO.

The third part of Drexel's approach to the takeover business was to join to its incredible financing skills the necessary first-rate investment banking advisory capabilities that would enable it to spread its net over the entire playing field. This plan made sense, too. Drexel's potential profit per transaction could only be maximized by adding to its other fees the large advisory fees that the top investment bankers had been dividing among themselves for some time. Having worked with Martin Siegel, one of the top merger investment bankers in 1986, on the Beatrice deal, Drexel not only realized that it had left a $15 million fee on the table (the amount earned by Kidder Peabody in advising KKR) but also realized why. There was no one at Drexel quite so experienced or skilled in merger tactics and maneuver as Siegel or with a reputation even close to his. On reflection, Drexel decided to recruit Siegel to build a first-rate merger advisory business. Siegel joined Drexel not long after the Beatrice deal. Drexel felt that it then had all the pieces in place to strive for a leadership position in the investment-banking industry, one from which it could become *the* leader, the J. P. Morgan of its day.

From Peak to Valley

In the summer of 1986 Drexel Burnham Lambert reached its zenith. Everything looked good and was getting better. Earnings were likely to double from the year before to $300 million, a total many in the firm regarded as unbelievable (Drexel's earnings would increase further in 1987, but that was after the firm's troubles had begun). Wall Street was coming to hold the firm in awe: such an amazing transit from middling to premier status, in such a short time. The firm had ranked fifth in overall U.S. underwritings in 1985 and was headed for fourth place in 1986. Drexel held first place in high-yield securities with a 45 percent market share and ranked first or second in convertible debt, straight industrial debt, straight and convertible preferred stock, and initial public offerings of common stock. It was also making rapid progress in municipal financing and in private placements.

Drexel's plans for moving more aggressively into mergers and acquisitions were coming together: Marty Siegel had joined the firm and was building a team equal to those of the powerhouse firms. Brokerage was good, the HITS were selling well, and all of the firm's parts were working together smoothly.

The firm's public image had never been better, despite its controversial product line and aggressive, competitive ways. It was seen as a success story, based on devoted commitment to a new kind of security and hard work. Like Salomon Brothers, which rose to prominence with the fixed-income market, Drexel had risen with high-yield securities and was confidently staking out its place among the industry leaders of the 1990s. It had also passed the reins of leadership from an aging Tubby Burnham to Frederick Joseph, a New Man himself, a former have-not investment banker at E. F. Hutton who had migrated to Drexel to become head of corporate finance and discovered what Michael Milken was doing and backed him. Milken's success helped Joseph achieve his. A former Harvard scholarship student and intercollegiate boxer, Joseph was young, good-looking (often photographed with one of his horses for a kind of Marlboro look), and flexible.

But, it was fleeting.

Before the beginning of that sunny year of 1986, Merrill Lynch received an anonymous letter, allegedly from an unhappy girlfriend, suggesting that two of its employees in Caracas, Venezuela, had been making a great deal of money from insider trading. Merrill Lynch investigated and discovered that three of its brokers had made many successful investments in stocks that had recently been subject to takeovers. The brokers were questioned and revealed that their good fortune was simply the result of piggybacking orders that came in periodically from an account in the Bahamas, the Nassau branch of a Swiss bank, Bank Leu. The group had noticed how successful the Bahamian account had been over the years and therefore had decided to place orders themselves in the same stocks.[7]

Merrill Lynch reported the discovery to the SEC. The SEC asked the Swiss banking authorities about the identity of the Bank Leu account that was doing the trading. The Swiss have agreed to disclose the names of such accounts if the U.S. government demonstrates it has good reason to suspect criminal activity. The Swiss came to this agreement very reluctantly, as it obviously pierces the veil of Swiss banking secrecy, but after several court cases, and reconsideration of the value of their banking operations in the United States, they consented. Now, when an American citizen or resident opens a Swiss bank account he must sign a waiver authorizing the bank to hand over any information requested by U.S. government authorities investigating suspected criminal activities. Such activities encompass money laundering, tax evasion, and violations of securities laws.

The request for information revealed that the owner of the account was one Dennis B. Levine of New York. The account had been active for about five years. Levine was an employee in the mergers-and-acquisitions department of Drexel Burnham, which he had only recently joined from another firm. The case was turned over to the office of the U.S. Attorney for the Southern District of New York, Rudolph Giuliani, for prosecution.

Levine was arrested in May 1986. He confessed to several charges of insider trading. Under an arrangement with a Swiss employee at Bank Leu, Bernard Meier, Levine would make untraceable collect calls to Nassau from public telephones to place orders in stocks about which he had insider information, fifty-four in all. The Swiss would place the orders under the name of the bank or disguised Panamanian accounts through brokerage offices of U.S. firms, such as the Merrill Lynch office in Caracas. Meier also placed orders in the stocks for himself. Levine agreed to cooperate with the prosecutors in exchange for favorable consideration at sentencing. He revealed the existence of a ring he had assembled of young lawyers and investment bankers who fed him information on the deals they were working on or found out about at their firms. These were all bright, hardworking professionals with very promising futures. They were paid pittances, if anything, for the information they passed along. All were disgraced; most went to jail. No one really knows why they allowed themselves to be drawn into the net. Perhaps they believed they could never be caught or were simply weak characters who couldn't resist the peer pressure to "help out" by doing what "everybody else was doing". Or, maybe they were driven by the desire to be thought of as "players" themselves, flattered and encouraged no doubt by the smooth, fast-talking pied piper of the Bahamas. Levine was in fact only a fringe player himself. He was a rumor collector, a glad-hander with lots of contacts, well dressed and glamorous but never at the center of the action. His network fed him information and he fed it to Ivan Boesky.

Boesky was an arbitrageur who made money betting on mergers. He was a totally self-made man, successful and flamboyant. He made and gave away millions. He sold interests in limited partnerships that would invest in arbitrage deals under his management. It was getting tough to make money in arbitrage, however, as too many cowboys were jumping in and ruining the profit opportunities. He needed an edge if he were going to be able to deliver the results all of his limited partners expected. He couldn't let them down—it wasn't just the money involved (though certainly it was that too); it was his reputation. If he fizzed out, they'd laugh at him or ignore him, something he dreaded possibly more than he knew. To win consistently he needed an edge. Levine was to be the edge.

Boesky was arrested and confessed to insider trading and other violations of securities laws. He agreed to a fine of $100 million and a jail sentence later set at three years. The fine staggered Wall Street—nothing like that had occurred before. The announcement had come shortly after the revelation of the ring of crooked Yuppies, which also had never happened before.

Next it was Boesky's turn to give evidence. He gave the prosecutors Marty Siegel, Levine's boss at Drexel Burnham newly arrived from Kidder Peabody, who secretly had been passed large amounts of cash on the street in exchange for information on deals. Another criminal, Boesky said, was Michael Milken.

Siegel confessed too and gave up other names. As the chain of arrests and disclosures continued, more information was gathered that pointed the prosecutors to Drexel and Milken, who denied everything. The government continued its investigation, interviewing hundreds of people and sifting through an overwhelming volume of trading data. Other figures, many of them prominent in Wall Street, were drawn in as well. Allegations of numerous violations of insider trading and other securities laws were made against Drexel and Milken; both would spend the better part of the next two years defending themselves.

Late in 1988 Drexel agreed to a settlement with the U.S. Attorney and the SEC in which it would pay a fine of $650 million, the largest penalty ever imposed on anyone for securities matters, and consent to various management and operational changes. Despite the settlement, Joseph remained defiant.

Milken was indicted on March 29, 1989, on ninety-eight felony counts that alleged that between 1984 and 1986 he had violated securities and mail fraud laws, engaged in insider trading and racketeering, and made false statements to the government. The government brought its action against Milken under the RICO (racketeering) provisions of the criminal codes, which permit the seizure of assets from the accused party and other unusually severe penalties. The government's charges involved maximum prison sentences of 520 years. Milken steadfastly denied all charges.

The government also announced that it was seeking forfeitures from Milken and his two co-defendants (his brother Lowell, a Drexel lawyer, and Bruce Newberg, a trader) totaling $1.8 billion. This extraordinary amount consisted of salaries and bonuses paid to the three men between 1984 and 1987, plus forfeiture of their ownership interests in the firm and all fees, profits, and other income derived from their activities at the firm.

The fees, trading profits, commissions, and other forfeitures for all the allegedly illegal activities totaled $58 million. Compensation paid by Drexel to the three men from 1984 to 1987 to be forfeited was $1.2 billion.

Milken's share of this amount was $1.1 billion.

The indictment disclosed that Drexel had paid Milken a salary and other compensation of $45 million in 1983; $123 million in 1984; $135 million in 1985; $295 million in 1986; and $550 million in 1987. It also disclosed that he owned 865,752 shares of Drexel Burnham stock worth about $98 million at book value (Drexel shares were not publicly traded).

At the time of the indictment, Milken was forty-two. His title was senior vice president; he was not a member of the firm's executive committee. He rarely traveled to New York or conferred with his colleagues there about management affairs. He was not really interested in them. Drexel reported earnings of $522.5 million for 1987, less than it had paid to Milken.

No one questioned his domination of the market that he had built little by little from scratch over the past twenty years. Indeed, Drexel was fortunate that a significant part of what Milken earned was paid to the firm; how else would it be able to earn $522.5 million in 1987? Milken had made the firm what it was, and had made its executives and shareholders rich. Accordingly, everyone seemed to agree that he should receive more than half of the firm's profits. He had in effect bought control of Drexel Burnham and "hired" Fred Joseph and the others to run it and to take most of the management burden of ownership from him.

As extraordinary as this revelation was, it was equaled by the length of time that this had been going on. Drexel had paid Milken $45 million in 1983, a year in which the new-issue volume was only $7.3 billion and Drexel's share generated a maximum of around $130 million of revenues (not profits) and junk had not yet been used for takeovers to any significant extent. The direct and indirect *trading* profits from junk had to have been quite large, equaling perhaps the profits from new issues, for the firm to pay him so much.

Michael Milken was like a character in a Joseph Conrad novel. He went off an innocent into the heart of a dark and unknown land, which he conquered and came to rule, but the process stripped him of his ability to comprehend reality. Milken's conquest was secured long before the period in which his offenses allegedly were committed. He was supremely powerful as far back as 1983 (when his compensation was at least ten times that of the average head of a major Wall Street firm), and most likely his power was greater than anyone else's at the firm long before then, perhaps as far back as 1978 when he was permitted to move "his" group to Beverly Hills. He had enough money and power to be whatever he wanted at the firm, to be whatever sort of industry spokesman he wanted to become or virtually anything else that most people aspire to after a successful career in Wall Street. He had the love and devotion of colleagues whom he had nurtured, and of clients whom he had helped, all of whom had become richer than they had ever dreamed. Two days after his indictment eighty-eight friends and clients joined together to run a full-page ad in *The New York Times* under the headline MICHAEL MILKEN, WE BELIEVE IN YOU. The group did not include any Drexel employees, who presumably were prevented from participating. He had all of this, and none of it depended on his being involved in comparatively small amounts of insider trading or other violations. However frequently these may have occurred they did not contribute very much to his wealth and influence.

Milken has always been described as brilliant but so intently focused on what he was doing that he lost track of everything else. One observer said of him:

> A man obsessed, he was like a nuclear physicist isolated at Los Alamos in 1944, so focused on the splitting of the atom, so assured that his work would help to win the war, that he couldn't see that he might be creating a lethal instrument capable of jeopardizing his own security.

And added

> Warned repeatedly by friends and colleagues, even by his own brother Lowell, to stay away from an obvious danger, the arbitrageur Ivan Boesky, because of the indecent and fraudulent aura which clung to him, Milken was mystified. "I don't understand what you're talking about," he would say, "Ivan's numbers always make a lot of sense."[8]

The ultimate effects on Milken of the era he created are yet to be seen. The visible effects, however, include his resignation from Drexel in early 1989 with further charges rumored against him. Milken's legal difficulties became the subject of heated argument between those who saw him as the symbol of all the evils of Wall Street in the 1980s, a menace to society, and those highly partisan supporters who saw him as a creative genius viciously persecuted by demagogic prosecutors. In the end, on April 24, 1990, Michael Milken, age 43, fearing further charges against him, entered into a plea bargain with the U.S. Attorney in which he admitted guilt to six felony counts of securities fraud and other charges in exchange for the dropping of all other charges. His sentencing, most likely to involve prison time, will occur in the fall.

As of the end of 1988 the total amount of junk bonds outstanding was estimated to be about $200 billion. Approximately $62 billion of these were thought to be held by insurance companies, $50 billion by mutual funds, $20 billion by pension funds, $20 billion by individuals, $12 billion by savings and loan institutions, and $36 billion by others, including a growing portion of foreign investors.[9]

The market, however, was starting to show signs that the euphoria that had supported it for so long might be waning.

Concern began to be registered in April 1989, when a study of junk-bond default rates by a group of Harvard professors was misinterpreted and *cumulative* ten-year default rates (the probability of a default on an average bond at any time during the entire life of the bond) were confused with the average *annual* default rates (annual defaults as a percentage of all junk bonds outstanding). Professor Altman had presented a paper titled "Mortality Rate and Bond Performance" in October 1987,[10] in which the cumulative default experience was first examined. This study provided a second way of looking at bond defaults. It concluded, as his earlier study had, that investments in single-B-rated securities over the period 1971–88, despite an average annual default rate of 1.5 to 2 percent (depending on the period) and a cumulative default rate of about 32 percent, would have earned about 44 percent more than investments in Treasury securities. The Harvard study was a substantially similar report, but in stressing the magnitude of the cumulative default rate the study was represented as contradicting Altman's work, something that if true would have upset the market greatly.

In time the controversy died, but it probably carried a few dozen junk bond investors away with it. In his study, however, Altman noted that default rates had been increasing in recent years and stressed that his work was not to be construed as predicting the default rates to be experienced in the future.

The total return on the five largest high-yield funds (which accounted for about $13 billion in assets) had been in decline for the past few years, dropping from a 25 to 30 percent return in 1985 to returns below 10 percent since 1987.[11] For the first six months of 1989, despite one of the strongest Treasury bond rallies in recent years, the junk-bond market weakened. The total return—that is, interest plus (or minus) price appreciation—on junk bonds tracked by First Boston's High Yield Index was 5.4 percent, while the total return on ten-year Treasuries was 11.2 percent.

A two-tier structure was developing, in which some of the large, well-known companies that had recently arranged LBOs or restructurings were in one tier and poorly known, less actively traded issues in the other tier were separated by a yield difference of 100 to 150 basis points. Actually a third tier of distressed companies for which the yield difference from the top tier was about 500 basis points also existed. Liquidity in second- and third-tier issues had dried up considerably, causing some issues to decline in price by as much as 40 percent as holders dumped them in their efforts to get out of their positions. Drexel had contributed to the problem directly by unilaterally deciding to liquidate about $300 million of its HITS (junk bond trust accounts sold as mutual funds to retail investors from 1984 to 1987) as a result of its decision to close down its retail brokerage business. Investors in the HITS suffered losses on the forced liquidations of up to 20 percent.

By mid-year 1989, weakness in the economy and increasing reports of bankruptcy by large issuers of junk securities were also frightening the market. In addition to the LBOs that had gone wrong for Revco, Fruehauf, Southland, and Resorts International, other bankruptcies for Eastern Airlines, Southmark Corp., and Integrated Resources and increasingly credible rumors of several others in trouble further soured the market. In September 1989, great concern began to build up about the solvency of Campeau Corporation, which had previously purchased Federated Department Stores ($6.7 billion) and Allied Stores ($3 billion), and was now considered to be unable to service the debt. Bloomingdale's was put up for sale, but to no avail. Others in trouble were earlier KKR buyout deals. SCI TV, a spin-off of Storer Broadcasting, announced a plan to restructure its $1.3 billion of debt, forcing holders of $500 million of its high-yield debt to exchange it for a package of new bonds and equity that investors valued at between twenty and seventy cents on the dollar. Later, Hillsborough Holdings, a subsidiary of Jim Walter Co., and Seaman's Furniture (both KKR companies), also announced that they could not meet their debt obligations and similarly would have to restructure them.

Forced debt restructurings were not the exclusive province of distressed LBO deals, however. Some simply reflected the terrible credit judgment of their underwriters in the case of new-issue clients. In July 1989, Memorex Telex, a Netherlands-based hi-tech computer firm, raised $557 million through two offerings underwritten by Drexel Burnham. Fewer than five months later, several "negative surprises" emerged, earnings crashed, and the company was in violation of its debt covenants. Its bonds were trading at about fifty cents on the dollar.[12] Several other Drexel deals, including a new issue for a bankrupt oil refinery that collapsed before Drexel could get it underwritten—leaving the firm with a worthless bridge loan—and poorly structured LBO financings for JPS Textile Group and West Point Pepperell, were generally regarded as disasters by the market.

Also, the scandals in the junk bond area involving Drexel and Milken had caused a number of pension fund and other more conservative investors to liquidate their positions. Investors in "guaranteed investment contracts" issued by a number of aggressive insurance companies, such as Drexel client Executive Life, began to worry that their contracts were excessively backed by junk bonds, so that business began to run off. Savings and loan institutions too had been required to liquidate all of their holdings in junk securities by 1994 as a result of new industry regulations that followed their $300 billion bailout by the taxpayers.

Indeed, regulators' worries became clearer when Columbia Savings & Loan announced a third-quarter loss of $226 million as a result of $350 million of write-downs on its $4.4 billion portfolio of high-yield bonds. Soon afterward, Thomas Spiegel, Columbia's chief executive, and one of Michael Milken's earliest converts, resigned.

The softness in the junk-bond market caused the SEC to become concerned that certain mutual funds and Wall Street dealers might be overvaluing issues carried on their books and announced that it was conducting an inquiry. A *New York Times* article had speculated that many such issues were carried at prices as high as 30 percent above their "true" value.[13]

Drexel announced in mid-1989 that defaults and troubled company exchange offers then accounted for about 5 percent of all junk bonds it had underwritten since 1977, a level twice as high as that reported in its 1988 High Yield Market Report, when it then pointed to default rates of 10.4 percent on Merrill Lynch underwritten deals and 16 percent on Salomon Brothers deals, both of which contained large issues in bankruptcy.[14] Later, Drexel also announced that it expected to make no money at all in 1989, reflecting its aggressive efforts to downsize and restructure the firm, but also the battering that its principal market was taking.

In August 1989 a Donaldson, Lufkin Jenrette index of active issues of junk bonds was trading at 540 basis points above Treasuries, an all-time high at the time. By year end the index would be trading at 650 basis points above Treasuries.

Indeed, as in the LBO market, a great deal of new supply of junk bonds had come on the market in the past two or three years, most of which was won by underwriters in competition and sold into a bull market that was convinced that junk-bond returns would be able to continue indefinitely at 25 percent or more. In 1989, however, the net returns on junk bonds were well below their interest coupons, indicating that significant capital losses had occurred. Liquidity was very spotty, and a renewed concern about quality had set in. Many investors, who had bought the basic Milken idea of greater risk-free value in junk bonds, were scurrying for the sidelines. Milken himself, having been forced to resign from Drexel and spending most of his time preparing his legal defenses and repairing his image, was not available to offer his considerable persuasive skills to stop the stampede. The perception was that junk bonds had come and gone, that in the bright sunlight all of the treasures in the junkyard were beginning to show the dents and tarnishes that had been overlooked.

The Death of Drexel

By the end of 1989, the junk-bond market had suffered a large-scale loss of confidence. Prices had dropped significantly during the year, though mainly for the second- and third-tier issues. At times like this, there is often a contrarian or two who will place large bets on the almost always correct notion that the market has panicked and sold through its realistic support level. There were few if any contrarians willing to support junk bonds in early 1990, however—there was still too much unresolved uncertainty. Things might still get a lot worse.

They did. Campeau declared bankruptcy. RJR notes were downgraded by Moody's, dropping its PIK securities to a price of 60; these were the reset securities that won the deal for KKR—if reset in January 1990 they would have to be replaced with permanent financing yielding 20 percent. Macy's had had a miserable Christmas and its bonds were being downgraded—to the B − range. First Boston and Shearson Lehman Hutton were constant topics of speculation: Would their huge holdings of unsellable bridge loans undermine the firms sufficiently to require help from their parents, Crédit Suisse and American Express, respectively? The answer turned out to be yes in both cases. Junk-bond prices would continue to free-fall through the first quarter of 1990.

The market collapse was the final blow to Drexel, which, unable to roll over its own commercial paper or to induce others to rescue it, threw in the towel and declared itself bankrupt on February 13, 1990, forcing the firm into liquidation.

Drexel's demise has been much analyzed; responsibility for its failure has been widely distributed, though the settlement with the government was generally thought to have been a fatal wounding of the firm. After draining its capital, wrecking its morale, casting it as a pariah within its industry, and exposing it to potentially hundreds of civil lawsuits, the settlement certainly was crucial. Perhaps the firm could have survived it, perhaps not. To do so, however, would most likely have required at least a decent market for its main products, high-yield securities. It could only hope to escape the grim fate that had awaited E. F. Hutton (which had pled guilty to hundreds of check-kiting schemes) by returning to profitability quickly. As almost all of its ability to earn profits were tied to its preeminent position in junk bonds, it was obviously in this area that the firm would have to stand up and be counted. Its success in selling the increasing-rate notes, and then the permanent subordinated notes for RJR-Nabisco, got the firm off to a good start in 1989. There were doubts that Drexel could handle such large financings without Milken, but it did.

As the year went on, however, and the junk market deteriorated further, it appears that Drexel found itself trapped. To protect its franchise, without which it might not be able to survive, it had to become the market of last resort for anyone wanting to sell junk securities. Few investors were buying; Drexel had to buy. Its trading inventories of junk securities rose. These securities could not be hedged against a rapidly falling market. When it folded, Drexel had over a billion dollars tied up in dealer inventories that were now worth far less than they had cost. Capital was disappearing in unrealized losses; creditors became nervous about Drexel's liquidity position. Despite the many months of clearly deteriorating market conditions, Drexel had not refinanced its short-term broker loans and commercial paper, which were being used to carry the growing inventory of devalued junk bonds. In the end the bankers withdrew. No one stepped in to buy up the firm at the last minute (as Shearson Lehman Brothers had done after Hutton's liquidity crisis following the crash of 1987), partly because of the unmeasurable civil liabilities still clinging to Drexel's skin. The Federal Reserve considered intervention, but saw no financial crisis following in the wake of its collapse, so it did nothing.

Fred Joseph carried the can. No one heard anything from Drexel's chairman, John Shad, or its other wise men, Roderick Hills, and Ralph Saul, put in by the SEC after the settlement to look after things. They were so intent on supervising compliance issues that they ignored Drexel's basic business problems. The firm took on increasingly lousy credits and built up its market exposures far beyond what sensible people would do, franchise or no franchise. Joseph was inundated, exhausted, and unable to say no to prima donnas who badgered him constantly for more money. He lost control of the firm; a condition that was probably evident long before its end. He desperately needed help in the chief executive's office and he didn't get it.

The Drexel bunch were about as picaresque as New Men get to be. They created great riches and fame for themselves during the eighties, but most will not have been able to retain much of it. This time the courts and/or the marketplace will expropriate most of their gains from them. Thus most will disappear from the scene and be forgotten. But, as always, they will be replaced by other New Men looking for their chances.

They will also be remembered for legitimizing the market for high-yield securities. Though things got carried away in the end, the basic principles of junk bonds still apply, and in due course some brave investors will appear again on the buy side of the market.

Indeed, the default rate for below-investment-grade straight debt issues for 1989, as calculated by Professor Altman, was 3.9 percent, a high rate to be sure but one that was lower than the default rates in three of the preceding nineteen years. The 1989 default rate, however, was nowhere near as high as the rate that market conditions were discounting in early 1990. Maybe the market knows something about a coming recession, or the true financial fragility of many of the overpriced, late-in-the-cycle LBOs that would tell us to expect a much higher default rate for 1990 and subsequent years. But at 17 to 20 percent yields, the default rates would have to more than double, to more than 10 percent, for the risk-adjusted rates to fall below Treasury returns.

Maybe we've come back to where we started from, and it's time to take another stroll around the junkyard.

III

UNDERPINNINGS OF THE NEW ORDER

8

ARE THE THEORIES
WRONG?

When I was a student in business school in the mid-1960s, we were taught that business management was no longer a seat-of-the-pants thing, it was now scientific. Business was all about achieving results, the maximum results possible for a prescribed set of goals and objectives. The manager's role was to provide leadership and "strategic direction" to an enterprise whose purpose was to "maximize" results by growing, functioning efficiently, and behaving responsibly in the face of complex demands from government and society. All businesses were made up of five functional elements that could be analyzed and studied rationally: marketing (in which you had to understand the customer, the market, and the "channels"), manufacturing (in which you had to understand queuing, reject rates, and "decision trees"), control (accounting, cost accounting, and "management information systems"), human behavior in organizations (in which psychological phenomena and "personality types" were appraised), and finally, finance.

Finance meant corporate finance, which was held up by two giant theoretical pillars: capital budgeting theory and optimal capital structure theory. Both were the product of many years of scholarly endeavor and were considered very sound. The first related to spending or investing the free cash flow and unutilized capital resources available to the company, either in dividends or in new projects. To know how to do this, you had to know the total amount of capital resources available and the "cost of capital." To know the total amount of resources available, you had to know how much you could borrow, and to know that, you had to know what the company's optimal capital structure was, that is, its best mixture of long-term debt and equity.

In simplified terms these theories led managers to follow a few basic rules of thumb. Internally generated funds were the cheapest source of capital. If they were not reinvested they would have to be paid out in dividends, in which case they would be subject to double taxation (first at the corporate level, then at the level of the individual receiving shareholder). The objective of the company was to grow and invest in new projects that would return more to the shareholder, after tax, than would receiving more dividends. As interest payments on debt were tax-deductible, there was an advantage to borrowing money whenever possible as long as the money was to be invested in a project that would return more, again after tax, than the company's basic cost of capital. The cost of capital was a single rate that blended the cost of debt and equity capital. Equity had to be counted too because a company had to issue equity from time to time to be able to continue to secure debt financing at favorable rates.

How much debt for every dollar of equity was a matter of capital structure. By the mid-1960s, a lot of serious work on the subject had been published: Franco Modigliani and Merton Miller wrote their famous piece, "The Cost of Capital, Corporation Finance, and the Theory of Investment," in 1958; John Lintner wrote *The Theory of Investment of the Firm* in 1951 and published "Dividends, Earnings, Leverage, Stock Prices and the Supply of Capital to Corporations" in 1962; Gordon Donaldson wrote *Corporate Debt Capacity* in 1961. There were many others who contributed sophisticated thoughts to the subject, which for many economists and mathematicians had become bewitchingly complex and therefore fascinating.

By the 1970s certainly, the business manager understood that what these eminent academicians were saying was that companies ought to borrow all they could, to take advantage of a very substantial government subsidy in the form of the tax deductibility of interest. The money so raised would be invested in projects ranked in order of their expected return on investment. As projects were approved, the best ones would be used up first, leaving progressively less attractive projects. After a while, the projects that would return more than the cost of capital were gone and further borrowing would cease. The benefit of the leverage was in being able to obtain financing beyond what internally generated funds could provide so as to be able to undertake all the high return-on-investment (ROI) projects that were available. Earnings would rise accordingly and the value of the firm would too.

Leverage, in other words, increased the value of the firm.

However, leverage involved risk and thus challenged the fiduciary concerns of the company's directors. So, in practice the upper limits of borrowing for mature publicly owned industrial companies were kept quite modest, in the area of 15 to 30 percent of total "capitalization," that is, the sum of its long-term debt and equity. For most such companies in fairly stable businesses, there was a substantial flow of internally generated funds and often a limited number of high ROI projects requiring only relatively small amounts of borrowing. In any case, many companies thought borrowing more than that would be unwise—it would be irresponsible, too risky— given the experiences of the 1930s. It was considered a point of high corporate honor in the 1960s to have been awarded a AAA or AA bond rating from Moody's or Standard & Poor's and, once received, such ratings should be preserved. They were content to pass up the occasional opportunity, perhaps, in the interest of sound business governance.

"Right," says my friend Ruth. "That sounds very reasonable, and it is backed, as you say, by respected scholarly opinion.

"So how can you justify today's ridiculous amounts of borrowings by companies—all these junk bonds? If a company can borrow 95 percent of its capitalization, how can there be any real limit on corporate borrowing? And if there is no limit, how do your academic experts make sense out of what's happening today?"

Are There Limits to Corporate Debt Capacity?

The merger boom of the sixties introduced the idea that projects did not have to be limited to further investments in one's own industry in order for the benefits of leverage to apply.

During the 1960s the perceived purpose of the American corporation changed. Immediately after the war corporations emphasized getting things back to normal and fulfilling consumers' pent-up demand for goods and the returning serviceman's need for a job. In the fifties, the emphasis seemed to be on battling with competitors for market share. In the sixties, with the advent of the institutional investor, the emphasis shifted again, this time to one of growth in earnings per share and thus in the capitalized value of those earnings as reflected in the company's stock price.

If a corporation, however, set for itself a growth objective of say 15 percent but its own industry was only growing at 10 percent, it would have to diversify into some other businesses growing at 20 percent or more to achieve the objective.

Thus the idea of the multi-industry company came into vogue. Buzz words like *synergy* and *conglomeration* entered the businessman's vocabulary. It might have been possible, instead of diversifying into widely different fields, to manage one's own business more scientifically so that it would grow faster than the industry average, but that would involve hard work over a long time to achieve the desired results assuming the basic economics of the industry would allow them. It was much faster to achieve the desired growth rate through acquisition, which in turn (like any other corporate investment project) was cheapest to finance with borrowings or, once the borrowing capacity was used up, with convertible preferred stock. All of a sudden, large amounts of borrowing, amounts that would substantially increase the debt ratios of many major companies, became justifiable.

A large supply of acquisitions that seemed to be worthwhile from an ROI point of view was available—after all, the number of projects that might return more than the cost of capital was unlimited if it didn't matter what kind of projects they were. Money, too, was abundant during most of the sixties: it could easily be borrowed at rates below the ROI that was expected, especially if there were no limits on your expectations. Thus, scientifically speaking, there was every reason to increase leverage to finance acquisitions. Accordingly, leverage rates did increase, but how much further could they go? What was the outer limit: the maximum amount that a multi-industry company could borrow?

This issue was probed in the late sixties by Nevins Baxter, who took up the question of excessive leverage in a paper titled "Leverage, Risk of Ruin and the Cost of Capital" published in 1967. He and others were beginning to focus on the risks and costs of bankruptcy as a limiting factor to corporations continuing to invest in projects of varying attractiveness that were financed with cheap borrowed money. Edward Altman joined in the study of these matters when he published a paper on predicting corporate bankruptcy in 1968, and, later with two colleagues, perfected his original work and devised an important methodology for identifying the bankruptcy risk of corporations. These efforts produced what came to be widely known as "Z-Scores" and "Zeta Analysis" techniques. Altman later applied his expertise to studying the default rates of high-yield bonds.[1]

These studies led to the notion of an outer limit to corporate borrowing for a given set of corporate performance measures. This limit would be reached when the debt burden achieved a level of bankruptcy risk such that the expected value of bankruptcy costs exceeded the benefits associated with debt financing.

In other words, the more that is borrowed, the greater are the risks and the associated expected costs of bankruptcy. This cost serves as a drag on useful borrowing. When the drag starts to exceed the benefits from borrowing, it is time to stop borrowing. This is the point of the optimal debt-to-capitalization ratio (see figure 1).

Bankruptcy risk is a fairly complicated thing to assess. Altman's Z-Score is an aggregation of many variables that yields an overall score reflecting a firm's current financial and operating profile, a kind of index of measurable factors that can ward off bankruptcy. The score, however, does not measure everything that might be relevant. For example, if a conglomerate keeps adding disparate businesses to its pile, the ability to manage the business decreases, as many have discovered. Occasionally conglomerates go off the deep end and take on something hopelessly beyond their capabilities, as James Ling discovered with Jones & Laughlin Steel. Market conditions, too, can make a difference in the ability of a company to protect itself against bankruptcy by raising prices or by selling assets, a condition that Campeau Corporation discovered in attempting to manage its Allied and Federated Department Stores LBOs. There are qualitative factors too that pertain to bankruptcy risk, and these should be taken into account along with the quantitative factors identified by Professor Altman.

Even so, Modigliani and Miller's and Altman's works suggested that there was more room for borrowing than most companies in the United States in the late 1970s and early 1980s were using. Modigliani, in fact, in an article published in February 1989 noted that he did not share the "common alarm concerning the extent and recent trends of corporate indebtedness."[2]

Figure 1

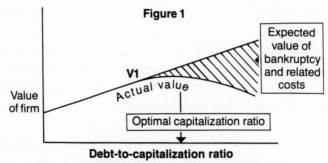

Theoretical value of firm (V1) = value of unleveraged firm + present value of tax benefits from borrowing

Companies began the 1980s somewhat underleveraged, which meant that they were not maximizing the values of their firms, a condition that was reflected in low stock prices. For some of these companies this meant that their stock prices were much lower than their potential "restructured" values. By the end of the 1980s, corporate leverage increased considerably as a consequence of mergers, LBOs, and self-restructurings, and the "underborrowing" gap was substantially closed. In some cases companies have gone the other way and overleveraged instead, with many defaults and forced recapitalizations under distress conditions the result.

Federal Reserve and Department of Commerce statistics demonstrate, for example, that aggregate corporate debt as a percentage of total capitalization rose gradually from a level of about 32 percent in the early 1950s to a peak of about 40 percent in 1972, then it dropped to about 35 percent in 1982 before rising sharply to 43 percent in 1988. The 1988 level, however, was actually less than 35 percent if equities were taken at market value.

Debt-service capacity went through a similar pattern, with gross interest paid as a percentage of cash flow peaking in the 1982–87 period at about 38 percent (23 percent if net interest only is considered). A Merrill Lynch quantitative research report in 1989 noted that the "chance of bankruptcy" (as determined by Altman's Z-Scores) for the S & P industrials has increased since 1980 to 10 percent after having dropped from 8.8 percent in 1974 to about 3 percent in 1980.[3]

Closing the underborrowing gap that existed in 1980 might explain an increase in debt as a percentage of total capitalization from, say, 35 percent to 45 or 50 percent. However, it still did not account for the extraordinary amounts of leverage being used by some operators whose borrowing levels reached 85 and 90 percent. Indeed, Professors Jensen and Kaplan calculated that the average LBO in the 1980s had a debt-to-total-asset ratio of 86 percent, or a six-to-one debt-to-equity ratio.

There was more to it than getting rid of the gap—two things actually, two new concepts.

One was the concept of *temporary debt*. This was debt extended by banks to be repaid relatively soon (within eighteen months usually) out of the proceeds of asset sales and other extraordinary steps taken by the new management after an LBO to free up cash. The money was borrowed by the LBO operator to assemble the cash package necessary to purchase the stock from the outgoing shareholders. In order to lend so much money, however, banks require that the LBO operator repay it first out of the funds it is first able to generate after it assumes control. Such a concept is little different from banks advancing seasonal working capital funds to a company that will pay it back within the current business cycle after inventories and receivables have been liquidated. Accordingly, that portion of the financing package advanced by banks as a takeover facility to be repaid out of asset sales, and so forth, should probably not be counted in looking at longer-term debt capacity, just as seasonal short-term borrowing would also not be counted. So a $5 million equity investment in a $100 million acquisition that represents 5 percent going in would be increased to a 10 percent investment after $50 million of temporary debt was repaid from sales of assets, and so on. In the case of the Beatrice LBO, for example, $6.4 billion of assets was sold and $1 billion of existing liabilities was transferred to others in the first year and a half, thereby reducing total capitalization to $1 billion or so against which equity of about $400 million (before exercising of warrants) was available, an equity ratio of 40 percent. A year earlier the equity ratio had been only 6 percent. The Beatrice case, of course, is an extreme example in which the purpose of the LBO seemed to be the liquidation of the company, not its continuation on a restructured basis.

The other concept was that of *tax-deductible equity*: that is, junk bonds and other forms of mezzanine debt financing. Interest payments on these securities were tax-deductible because legally they were bonds: they had a preferred claim over equity securities in liquidation, and they of course required full repayment of the principal amount of the bonds on a certain date along with annual interest payments until then. If required payments were not made, then holders of these securities could force the company into bankruptcy. Still, mezzanine financing was designed to have an appeal to investors that would be very similar to the appeal of equities. It was similar also to the use of preferred stock in the nineteenth century before taxes to be avoided through deductions existed.

At the time of issuance of the mezzanine securities, their asset coverage was poor and most of the company's cash flow was used to cover interest charges on senior securities, so, like that of equities, the real value of the securities would have to derive from events that had to happen in the future, giving them a speculative character. The junk bond investor looked to the high coupon rate and the possibility of capital gains for a return that he expected to be commensurate with the risk he was taking, that is, a return commensurate with an equity return. In Chapter 7, an illustration was given showing how annualized returns of 20 percent or more could be achieved by combining high-interest-rate coupons with market value increases in bonds that had been upgraded by the market as a result of the issuer's survival and success in servicing debt during the difficult first few years.

Mezzanine securities are subordinated in right of payment to the company's senior debt (bank debt and pre-LBO senior debt outstanding). This means that all the assets in the company in the event of liquidation have to be used first to repay senior debt before they can be used to repay the junk bonds. As far as the banks and senior debtholders are concerned the junk bonds are virtually the same thing as equity, though banks know to be careful in all aspects of documentation to preclude subordinated bondholders from worming their way into senior debtholders' territory when an actual bankruptcy occurs.

A recent study by First Boston Corporation showed that representative capitalizations of companies with junk bonds outstanding in 1987 and 1988 had about 60 percent in the form of senior debt (40 percent bank loans, 20 percent senior debt), subordinated debt of about 20 percent, deferred-interest obligations (from PIKs and deep discount bonds) of 7 percent, and equity (common and preferred stock) of 13 percent. If the deferred payments were not counted as part of capitalization, then the senior debt would represent 65 percent, subordinated 21, and equity 14. This study included many companies that had been the subject of an LBO or a self-recapitalization at some time in recent years.

The First Boston study demonstrated that once temporary debt was paid down, the resulting capital structure for highly leveraged, noninvestment-grade companies was not substantially different from the lower end of investment-grade companies insofar as *senior* debt is concerned.

Thus what we have is a sort of reconciliation of the differences between the traditional capital structure thinking, as updated by Altman and others, and the reality reflected by today's markets. Borrowing capacity is possible in many investment-grade companies of up to 50 or 60 percent of total capitalization without either aggravating the gods of bankruptcy unduly or inducing the rating agencies to downgrade the companies to below investment grade. Even some LBOs, after one or two years, when temporary debt has been repaid, end up with about the same ratio of *senior* debt to total capitalization as BBB-rated companies have. The rating agencies do not of course immediately upgrade ratings on companies just because their senior debt to capitalization ratios and Z-Scores improve: they like to be sure that the companies have their operating problems under control and have overall debt-service-to-cash-flow ratios that no longer make the company highly exposed to market risk. They also seek assurances on plans for further disposals and new investments among other matters. They also want to be sure that, if upgraded, the company could hold the new rating for several years at least.

"Okay," says Ruth, "I can see that for senior debt maybe reality is not so far adrift as I thought. But what about all that subordinated debt? Debt is debt, isn't it?"

It is the subordinated debt and the equity accounts that make up the real difference between the capital structures of investment-grade and noninvestment-grade companies. In the investment-grade company the equity is predominantly in the form of common stock (or securities convertible into common stock). In the noninvestment-grade company the equity is divided into tax-deductible equity and straight equity.

Tax-deductible equity provides three important advantages to the company issuing it. First, of course, it may deduct interest payments against present and future income, thereby reducing cash payments for taxes. Second, the company is not obliged to pay more than the interest and principal due on the securities to the investor: the capital gains that the investor seeks come from the market's repricing of the securities because of successful debt reduction and other programs that follow the LBO, that is, the company is not required to share future earnings with the holder of the securities. Of course, these securities have a priority claim on the company's cash flow relative to the common stockholders until they are redeemed, but afterward all of the cash and the earnings can be retained by the equity investor.

The third benefit provided by tax-deductible equity is its capacity, in aggregate, to enhance the market value of the company. In substituting a variety of different equitylike securities for most of the company's common stock, investors are offered a choice of different instruments with which to maximize their objectives while minimizing their concerns. As in the case of the restructuring of the Sugar Trust in the 1890s, offering the choice (including the opportunity to purchase packages of securities tailored to suit an investor exactly) tends to raise the price that investors are willing to pay for them.

Enhancing Values

Thus the equity account can be replaced by a picnic spread of common stock, preferred stock, junior subordinated securities, pay-in-kind securities, senior subordinated securities and warrants, and options in any or all of them to give each investor exactly what he is looking for in terms of yield, expected return, speculative quality, volatility, security, and waiting period. Each security has substantially different characteristics from the others. A holder of subordinated debt, for example, is paid out before a holder of common stock, though his theoretical maximum return is substantially less than that of the holder of the common stock. The investor is prepared to pay a premium to get exactly what he wants, and thus the fragmentation of the nonsenior debt and equity accounts results in an aggregate market value that is potentially greater than the market value of the common stock alone.

It is useful to think in terms of the total market value of a company when considering how values are enhanced or shifted between different securities. The total market value is the combination of the market value of all of a company's outstanding common stock *and* the market value of all other loans and securities that may be outstanding, namely debt or preferred stock.

Consider the case of a company that before acquisition by an LBO group had a *total market* value of 100 (say, 80 for its common stock and 20 for its outstanding debt) and was acquired for 150. The old debt would remain outstanding and become a "fallen angel," so its market value would drop, say, by 25 percent, to 15, leaving the common stock valued at 135. The old equity holder would see his investment rise nearly 70 percent, from 80 to 135, because of the premium paid for control of the company. The disparity in what happened to the debt and the equity investors demonstrates the good sense for all holders of corporate debt of buying a few shares of common stock as a hedge against the risk of the bonds' being suddenly downgraded in a takeover.

The new company (the acquisition vehicle) will have to find 135 to pay for the acquisition. It arranges borrowing from banks of 60, (which together with the 15 of outstanding debt comprises a senior debt tier of 75, which is 50 percent of total capitalization of 150), an amount that is actually somewhat less than the preacquisition market value of the company's common stock (80). The senior debtholder thus in effect has the preacquisition value of the company's net worth as reasonable collateral for his loan. For a great many healthy companies liquidation value is significantly greater than preacquisition market value; that is, the breakup value was greater than the stock price before the company came into play. So the value of the common stock as collateral—that is, first crack at all the assets of the com-

	MARKET VALUE			BOOK VALUE	
	Before LBO	After LBO	Percentage change	After LBO	Percentage of total
OLD CAPITAL STRUCTURE					
Old senior debt	20	15	−25%		
Old equity	80	135	+69		
Total	100	150	+50		
NEW CAPITAL STRUCTURE					
Senior debt outstanding		15		20	13%
Senior bank debt		60		60	39
Total senior debt		80		80	52
Mezzanine Financing ("tax-deductible equity")		65		65	42
Equity		10		10	6
Total Capitalization		150		155	100%

pany,—is comparatively high in relation to the principal amount of the senior debt.

The LBO group puts in 10 of equity. The difference between the acquisition price (135) and the total contributed so far by banks (60) and equity investors (10) is 65. This is the amount to be raised in the form of tax-deductible equity. The new capitalization, at accounting (book) values totals 155: 80 senior debt (bank debt, 60, plus the par value of preacquisition debt, 20) or 52 percent of the new capitalization; 65, subordinated debt, 42 percent of capitalization; and 10 in common stock, representing 6 percent.

In this transaction the magician's wand has waved twice over the preacquisition company to transform it into its new state. First, the old company was leveraged up in the conventional way: a senior debt ratio of 20 percent was replaced by one of 52 percent. If no acquisition was involved, the company might have increased borrowing to buy back its own stock, increasing its senior debt by 60 and its debt ratio to 52 percent. But in the case of the LBO, the second passing of the wand involved the creation of 65 in subordinated debt, or tax-deductible equity, which leveraged the conventional equity of the company further. On the one hand total debt now amounted to 145, or 90 percent of the post-LBO capitalization

—surely a lot of debt. On the other hand, LBO equity plus tax-deductible equity equaled 75, or 48 percent of total capitalization—surely a respectable amount.

But investors had to be attracted to the tax-deductible equity. Dollar for dollar, they were taking the most risk. Why would they do it?

Because the market saw the prospects for change from the re-structuring of the company that would accrue benefits to all of the equity holders: the holders of common stock would benefit over time from the large amount of increased leverage, the tax-deductible eq-uity investors from the high interest received in the short run and from the opportunity for quick capital gains should the market up-grade the subordinated debt as senior debt is repaid. The "new equity" investors (the equity and the tax-deductible equity investors) will benefit by the prospective *deleveraging* of the now fully leveraged corporation. For every dollar of debt repaid, the market should increase the valuation of the equity, though initially of course the tax-deductible equity, with a substantial repayment schedule, will capture most of the benefit.

Riding the Leverage Curve

The equity investors in the preacquisition company, had benefited by the increasing of leverage up to the point of the optimal capital-ization ratio. For every dollar of new assets put to work, earnings would be increased by, say ten cents, which, times a price-earnings ratio of, say, 10, meant that the market value of the equity of the company would increase by the amount of the money borrowed—for a while anyway. After the optimal capitalization ratio was reached, things would start to go the other way, and the equity account would decrease by more than the benefits from borrowing, as figure 1 (page 260) illustrates.

LBOs and their high total debt ratios have taught us something new about value enhancement from leverage. In an LBO, total debt exceeds the optimal capitalization ratio by a large amount. Ordinarily this could not be done, because value would start to decline as additional debt was added beyond the optimal point. But in an LBO, suddenly, the initial shareholders are bought out and replaced by new shareholders who have created a new corporate structure in which the debt ratio is 90 percent. How can this work to create enhanced value for the new shareholders?

First, the new shareholders account for only 10 percent or less of the new market value—the rest of the market value is contained in the debt. Second, some of the debt is temporary debt that will be repaid quickly out of the sale of assets. And third, the company's operating policies will be changed to direct all free cash flow to the retirement of the rest of the debt as soon as possible. Thus value can be created by turning the new debt into equity, that is by reducing the debt-to-equity ratio. The increased value will be in part from increases in book value and in part from increased market value.

It all depends on which side of the optimal capitalization point you are. You start from one side or the other: either you are *moving up* the leverage curve to the optimal point, beyond which it does not make sense to pass, or you start from the fully leveraged, beyond-optimal, position and try to make money by repaying debt, that is, by *moving down* the leverage curve.

While moving up the curve the enhancement in the total value of the company (the value of its debt and equity combined) accrues disproportionately to the benefit of the equity investor, as shown in figure 2 between points A and B. Total value continues to increase past the optimal capitalization ratio (between points B and C) because the incremental debt has been borrowed to buy out the old shareholders in an LBO at value C, which reflects a control premium for the old shareholder. While moving down the leverage curve (from points C to B), the enhanced value of the company is returned to the common stock investor. You can make money either way.

Clever operators like KKR know that by waving their wands they can enhance the value of companies they wish to pursue, by increasing leverage and by recapitalizing the equity of the firm. The enhancement, which is almost entirely attributed to the nonsenior

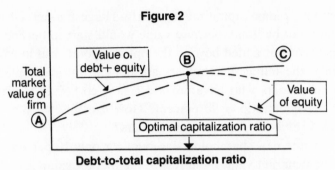

Figure 2

Debt-to-total capitalization ratio

Total market value of firm rises from B to C because of control premium paid to acquire the firm in an LBO for a price of C, otherwise value would begin to stabilize or decrease if the debt ratio increased beyond B.

debt accounts, the equity and the tax-deductible equity accounts, enables them to pay such high prices for targets, even in competition with others. Competitors, of course, do the same so the ability of one side to out-enhance the other is often what makes the difference. In the RJR-Nabisco transaction, for example, the successful bidders ended up with five different securities below the senior debt.

"In other words, the lesson from all this theory is that you can enhance the value of a company while nearly bankrupting it?" asks Ruth.

Well, yes. RJR-Nabisco was stuck at a stock price of about $55, after leveraging, acquiring, and doing a lot of other things that management thought should appeal to investors. Perhaps it had reached the optimal value of the firm for its stockholders as Ross Johnson believed it had. Perhaps the market would pay more for the company's parts than for its whole as he and many others believed. If so, shareholders' value would be increased by breaking it up. In the end the original RJR-Nabisco shareholder had his value enhanced to nearly twice what it had been before. The new shareholders, KKR, secured the financing they needed from banks and subordinated and preferred investors who expected high, equitylike returns. At the end of the first year (May 1990), senior debt had been reduced by 37 percent, indicating that approximately $6.5 billion of the $17.5 billion of senior debt originally outstanding was temporary debt.

Altogether senior debt outstanding had been reduced to about 46 percent of capitalization. The year's results had generally been favorable, but the collapse of the junk securities market and the disappearance of LBOs meant that RJR could not sell off assets as freely as it had bought them, and the yield on its PIK reset securities had climbed to nearly 20 percent, triggering a downgrading of the rest of the company's debt. So even though the company was moving down the leverage curve, other factors were at play too, which prevented much of an overall increase in the value of the shares in RJR owned by KKR. Or put another way, the risk of bankruptcy had increased and that changed the curve that the company was moving down on. Even so, as long as it continues to move in the direction of reducing leverage, its value will be greater than if it were not moving at all.

What Are Stocks Worth?

Theorists have contributed a lot to the understanding of securities valuation and portfolio management. Most of the early ones, such as John Maynard Keynes in the 1920s and Benjamin Graham and David Dodd in the 1930s, insisted that investment management was as much an art as a science, but latter-day scholars have relied more heavily on the scientific part in attempting to answer the most ancient and fundamental question of finance: What is it worth?

With apologies to my academic colleagues, I will venture to say that there are only two theoretical approaches to securities valuation. First is the idea of an "intrinsic value" originally put forward by Graham and Dodd in 1934 and sharpened over the years by the thoughts of many others. The root of intrinsic value was the future earning power of a company; everything else sprang from that. In 1938 John Burr Williams noted that the investment value of a stock was the present worth of all the *dividends* to be paid on it, not on its future earnings: dividends, not earnings is what you actually get. Williams also argued that a stock's intrinsic value (the future dividends) should not be mixed up with its marketability. Its value was what it was; the market may or may not know it.[4]

The second approach involves the assessment of the value of a security in the context of a portfolio of other securities. This is a "relative value" approach. According to this way of looking at stocks and bonds, what counts is one's whole portfolio. A stock or bond will be valued relative to similar securities: which one has the higher yield, or the lowest price-earnings ratio, or the greater volatility, or whatever. Portfolio managers are looking for the highest risk-adjusted rate of return and invest accordingly; intrinsic value doesn't really enter into it.

The ultimate refinement in portfolio theory is that as large numbers of players (investors or money managers) of substantially similar backgrounds and investment dispositions compete with each other against common standards of performance in an environment of equal access to information, the market itself takes over and runs the portfolio on autopilot. This is the "perfect market" in which all relevant information about a security, past, present, and future, is already discounted in its price. In a perfect market there are no particular advantages to one stock or another—all can and do fit in. Everyone becomes an investor in a common pool of investments. You may as well pick your stocks with a dart board as through analysis. Intrinsic value? It's already discounted in the price.

This line of thinking has led to an abandonment of active portfolio management by some large, performance-oriented institutional investors unable regularly to "beat the market" to put their money instead into "market index funds" so they at least can tie, if not beat it. One savvy market observer, Charles Ellis, managing partner of Greenwich Research Associates, calls trying to beat the market averages the "loser's game," and the only way to win at it, he says, is to index.

"In other words," said Ruth, "the market knows everything so just relax and leave the investing to it. That seems like saying everybody may as well go work for the government where you don't move ahead any faster than anyone else but also no slower.

"For this we pay you all those fees you earn?"

Ruth is reminded that since the 1960s institutional investors have dominated securities markets in the United States, and these investors are for the most part playing by the same rules: to invest as prudent men would but to do so on a basis that makes the people who give them funds to manage happy that they are getting the right mix of safety and performance. Hence these look-alike investors have made themselves into a perfect market, where everything ticks away in a nice orderly way like a Swiss watch. A triumph of theory: the results seem to confirm it.

"But what if the makeup of the investors changes?" asks Ruth. "What if this lockstep group of institutions has to operate in the same market with a bunch of newcomers, whose approach to valuation of securities is different?"

Changing Investors

One old hand in the stock market, Dean LeBaron, a senior trustee of Batterymarch Financial Management, offers a sensible observation.[5] He points out that since the late 1940s the stock market has been principally dominated by three different types of investors, each with different interests and behavior and different methodologies and tools for valuation of stocks. Until the late sixties,

> individual investors were the dominant force in setting stock prices. This was the era of the stock-picker, the research analyst, and the "star" portfolio manager. Passions ran high, and investors tended to "fall in love" with stocks. They were impatient with bad news and often obsessed with getting "the latest story."

Stock valuations in the sixties were extremely high: price-earnings ratios about fifty times earnings were not uncommon then. However, after the 1969 market decline and the dreary seventies, individuals began a steady twenty-year liquidation of their holdings of common stocks.

Next, from the sixties until the early eighties, came the time of the institutional investor as the dominant price-setting influence. LeBaron describes them as

Applying quantitative techniques to financial databases, they used dividend discount models and price screens based on academic research to set the prices of stock to within a few basis points, based on key value measures. These institutions are dispassionate: they do not care about control, they just want cheap stocks that go up. Their activity has made the market more efficient relative to their popular measures of value: price/earnings, price/book, yield and so forth. Their activity also set the stage for a fresh perspective on value.

In short with individuals departing the market, the gap was filled by institutions, which had a very different way of valuing stocks. Values had to be realigned from the euphoric, irrational sixties. During most of the seventies they were—downward.

In the eighties, LeBaron says, corporations took over from institutions as having the principal influence in valuing corporations. During the period from 1982 to 1988, U.S. corporations acquired more than $580 billion of corporate stocks (excluding the purchase of shares in privately held companies, or corporate divisions or assets); institutional investors at the same time bought (net of sales) only about $230 billion.

The corporate sector was trying to realign itself following the many changes that had affected its competitive environment over the years. It discovered restructuring. But it also realized that one reason for the misalignment of values was that the stock market, dominated by bargain-hunting institutions, was placing too low a value on their shares. The corporations, therefore, began to value each other— their own way, not the way institutions did. Corporations look at different things in measuring what counts, for example, liquidation value, replacement value, and undedicated cash flow. Instead of looking at price-earnings ratios and dividend yields, says LeBaron,

> they analyzed off-balance sheet items (pension assets and li-
> abilities, LIFO reserves, tax losses); tax considerations (the
> write-up of acquired assets, spinoff of tax shelters, the capture
> of tax shield from debt leverage); and "soft" assets (the control
> premium, market share, goodwill, and potential synergy).

LeBaron made these points in a paper describing a new valuation model that institutions might use in selecting investments. He calls the practice of valuing companies the way corporations seeking to restructure them would the "Chop Shop" method. The technique involves placing a market value on the various parts to see if the market will sell the stock to you for less than the value of their sum, like a closed-end investment company. In time, as other institutions adjust their methods of valuation to those used by the corporations, they will contribute to a general raising of prices for the whole market as corporate valuations are generally higher than institutional valuations. Indeed, a research report published by Steve Einhorn of Goldman Sachs in July/August 1989 indicated that over the last five years corporate demand for shares had lifted prices by 20 percent. Rising market prices reduce misalignments, and as the misalignments are reduced so will be the opportunities for restructuring and thus the number of new deals.

"But how can I know what a stock like RJR-Nabisco is really worth at any given time? How do I know whether the investors are changing or not? How do I know what to do when an offer comes in that is above the market?

"I mean we've got its intrinsic value—which may be more or less depending on who's valuing it—and its market value (which is supposed to discount everything to the present, including a bid for 109), and we've got investment bankers talking about 'adequate' and 'fair' values. The courts apparently have a view of whether a bid is way off or not and therefore whether it constitutes a 'threat' to the stockholders. The company's own financial statements, certified by independent accountants, report its 'book value,' or net accounting value. The difference between all these is huge. RJR had a book value of $25.24 per share and a market value of $55 when the gun went off. Its all-time high stock price was $71. Johnson made what he says was a fair offer at $75, and this was immediately topped by KKR with an offer of $90, which the company said was inadequate. Finally an offer of $109 won the day, which some people said was too much and would cause vastly excessive levels of debt to be issued that would bankrupt the country. It sounds like valuation is strictly in the eye of the beholder, or otherwise a hostage to an auction process looking for the last crazy bidder, like when we sold my grandmother's painting at Sotheby's.

"So does all this mean that the market is more perfect or less perfect than your theoretical people thought it was?"

That's a good question, Ruth. Things can be pretty confusing during periods of great changes in the way things are seen to work.

"Yeah, it's getting to be that you don't know what the stocks you own are worth anymore."

9

REFORMING THE SYSTEM

"It's perception versus reality." David Aylward, executive director of Alliance for Capital Access, a lobbying organization that opposes regulation limiting the free access of junk bonds to the market, was explaining the current mood in Washington to those attending a high-yield bond conference in September 1989.

"Some federal regulators and politicians have been carried away by the fiery rhetoric from critics of mergers and acquisitions and of the high-yield bond market," he noted, "and right now, we are in the midst of another wave of near-hysteria about corporate debt and junk bonds. At no time has the gap between perception and reality been greater in Washington.

"And as anyone will tell you, perception is often the stronger force, especially in Washington."

The perception that Aylward was referring to was that easy money and light-handed regulation had fueled takeover activity to such excesses of leverage and greed that it endangered the entire economy and the livelihood of millions. Sharp financial operators were behind it all—looking for ways to divert millions into their own pockets from a lot of fancy restructurings that ordinary people

281

couldn't understand but nevertheless would be made to pay for in the end. Just like the S & Ls.

It was true that since 1980 the corporate debt level had increased substantially, that takeovers had increased, that raids were common and often successful, that some misconduct had occurred in high places, and that by the end of the decade many of the restructurings hailed a few years before as the best way to invigorate American industry would collapse into bankruptcy.

"The facts, however, are on our side," continued Aylward. Washington mainly seems consumed by "unfounded fears."

The fact was that there was substantial evidence supplied by academic studies and the Federal Reserve itself to support the notion that restructuring as a whole, through takeovers and recapitalizations, was increasing American productivity and competitiveness: inescapable evidence that on balance, over a ten-year period, the merger and LBO boom of the 1980s had been good for the country and the economy.[1]

Though debt was much greater than in the early 1980s and this worried Alan Greenspan and many others, the debt mainly was way up in relation to a historically low point in American borrowing, and the ratio of the debt to the market value of corporate equities was not especially high at all. There were some blockbuster defaults, and near-defaults, such as Revco, Fruehauf, Hillsborough Holdings, Campeau, and Southland, but defaults were expected. The whole idea behind junk bonds was that the return after the defaults were taken into account would exceed returns on Treasuries and other assets. Lots of studies were made to dispute the point, even when steep recession scenarios were included, and none could.[2] You were supposed to have defaults, and in some years these might reach 3 or 4 percent of the total of all noninvestment-grade securities outstanding, but in other years defaults would be less. On average, they would work out to be between 1.5 and 2 percent before recoveries, a rate much lower than the average difference between the yields on these bonds and Treasuries.

The "human default rate" was another matter. The misconduct of professionals has been far less than the perception. Fewer than fifty Wall Streeters have been convicted of serious securities law violations during the last decade. This is certainly a low default rate considering the 200,000 or so employees of Wall Street investment banks, law firms, commercial banks, and other professional organizations that might have had access to inside information. Insider trading, in any case, wasn't the same sort of thing as taking bribes or looting companies. It was nothing like what had happened in the S & L industry (to which many congressmen had ties, some proving to be very embarrassing) or what was coming to be revealed at the Department of Housing and Urban Development. In any case, the system worked: the Wall Street offenders were caught, prosecuted, and sentenced.

Finally, there were plenty of signs by December 1989 that the great merger and LBO boom of the 1980s was running out of steam and beginning to return things to "normal." Normal, of course, was something quite different from what it had been ten years before. It was now understood, for example, that there was such a thing as management entrenchment and that the same old folks did not always get the most out of the companies they managed. Different attitudes about employee incentives, employee ownership, and streamlining of corporate expenditures now existed. Raiders may be bad—though some of them, such as Boone Pickens, Ted Turner, and Sir James Goldsmith, have become antiestablishment folk heroes to many people—but bloated do-nothing corporations aren't so great either. Anyway, if the boom was subsiding, maybe all the attention to tighter regulation to slow it down was unnecessary.

Still, said Aylward, "Our PR is terrible." The industry (Wall Street, and the junk bond industry in particular) is getting blamed for everything. "We are being held to a much higher standard than any other industry."

Reagan Era Regulation

Not, however, for the first time. Three preceding merger booms concluded with heightened regulation. Antitrust enforcement activity followed the 1898–1904 boom. The twenties of course ended in a dreadful worldwide depression that was generally thought to have been caused by the market crash of 1929. After the crash, the Banking Act of 1933 and the Securities Acts of 1933 and 1934 were enacted, changing dramatically the ways in which financial activities were carried out thereafter. In the 1960s the dramatic growth in hostile tender offers resulted in the Williams Act, which regulated the process. While the boom was on in the 1980s, nothing much happened in the regulatory field, despite the deteriorating PR and the largest market crash of all time in October 1987.

If anything, regulation diminished during the 1980s. Antitrust enforcement dropped off to nothing. Regulations restricting (some say, protecting) the oil and gas, transportation, broadcasting, banking, insurance, and savings and loan industries were weakened or removed, allowing greater competition and combinations among companies in these fields. The Reagan administration believed that free markets worked better than regulated ones and that government should interfere in business and finance as little as possible. At the same time it cut back government expenditures so law-enforcement and watchdog agencies found it difficult to keep up with all the activities of their charges.

Periodically, however, events would upset powerful constituents of powerful politicians. The takeover and LBO boom upset the heads of many large corporations, who complained to friends in Washington. Usually these friends listened sympathetically but did little. "The White House is for free markets; on balance that's the best policy," they would be told. In order to influence the process in the 1980s, when the regulators were sitting on their hands, you had to go around them. You had to make a lot of noise, get a lot of press attention, make a lot of contributions, and put congressmen in awkward positions where they had to take public positions they did not always agree with. That was the way a lot of business was done in Washington, but generally not matters involving highly complex issues of business, economics, and finance, which were unfamiliar to most congressmen. It was also difficult to manage the influence process once it was begun. How a particular piece of legislation would turn out no one could say, so the main emphasis came to be the influencing of attitudes.

The early rounds in the battle of the attitudes were won by the establishment types who wanted to prevent the Huns from getting over their walls. Raiders and takeovers were back again, even though the bid for Electric Storage Battery by International Nickel in 1974 opened the door for establishment companies to join the raiders, which many did. The process was all wrong, the antiraiders said. Raiders could get away with murder under the present system. Just look at the Bendix–Martin Marietta–United Technologies–Allied Industries affair in 1982, when one blue-chip company, Martin Marietta, when raided by another, tendered for the raider's stock in response, ultimately resulting in its own overleveraging and breakup. The whole thing was ugly and unseemly, like a nasty brawl at a church picnic involving four respected vestrymen. The process through which mergers and takeovers occur should be changed, they argued at the time; many federal reforms were proposed and discussed, most of these getting in each other's way. Finally a consensus emerged: the SEC, which understood the processes better than any other governmental body, should be the one to change it.

So it was left that the SEC would handle merger and takeover policies. In early 1983 it appointed an eighteen-member Advisory Committee on Tender Offers to make recommendations. The committee was made up of professionals from the mergers-and-acquisitions business. Marty Lipton and his counterpart from Skadden Arps, Joe Flom, were included. So were leading players from the investment bankers. The committee was asked to come up with its report within four months, and it did. Although the report was introduced with the preamble "There is insufficient basis for concluding that takeovers are either per se beneficial or detrimental to the economy," it proceeded to make about fifty sensible recommendations.

By the time the Advisory Committee was considering its recommendations, it had become clear that the regulated tender offer process installed by the Williams Act in 1968 was not sufficient on its own to moderate the practices that had emerged during the past few years. The Williams Act, for example, never anticipated greenmail, two-tiered front-end loaded offers, golden parachutes, the Pac Man defense, and many other innovations that had been introduced by the opposing sides in current takeover battles. In most aspects of takeovers there were simply no rules and contests were decided by combat, with the strongest or boldest or smartest party emerging after the fray as victor. Takeovers, in the United States, were coming to be ruled only by laissez faire.

Not so in Britain, which also had a long history of and much current activity in takeovers, a great many of them hostile. Since 1981 when Goldman Sachs became involved in the defense of Thomas Tilling plc, which was being bid for by BTR plc, two British companies, U.S. firms had followed developments in the U.K. mergers-and-acquisitions market closely. This market at the time was "self-regulated" (it is not now) under a system in which "the City," that is, Britain's equivalent of Wall Street, provided members of a Takeover Panel who would referee the conduct of behavior of both sides during a takeover. The panel, which was made up of experienced professionals on secondment from their firms for a year or two, lived by the idea that its job was to maintain a level playing field. There were certain published rules and procedures that all must follow, but the panel conducted hearings and made decisions on the spot on what was permissible in all gray areas, of which there were of course many. To maintain a level field, the panel lived by four basic ideas: fair and prompt disclosure of stakes had to be made, offers had to be real and fully capable of being financed as described, once a stakeholding of 30 percent had been accumulated an offer must be made to all shareholders, and the target company had to let the shareholders decide the outcome; that is, management could not frustrate a bid to the shareholders if all the rules were followed. The emphasis then in contested deals came to be on price, whether shareholders would be better off selling out now or hanging on for management to improve values later, and, inevitably, on loyalty. Most of the Advisory Committee members were familiar with these British rules and appreciated their effectiveness.

Among the committee's recommendations were several powerful and very significant proposals: an acquirer would be prevented from crossing the 5 percent stakeholding level until 48 hours *after* public disclosure of his plans to do so, rather than having an interval of ten days between acquisition and disclosure. Acquisitions of stake-holdings of 20 percent would require an offer to *all* shareholders. Pac Man defenses would be prevented if a fully financed cash offer were made for a company. Golden parachutes could not be issued to management once a tender offer had commenced. Neither green-mail payments nor the issuance of new shares as a defensive measure would be permitted without shareholder approval. Partial and two-tiered offers would be permitted only if all shareholders received the highest price paid, and the time of the first-tier offer were extended.

When the Advisory Committee's report was published, it included several dissenting opinions, but the recommendations adopted were those of the majority. They were generally considered to be workable, substantive, and pragmatic. They had taken a page or two out of the British book, but they were suited to the American market. It was one of the few times since Joseph Kennedy had been made head of the SEC in 1934 that industry opinions would be sought out to improve rule making.

Naturally, the recommendations went nowhere.

Congress had held many hearings, had many proposals of its own on restricting takeovers. There were ideas floated to restrict income tax deductions for money borrowed for acquisitions or for junk bonds, proposals for revising the Williams Act, proposals for restricting hostile offers, for a lot of things. They swirled around in the air, looking only for some leadership to roost on. Few topics were as widely and vocally considered as these financial issues. Naturally the SEC, charged with regulating the markets and armed with its advice, was asked to testify and contribute to the debate and to its resolution. It did so very cautiously, taking eight months to offer a lukewarm endorsement of its own Advisory Committee's proposals. The SEC waffled on almost everything, evidently hearing non-interfering free-market drumbeats from the direction of Pennsylvania Avenue. As John Brooks put it in *The Takeover Game* in 1987:

> With such a legislative storm wind blowing, could the administration's wall of inaction stand? It could. In May 1985 the SEC voted, unanimously . . . , not to seek new legislation,

and withdrew all of its previous proposals for change (they were now "obsolete," Chairman [John] Shad said). . . . This probably marked the turning point. With the whole executive panoply of economic power arrayed against change, and with the SEC now solidly in the laissez-faire camp, Congress began to lose heart. In June there was a growing feeling among legislators that what was needed was not new laws but more vigorous enforcement of existing ones. Even [then Congressman Tim] Worth, the man most visibly at the cutting edge of legislative reform, was saying, "The more I know about the issue, the less sure I am about what to do."[3]

Paul Volcker, then chairman of the Federal Reserve, wasn't unsure about what to do. The Fed had authority to set margin rules that determined how much borrowing could underlie purchases of stocks. Volcker believed that hostile raids to be financed entirely by pledging the target's assets were destabilizing and led to inappropriate use of the banking system. In December 1985, the Fed governors voted (three to two) to propose a 50 percent margin limit on such transactions. If the rule had been in place during 1985 it would have prevented several large hostile takeovers that occurred during the year from being completed on the terms offered. The margin restriction would not apply, however, to transactions that were approved by the target company's board of directors.

There was much objection to the Fed's proposal, and indeed an astonishing degree of criticism from sister agencies of the U.S. government. In what appeared to all to be a coordinated attack on the Volcker block among the Fed's governors by the administration, opposition to the proposal appeared suddenly from the departments of Justice, Treasury, Labor, and Commerce, and from the Office of Management and Budget, the Council of Economic Advisers, and the SEC. The proposal, they said, would cripple the free-market system.

The Fed hung in there and in January 1986 voted to adopt the proposal, again three to two. The new regulation was largely intended to be symbolic at best because of the ease with which it could be circumvented (by substituting preferred stock for borrowings, for example), but the strong across-the-board opposition of the rest of the executive branch certainly weakened the symbol.[4]

There were other struggles too in the early 1980s that derived from the takeover boom. Several state legislatures passed laws that made it very difficult to acquire a state-chartered company on an unfriendly basis. The Supreme Court later ruled that many of the actions so taken were unconstitutional, but states still seemed to be willing to enact local laws to protect favored companies from attack. At the heart of this debate, of course, lay the question of whether the commercial system of the United States was to be operated on a federal basis or on a state-by-state basis. The states argued that the federal government wasn't *doing* anything, so they had to. Finally Indiana passed a takeover statute that almost everyone thought was fair and level and did not attempt to infringe on federal prerogatives, and this statute was adopted by several other states.

By the end of 1986 regulatory inactivity at the federal level had been accepted as being the way things were going to be. By then, of course, the poison pill had become popular, and the battlefield, as Marty Lipton said, was moving into the courthouse.

Then came the crash.

Nineteen twenty-nine was revisited again and again. This time too it had been excessive speculation that had driven the market to break, and when it did there was nothing under it. The crash was a warning: the financial markets had to be reined in or the economy would collapse. The principal culprit many observers claimed was "program trading," another product of Wall Street that seemed to serve no useful purpose but to enrich the players there who couldn't see how their actions were eroding the integrity of the market as a whole. President Reagan appointed Nicholas Brady (now secretary of the Treasury) to head a presidential commission to look into the causes of the crash and to recommend corrective actions. The New York Stock Exchange, the Chicago Mercantile Exchange, the SEC, and the Government Accounting Office also conducted studies of their own, but the Brady commission outranked the others. Brady recruited Professor Robert Glauber of the Harvard Business School (now under secretary of the Treasury) as the commission's chief of staff. The commission focused mainly on technical matters, such as the fact that shares were traded on one exchange, and futures and options in those shares, and in Dow Jones and other indices, were traded on other exchanges that were subject to substantially different regulation and margin requirements.

Program trading involves computer-ordered trading when certain gaps open up between the values of individual stocks and their "synthetic" value, which can be created through purchases or sales of options and futures in the stock. Closing such gaps (between the cash and the futures markets) is a normal function of efficient markets. Similar actions affect all money markets and foreign-exchange and commodities markets. In today's stock-market environment, in which market data of all types can be communicated instantly to thousands of players, the devising of computer programs to buy or sell positions to close gaps in stock prices is a natural enough function of financial traders.

The traders also devised a means of hedging a portfolio by selling stock index futures. This is the same as "shorting" the whole market via one of its market indices, but with futures not with cash. If the market went up you lost on your futures, but you made money on your main portfolio. If the market went down, the profits from the futures position would be a cushion against the market decline for the rest of the portfolio, thus creating a kind of "portfolio insurance."

Large-scale hedging, however, could depress the index, possibly below the value of the underlying stocks. Arbitrageurs (or their computer autopilots) would see the gap and sell the stocks, buying the index. Technical considerations, not fundamental values, were driving the market and amplifying the volatility of individual stocks as these were jerked around to stay in alignment with the indices. Thus Brady concluded that technical factors had gone berserk during October and been principally responsible for the 508-point loss on October 19, though he also pointed to rumors of Congress's deciding to withdraw the tax deductibility of interest on takeover debt, conflict with the Germans over interest rates, and other factors, presumably including the fact that interest rates had risen more than 100 basis points since May, the dollar had collapsed, and the twin deficits were still building with no relief in sight—all without a correction in the soaring stock prices.

The remedy, the Brady commission said, was to adopt a three-point program: use a system of "circuit breakers" that would stop trading in stocks when the market appeared to be running away with itself, presumably because of technical factors; integrate the regulatory supervision of cash and futures markets under one powerful head, such as the chairman of the Federal Reserve, who would be responsible for all equity markets and futures exchanges; and stick with the "specialist" system used to support the auction market of the New York Stock Exchange.

None of these proposals was adopted or even seriously considered. There was substantial objection to the idea of closing the markets to make them work better. Markets worked when they were open, not closed. A continuous market had the best chance of rectifying imbalances, and program trading (though perhaps needing to be restrained until the exchanges' clearing systems could handle the volume in trading that was produced) was a system for arbitraging out market imperfections, one that made the market *more* efficient. Circuit breakers, their critics claimed, were an arbitrary means of imposing restrictions on the market that would only lead to illiquidity and other undesired imperfections.

There also seemed to be no appetite anywhere for creating a czar of equities and futures markets, and Alan Greenspan had had enough experience in Washington resolutely to disclaim any interest in the job.

The stock-exchange specialists, something of an anachronism in these days, continued along as before. The short-term money markets; the government, corporate, and municipal bond markets; the foreign-exchange markets; the commodities markets; the over-the-counter stock markets (now accounting for about 40 percent of all U.S. stock trading); the new U.K. stock market that was designed from scratch in 1984; and just about all other markets function effectively without specialists. The trading capital behind the market in equities, as in all other securities, is with the large-scale market-makers, not the specialists. Still, the specialists weren't to blame for the crash, so why not support them?

By the early part of 1988 it was apparent that the stock markets were coming back to life, that mergers were more active than ever, and that the recession in the economy predicted by many (as a result of the loss of a trillion dollars of wealth from the crash) was not going to happen. Soon after the Brady report was presented it was forgotten. Soon after that the RJR-Nabisco deal surfaced and attention shifted again to mergers, takeovers, LBOs, and junk.

According to David Aylward, before the RJR deal he felt no fear of new regulation being imposed on takeovers or their financing. Congress was thinking about other things, but afterward, Washington "exploded with fear" of abuses from the actions of securities dealers. It is true, he added, that Congress had wanted to divert attention from its aborted pay rise; Jim Wright's various conflicts of interest; the deteriorating condition of the S & L's, in which many congressmen were involved; the Tony Coelho affair; and no doubt other things.

The emphasis instead was given to taking another hard look at the scoundrels in New York, Beverly Hills, and elsewhere. Perhaps RJR was a convenient offender, or maybe enough time had gone by without anything happening that a new effort at reform was appropriate. Several areas were ripe for action.

One was the restraint of hostile takeovers through reform of the tender-offer process. In August 1989, after several months of hearings and consideration, Congressman Edward Markey, chairman of the House Subcommittee on Telecommunications and Finance (and successor to Tim Worth, now moved to the Senate), unveiled an outline of a bill that would require "firm" financing to be in place before a public offer for a company (which would put it in play) could be announced. The bill would also close the ten-day window, extend the minimum tender-offer period, prohibit greenmail and two-tiered tender offers, and require a "community impact" statement (a congressional favorite) to assess the damage a takeover might cause affected communities, among other requirements for fuller disclosures of various types by the principals.

Proposals for rescinding the tax deductibility of interest on acquisition debt were revived. Several attempts have been made to do this without success. The issue is more complex than it seems: What is a "good" acquisition or a "bad" one? How do you know what the money being borrowed is really being used for? What is an acquisition? All of these questions lead to the creation of loopholes that ultimately defeat the purpose of the legislation. There appears, however, to be an overriding impression that the tax code is subsidizing the very kind of acquisition activity Congress is trying to curtail. Two proposals were hot in the autumn of 1989: a disallowance of interest deductions on pay-in-kind securities or those issued with substantial original issue discounts, such as zero-coupon junk bonds. Such securities, argued Dan Rostenkowski, chairman of the House Ways and Means Committee, are essentially equities and should be taxed as equities. The other proposal, one introduced by Senator Lloyd Bentsen, chairman of the Senate Finance Committee, sought to eliminate certain net operating loss tax "carrybacks" that result from losses incurred as a result of large amounts of takeover interest expense. The provision would prevent refunds of taxes paid in prior years because of losses incurred as a result of an acquisition, though accumulation of tax credits for future years would not be affected by the bill. The Bentsen proposal was incorporated in the capital-gains tax-reduction bill approved by the House Ways and Means Committee on September 14, 1989, though (oddly) the Rostenkowski proposal was not.

In any case, the capital-gains tax-reduction bill failed in Congress, but both the Rostenkowski and Bentsen proposals were adopted in the year-end revenue bill passed by the Congress in late November.

There were also efforts to legislate restrictions on investments that could be made by regulated financial institutions. Such restrictions would limit investment in junk bonds by S & Ls, pension funds, and insurance companies. In the former case, after a three-year consideration of the subject, Congress passed its S & L bailout bill with a provision requiring all insured S & Ls to divest themselves of all of their holdings in junk securities over the next five years. Pension funds are not yet restricted as to how many junk bonds they may own. Insurance companies are regulated by state insurance commissions, the most potent of which is the New York State Commission, which ruled in 1987 to restrict junk bonds to 20 percent of permitted assets.

And, finally, there were proposals to repeal the Glass-Steagall provisions of the Banking Act of 1933, the provisions that require the separation of commercial and investment banking and that were nearly done away with in 1988. Commercial banks have long sought the opportunity to compete in securities markets, and securities firms have long sought to exclude them. The provisions separating the two have been eroded little by little over the years, and many think the time is near when the separation will be ended, driving many banks into many of the different businesses of the investment banks, including the underwriting of junk bonds, which would be used to fund out "temporary" debt extended by the banks themselves. In November 1989 the Securities Industry Association announced at its annual conference that it was dropping its resistance to Glass-Steagall revision, providing that satisfactory "firewalls" be required for banks to ensure that the securities affiliates of banks not receive any of the direct, or indirect, benefits of federal deposit insurance.

Who Should Regulate?

Financial regulation in the United States is a messy business. Banks, for example, are either state-chartered or nationally chartered and are either members of the Federal Reserve system or not members. States regulate state-chartered banks; the Federal Reserve, through twelve regional banks, regulates member banks; and the Comptroller of the Currency regulates the rest. The Federal Deposit Insurance Corporation, which reports to the Treasury Department, insures the deposits of commercial banks and has now taken over from the

Federal Savings and Loan Insurance Corporation in insuring deposits of S & Ls. Securities firms, on the other hand, are regulated by the SEC, the National Association of Securities Dealers, and the rules of the various stock exchanges. Their securities customers are insured against loss by the Securities Investors Protection Corporation. They are also regulated by the Commodities Futures Trading Commission, with respect to business in commodities, currencies, and futures and options.

Banks are subject to new, stringent capital adequacy regulations, agreed on by the central banks of the twelve leading industrial countries in 1988. Securities firms that are involved in many of the same businesses as banks (trading government and municipal securities and foreign exchange, handling short-term funds for customers, and underwriting swaps and other intermarket contracts) are not subject to capital restrictions other than modest and somewhat outdated ones imposed by the New York Stock Exchange. The Federal Reserve regulates margin requirements for the stock market but otherwise does not wish to be involved in securities firm matters. However, the short-term commercial paper market of over $500 billion and money-market funds of various types nearly equaling this sum, which represent a large proportion of total liquid financial assets in circulation, exist outside the direct regulatory powers of the Federal Reserve.

Things are not much tidier in Congress, where each house has several committees that are involved with financial regulatory matters. Each house has a Banking Committee and each a Finance Committee (in the House it is Ways and Means, which specializes in tax legislation). Each also has various strays, such as Congressman Markey's committee, which is a subcommittee of the powerful House Energy and Commerce Committee chaired by Congressman John Dingell, himself a frequent spokesman on securities regulatory matters.

Tax issues, in particular, are extremely political and unpredictable, as evidenced by the fact that the recent proposal to reduce capital-gains taxes, which was opposed by the committee's chairman, got through somehow but included a provision restricting tax loss carrybacks resulting from leveraged acquisitions that was supported by the chairman of the Senate Finance Committee, while not including Rostenkowski's own proposal on limiting deductibility of deep discount junk bonds. In these matters you never know what you're going to get.

The executive branch is almost as bad at dispersing responsibility for financial matters as the legislative branch. The Office of Management and Budget, always a powerful place, may wield influence in almost any area it wishes, especially if the economic ideology of the day is not being followed. The Treasury Department periodically offers ideas and proposals on tax and regulatory matters, though these often seem to go nowhere. The Council of Economic Advisers frequently has something to say about free markets, which might quickly be contradicted by the Commerce Department or the Special Trade Representative. The Labor Department supervises pension funds without attempting to interfere with junk bond investments, which the Treasury department dislikes. It is almost impossible to develop a coordinated set of policies aimed at comprehensive regulation of the financial services area, except perhaps after a disaster like the Great Depression. We have to live with things the way they are, that is, in an environment that lacks an effective and cohesive national banking and financial policy.

Unless, of course, you believe that we already have such a policy, a policy of keeping regulation at a minimum by keeping the regulators and would-be regulators confused about who has which power to do what. Vesting one or another of these bodies with enough power really to do the job might backfire in an orgy of overregulation or worse. Instead, real problems are handled on an ad hoc basis as they arise by the agencies best able to react, such as the Federal Reserve, the Treasury, and the SEC. Noncrisis problems tend to be handled by the courts, which, in the absence of a complete set of federal regulations regarding takeovers, write the rules as they go along and thus develop case law. Given that there is no single regulatory body with power to adjudicate takeover disputes, as there is in Britain, issues in conflict have no place to go but to the courts.

This has been our system for a long time, and in many ways it works well, despite the fact that it is very frustrating and upsetting to the tidy-minded among us.

In many respects the principal regulatory institution with respect to takeovers today is the Delaware Chancery Court. The rulings of the Delaware courts have actually cured a number of the abuses that proposed takeover regulations were aimed at preventing. By allowing the poison pill to become a relatively fixed element of every company's defenses, the period of time over which the change of control can occur has been greatly extended. Shareholders are arguably better protected by the pill and by the enhanced business-judgment doctrine, which also prevents abuses by management, than they would be by some particular regulation that no doubt could be gotten around once the players became used to it. Certainly shareholders cannot be stampeded into accepting a hurry-up offer at a low price (which would constitute a major "threat" to the company) any longer, nor can management decide unilaterally to foist a deal of its own on the stockholders without a vote. Greenmail has virtually disappeared since the poison pill, and the courts have even restricted the terms of golden parachutes. Little by little perhaps, but ultimately, many of the reforms long thought necessary, and some valuable ones that had not been, have been put in place by the judiciary. And these reforms are harder to get around because questions of judgment are involved, not just adherence to a particular set of rules.

Lawyers receive their share of abuse in this the world's most litigious country, but the role they play is similar to that of the arbitrageur closing the gap on a market misalignment. Suit is followed by suit until reason prevails and misalignments are removed. This no doubt overstated tribute to the legal end of the takeover business is easier to make because of the superior degree of competence generally found in Delaware (where the Court of Chancery actually specializes in takeover law) but not always found in other states, as Texaco discovered in Texas.

What Should Be Regulated?

Congressman Markey's proposed bill has three basic parts. It wants to increase the amount of disclosure that bidders have to make and to slow the acquisition process by extending the minimum tender-offer period and by requiring lengthy reports justifying the intentions of the bidders and assessing community impact. These provisions are unnecessary: the SEC already has the power to require further disclosure (and to close the still open ten-day window) if it wishes to use it, and the poison pill has already slowed the process considerably. The extra reports do not seem to bear on the issues except to the extent that they delay transactions—which we no longer need them to do.

The third part of his bill is perhaps the most important. It requires that bidders have firm financing in place before they announce their deal. Bidders can easily comply with this rule, as Boone Pickens and others did in their early appearances on the scene. However, paying a commitment fee for what could be several months is quite expensive, and if a large self-financing corporate bidder should emerge from the process it might have an advantage in arriving at the highest price. Does Congressman Markey really want to provide such an edge for the corporate buyer—as a matter of regulation—when the shareholders, the community, everybody might prefer the first bidder, a management-led, fair-price ESOP buyout, for example? Would the real result, an unintended one, be that LBO and management-led groups elect instead not to compete for the acquisition but instead to wait for the postacquisition restructuring of companies? The effect is only to remove the LBO player as a direct competitor in the bidding.

"But," Congressman Markey might say, "it may still be better to restrict the competition than to have to bail out a whole financial system that has collapsed because of excessive amounts of very risky debt to takeover operators, the lesser of two evils."

Worrying About the Banks

What Congressman Markey means is that banks may get stuck with too much acquisition debt, as they did with Latin American credits, and have to be bailed out like the S & Ls. The banks have a kind of herd instinct. Once one or two of them start running off in one direction, the others follow. Partly this is because they share similar goals and objectives and business often comes on them in waves. The Latin American loan situation developed when the countries had a huge desire to borrow at a time when the banks needed to put large loans on their books. This was similarly the case with oil-patch loans, real estate investment trusts, REITs, and other sectors in which the banks had been surprised by large, sudden loan losses. The S & Ls were quite different, really, as the basic economics of mortgage lending had been changed by deregulation and rising interest rates.

Still, the surprise aspect is what had people concerned about the banks' growing involvement in LBO financing. The banks always seemed to be getting surprised by the collapse of one sector or another to which they had committed large amounts of loans. Often these large commitments were justified on the grounds that they produced superior returns that would enable the banks to fund their loan-loss reserves quickly to protect themselves against any problems. In any case, the banks said, they were on top of all these credits and were confident that their judgments would prove to be right. One after another, of course, they proved to be wrong. No wonder people were skeptical when LBOs became the rage.

The principal worry was the standard one about what happens to LBOs in a major recession or in an inflationary period when interest rates go up to 20 percent again. LBO companies, being so dependent on favorable conditions to manage the pay-down of their debt, could be devastated by either scenario, both of which had occurred within the last ten years. Even though many LBOs had some protection in the form of "interest rate caps," in which options that put a ceiling on interest rates had been purchased, either a recession or an inflationary economy would constitute a systemic risk to the banks, in which all the LBOs would be headed down the tubes at the same time.

Further, there were a number of technical worries. The large, sophisticated banks were enjoying the boom enormously. They could originate new loans, earn the gigantic arrangement fees being paid, and then sell down their loans to country and foreign banks as they had done so often with Third World debt. They would hope to retain only a small part of the loans they were responsible for, even a small part of their initial retentions. Their lawyers would handle the documentation and their experts the credit analysis. The country banks had no capability to perform these functions for themselves so they had to rely entirely on the originating banks. A lot of the risk, in other words, was being passed down into the system by the handful of banks in New York who originated the loans. These banks, of course, competed with each other for the origination mandates, and in doing so they sliced rates or eased up on some of the terms, as they did in the UAL case. Also the LBO originators were pushing up acquisition prices, relying more heavily on junk to complete their deals, and the originating banks were going along with them. What if the originators got carried away and started pumping defective paper through the system? No one would know until much later, as was the case with the REITs and with the famous Continental Illinois oil loan syndications.

Meanwhile, the amount of the new lending done by banks for LBOs was mounting quickly, and these sums began to be reported in terms of the percentage of banks' stockholder's equity that they represented. By the end of 1988, Bankers Trust and Wells Fargo reported LBO loans in excess of their book value. A Federal Reserve study in mid-1988 showed LBO loans to account for about 10 percent of all commercial loans of large banks (that is, those with assets above $7.5 billion), up from virtually nothing a few years before.

The regulators began to make public statements expressing their concerns about LBO lending and urging banks to be cautious. Alan Greenspan put banks on notice that he was watching things. In December 1988 the Comptroller of the Currency issued an examination circular to all national banks requiring them to tighten their supervision and controls over LBO loans. In February 1989 the Fed published detailed and lengthy new bank examination guidelines for LBO debt that required, among other things, that banks establish specific credit review and approval procedures for LBO loans, set consolidated lending limits, and set limits and standards for purchasing loan participations from other banks.

Also, one of the Wall Street firms that specialized in bank securities, Keefe Bruyette & Woods, published an "open letter" in the autumn of 1988 asking the banks to increase their disclosure of information related to LBO debt so the market could analyze its effect on the banks. Somewhat to everyone's surprise, Bankers Trust responded by inviting analysts to a special, very informative presentation on its LBO debt originations, syndications, and retentions.

Anxiety regarding the banks' involvement in LBO loans reached a peak when the $17.5 billion RJR facility was organized in early 1989. Most banks believed that the senior debt exposure in that deal was modest, even comfortable: coverage ratios were pretty good; the assets to be sold were first-rate; the junk bond takeout was dicey perhaps, but it wouldn't affect the banks directly. The junk would take out short-term junk notes, not part of the takeover credit facility as was the usual case. There were problems, however. First there was terrible publicity on the RJR deal, and many banks dreaded the reaction of their own board of directors when they announced their participation. Some thought the Fed would clamp down on the banks as a result of this deal and maybe they were killing the golden goose. Mainly, though, the concern was about sell-downs. The banks would have to agree to a substantial delay in being able to sell down part of their own participation to other, correspondent banks. There would be very limited liquidity in this loan for the first year or so.

Because of these concerns, there was some nervousness that the RJR banking commitment, $17.5 billion, might not make it. If all banks limited their average LBO loan commitment to 5 percent of their lending limits (the top eleven U.S. banks originating LBO loans averaged 6 percent of their lending limit per credit in 1988), then banks with aggregate lending limits of $360 billion would have to be found (the top eleven banks had combined lending limits of approximately $5 billion).[5] In the end the deal was saved by extensive participation by foreign banks who took 65 percent of the credit.

After the RJR deal, however, things calmed down somewhat. The Bankers Trust disclosure had been emulated by other banks. The analysts were reassured. The regulatory tightening and the slowdown in new LBO credit origination following RJR helped. In late November 1988 Salomon Brothers came out with a research report in which it announced, "The size and scope of potential problems are manageable," and "Nonperforming LBO assets are minimal and actual loan losses are virtually nonexistent." A later Goldman Sachs report pointed out that banks have been making loans, including takeover loans, to highly leveraged companies for a very long time and their experience with diversified portfolios of this sort was considerable. The report further stressed, "LBO credit risk is extraordinarily low," because of the small amount of the lending given over to LBO loans and the reassuring effect of their experience with the Revco bankruptcy in which no charge-offs were expected. The report continued to stress that the LBO portfolios were not concentrated in any industry sector and that the banks were not unduly relying on them to build up their profits and retained earnings as only 8 percent of net income in 1988 was attributed to LBOs. These loans, however, produced average returns on assets of about 300 basis points, as compared to overall bank loans, which averaged about 100 basis points.[6]

In any event these banks are regulated by the Federal Reserve, whose chairman has expressed concerns on several occasions similar to those of Congressman Markey. The Fed possesses the power to restrict banks' activity in LBO loans further if it feels the need, from a bank safety point of view, to do so. So far it hasn't, but in late October 1989, it moved a bit further in that direction with its adoption (along with all other federal bank regulatory agencies) for supervisory purposes of a new definition of "Highly Leveraged Transactions" (HLTs).

The rest of the traditional financial system does not appear to be excessively exposed to LBOs or to junk debt. The S & Ls, despite the convincing studies done for Mr. Aylward by Wharton Econometrics and DRI, have already been required to divest themselves of all junk bond holdings, which were not more than about $16 billion for the entire industry. Pension funds are protected from imprudent investments by their trustees both by the Labor Department and by the Employee Retirement Income Security Act (ERISA), which make trustees liable for decisions that might seem "imprudent." Pension fund holdings of junk bonds are only a modest amount of total pension fund assets, generally well less than 10 percent. Life insurance companies will have to limit junk-bond investments to a maximum of 20 percent of assets if they want to sell insurance in New York State, as virtually all do. Some other insurance companies, particularly casualty insurers, are not restricted but are still subject to regulation by state insurance commissioners. Mutual funds are not restricted at all but have to react to market conditions to attract and retain investors. One large mutual fund, for example, ran ads when the junk market slumped in September 1989 pointing out that the fund did not own any junk bonds at all. Anyway Congressman Markey doesn't have to worry about bailing out high-yield mutual funds.

"Well, anyway," Congressman Rostenkowski and Senator Bentsen might add, "even if we don't do what Markey proposes, we've still got the problem of these LBOs and other leveraged deals depending on a handout from Uncle Sam in order to get their prices up to levels that might be competitive with qualified bidders. They can play in the game if they want to, but we do not see any good reason for the U.S. taxpayer to put up their table stakes."

The "handout" is in the form of tax loss carrybacks and the ability to deduct from future income interest payments made on subordinated debt. They have a point. The tax code is filled with unintended subsidies, and the job of the IRS is to detect and correct them when they can. However, these matters are always complex and often cut more ways than one. For example, in the Rostenkowski proposal regarding "original issue discount" (that is, the zero-coupon and related bonds) securities, even though at present the bidder gets the tax deduction from the deferred income securities, the investor has to pay taxes on the income implicitly received (unless, of course the investor is not a taxpayer, that is, a pension fund). In the end the Treasury will probably make money on the combined taxes paid by everyone involved in LBOs, as demonstrated earlier for RJR-Nabisco. In any case, adopting the tax provisions proposed by Rostenkowski and Bentsen does not seem to be enough to prevent bidders from bidding. They will just come up with something else.

The deductibility of interest is by far the most important reason that LBOs are possible. As Modigliani and Miller advised us, the tax factor is what makes debt cheap and thus makes it sensible to borrow as much as you can. Congress decided long ago that it was a good idea to have companies and individuals borrow money to make new investments, and therefore the deductibility of interest payments has been as sacred a cow as there is in the United States. But Congress did not intend securities that resembled equities to be classified as debt so as to capture the tax benefits inappropriately. Congress, however, did not expect matters to become so complicated, forcing it to have to deal with such questions as What is debt? How does it differ from tax deductible equity? to which an answer that will appeal to a majority of members voting may be difficult to find. If it wanted to, it could shut down junk bonds altogether by classifying them as equity-type securities not entitled to deductions. It has not done so partly because it is not so sure that junk bonds, and the restructuring they finance, are all that bad for the economy. Indeed they may do some good.

Congress, of course, is the biggest gorilla of all. It can do absolutely whatever it wants. Mostly, at least with respect to financial matters, it doesn't do anything at all—which is probably the right outcome in most cases—though it growls and threatens and beats its chest from time to time to remind everyone of its crude but awesome power. For the most part Congress has been happy letting those supervising the regulatory agencies do their jobs in determining the details of what protected institutions shall be permitted to do or not do. Occasionally, something like the S & L crisis comes along, which demonstrates just how foolish it is to leave the regulators completely alone to do their jobs, but even when Congress's various antennae are tuned to maximum watchfulness, its members are aware that they can make matters worse with the wrong legislation. Senator Bentsen acknowledged in March 1989, before his modest technical proposal on carrybacks, that his committee had "not found what I believe to be an effective way to address LBOs and junk bond financed acquisitions, and the odds are that unless we find something we will not move on it in our committee. I don't want to devise a cure," he added, "that is worse than the condition."[7]

The Bush administration has not added much to the debate so far. During the RJR deal the president-elect commented about the upsetting effect these transactions produced and mentioned that tax laws might be changed to return matters to normal. Since then, the administration has gone quiet on the subject. Without the sort of focus and leadership than only the administration can provide, most congressional initiatives have long odds against approval.

Secretary Brady, a quintessential old-school investment banker, is known to be a strong opponent of hostile takeovers and junk financing, which he believes force management to focus on very short-term results. This prevents them from making the right decisions to maximize the long-term values of their corporations, which is the only way, Brady believes, that they are going to be competitive with the Japanese and others. Lifting the time horizons of American management, he says, is one of his main jobs in his present office. Still, since in office he has given out very mixed signals on regulation of takeovers and junk financing, perhaps deliberately, to keep the issues unfocused. His preferred solution to the problem of returning order and discipline to the financial markets is to change the tax code to discontinue taxing dividend income received by investors in common stocks. By abolishing the "double taxation" of corporate profits, the relative advantages of debt over equity would be reduced and LBOs would lose some of their steam. He admits, however, that there is no money in any current or foreseeable fiscal budget to accomplish this reform. So instead he urges support for the initiative to reduce capital-gains taxes. The Treasury has been silent otherwise on takeover regulation.

Accordingly, meaningful changes in federal takeover and financing regulations, ones that would alter materially the flow of transactions, did not appear likely in mid-1990.

This was not the case on the state level, however. Earlier in the year, a Pennsylvania company, Armstrong World Industries, had come under the guns of the Belzbergs, a well-known group of Canadian raiders. Armstrong raised a fuss, of course, and attracted support from state legislators, who had been motivated to prevent an opposed takeover of a great Pennsylvanian institution by an ugly band of corporate terrorists. Subsequently, the state passed an anti-takeover statute that provided for the recapture of arbitrage profits and other restrictive features, but most important, contained a fiduciary duties provision that permits directors to consider other constituencies' interests above those of shareholders. The Belzbergs withdrew and Armstrong was saved, but not from controversy: much criticism of the legislation as favoring entrenched management ensued, including a comment by the manager of Pennsylvania's state employee pension funds that the legislation was causing him to rethink the desirability of investing in any Pennsylvania company.

The Pennsylvania legislation was also an inspiration for a similar law passed in Massachusetts when the Norton Co. was tendered for by British conglomerate BTR plc. In the Massachusetts case, the law was rushed through just in time for Norton to accept a higher, "friendly" offer from Rhone Poulenc, a large French industrial corporation. In April 1990, Ohio also passed a law similar to Pennsylvania's, its principal sponsor noting that if the law had been in place it would have prevented the "Campeau fiasco," meaning the acquisition of Federated Department Stores, an Ohio corporation, by Robert Campeau.

But in a broader context, what makes the most sense? How much regulation should there be, and of what by whom?

Certainly the banking system has to continue to be safeguarded by regulation as long as the taxpayer is going to guarantee the banks' deposits. The Federal Reserve has the greatest influence in this sector, and it has already taken steps to ensure that HLTs are subject to intensified attention from the management of banks and from their examiners. Banks are also looked after by the FDIC and, quite important, inspected and pawed over regularly by the analyst community on Wall Street. If Congress is unhappy about some aspect of bank involvement in HLTs, then it can call in the regulators and make their feelings known directly. If they do this often enough, the regulators will turn up the heat on the banks. The main point, however, is that the regulators have the power to reduce bank participations in LBO lending and are watching HLT exposures carefully. So far they have not felt it appropriate to do more than tighten procedures and issue generalized warnings. Some increased concern had developed about banks' HLT exposure by mid 1990, because of the collapse of Campeau and other large transactions, but still learned opinion was not overly concerned about the banks.

Other insured or protected institutions, such as S & Ls, insurance companies, and pension funds, have already begun to reflect the concerns of the times by restricting ownership of junk bonds to a modest percentage of total assets. Only a few of these institutions have yet suffered from excessive exposure to low-grade bonds. Plunging market values in 1990 caused a great deal of distress, of course, but the number of defaults experienced was small and has not caused major loan losses. This is partly because of the inherent economics of junk securities and partly because all the institutions involved own a portfolio of at least fifteen or twenty bonds; such diversification protects the owners from any single disaster. The concern for these institutions is not whether they buy junk securities at all but whether at some time in the future they should be found to have excessively concentrated their assets in them. This seems unlikely in the present environment.

Regulation to protect equity investors has never really been contemplated. These investors are the "speculators" who are supposed to protect themselves. Adverse market developments in the high-yield bond markets have no doubt discouraged some individual investors from purchasing mutual funds that specialize in junk securities. The same may be true also for investors in LBO funds, where it appears that high annual rates of return may be a thing of the past. With lowering returns there can only follow a lowering of the enthusiasm for these funds among investors, and in time some reduction in the supply of funds made available to operators over the past few years.

When mezzanine finance goes off the boil, it becomes more difficult for LBO arrangers to compete with the larger industrial companies in the target's same industry. These companies expect to finance acquisitions without resorting to junk securities, so that their highest offer in an auction may not be as high as that of an LBO group with access to large amounts of highly priced mezzanine financing. In the RJR deal, for example, one bidding group that dropped out early was a consortium of industrial companies led by Procter & Gamble that could not see a price higher than the low $90s. Both the management LBO and the KKR group ended up at about $109, largely because of the expected market valuations of the various mezzanine securities they were intending to sell. If these begin to meet resistance in the market, the value of mezzanine packages like KKR's for RJR will decline, perhaps below the level at which the highest-priced bidder is likely to be an industrial. During 1990 the few large deals that occurred, tender offers for Great Northern Nekoosa, American General and Norton Co., were made by established corporations; entrepreneurial bids did not appear at all except in some unsuccessful proxy fights waged for Lockheed, USX and a few others. In other words, the market regulates, too, perhaps more powerfully than anything else.

The SEC certainly has a role in regulating takeovers. Its principal job is to ensure that the markets function in ways that are fair for all investors. Its principal means of ensuring this has been through regulations concerning disclosure of information that tends to affect prices of securities. These regulations deal with both the content and the timing of disclosure. They have been quite effective over the years. The U.S. market has the best and most timely disclosure of important information of any market and accordingly has been able to create the most efficient and widely used capital market the world has ever seen. The SEC has all the power it needs to close windows that have been too long open or to require more time for all investors to get the word in takeover situations before they have to act. The SEC is not empowered to act as an adjudication body, so it leaves the resolution of many matters concerning the fairness of takeover practices to the courts. The courts have certainly lived up to the tasks they have inherited during the past decade of turbulent activity, including the tasks associated with the prosecution and sentencing of those accused of securities law violations. Here, too, case law has contributed to a better understanding of what it is that is to be considered a violation of the law. Strict enforcement and the visible effects of the punishments and disgrace inflicted on the offenders have also left an indelible message with the market.

It could be that through the interaction of regulators, courts, and investors, over a period of several years, we have actually regulated the market in takeovers and speculative securities much more efficiently than one might have thought. Demand for the securities that are created by restructuring situations has been affected by restraints on certain important investors and banks and by caution induced by high price levels in the market.

Without aggressive regulation by the SEC, the principal points of conflict in owner-manager disputes have been shifted to the courts, which are better able to deal with judgmental factors. The standards of fairness have been raised, for both investors and defenders, to a level that greatly exceeds that which existed at the beginning of the decade.

Tax laws favoring leverage in corporate capital structures haven't been altered through this period in response to public anxieties, which might have snuffed out the most powerful force permitting the beneficial and needed restructuring of American industry.

Finally there is the matter of permissive antitrust policies, which symbolized the Reagan administration's approach to economic regulation more than anything else. Through almost all of this century, antitrust regulation has restrained corporate mergers and takeovers. At times, such as during the latter part of the 1960s, the restraints have been considerable. During the Reagan years, however, the Justice Department and the Federal Trade Commission were staffed with those who were appointed in order to administer with a light hand. Many combinations that might have been prevented in other times were permitted, and few companies were free to sit back and relax while motoring through the eighties, because of the threat to their independence that the loose enforcement implied. Many shake-ups and self-restructurings resulted. Now, however, it appears that the pendulum may be set to reverse its direction. The new Bush-appointed commissioner of the FTC, Janet Steiger, has ordered a change in FTC merger policy, which, she says, will increase its vigilance in reviewing mergers and will view more skeptically claims that business combinations increase corporate efficiency.

It is a marvel that in our ostensibly chaotic system of multiple regulation, litigation, and congressional interference there has emerged, after a decade that many will remember later as one of radical change in the American financial landscape, what in the end looks like an eminently sensible and workable base for regulating complex takeover and related financial transactions. Maybe, after all, there is an "invisible hand" that guides our humble institutions safely through such times as these.

10

THIS, TOO, SHALL PASS, OR WILL IT?

Boy Scouts are taught that to make a campfire you must have fuel, such as dry wood; oxygen, which is contained in the air around them; and flame from a match or burning tinder. They are also taught the basic technology of fire building, that is, the science of arranging the kindling and logs and striking the match. Most learn quickly how to do this and are able to get small fires started. Their objective is always, it seems, to build up the fire into a great crackling blaze worthy of their efforts. To do this they must continue urgently to add fuel to the fire. However, the fuel that must be gathered from an ever-diminishing supply of locally available dry wood is also being sought by other fire builders and it soon becomes scarce. In time the quest for fuel becomes a drag—the good stuff is too far away—and they ask each other, "Why not burn greenwood or these slightly wet logs instead?" The fire banks, burning more leisurely. The fire tender becomes bored and goes off to do other things. Keeping a fire going at full blaze is a lot of work: experienced scouts know it is not really worth all the trouble. Anyway, new boys always seem to be available to get the next blaze going.

There are fire-building analogies in the great deal-making era of the 1980s, one of the most fabulous blazes of our century. To get it going, fuel, flame, and oxygen were also needed.

The fuel, in the form of undervalued companies and assets, was available in abundance. Many of the companies that would be targets in the merger boom of the eighties were in need of restructuring, particularly the conglomerates, which had no particular rationale for existing the way they did, and all had been dried out by the recession and low stock prices of the early 1980s.

The source of heat for the conflagration was in the market. As interest rates declined and the stock market more than doubled between 1982 and 1987, financial energy was released in the United States, and in all other wealthy countries, as never before. The flames became incandescent as investors, excited by all the action and opportunity, bid higher and higher prices for the same assets they had scorned only a few years before.

And the air was almost pure oxygen. The Reagan spirit carried the times and the atmosphere was solidly probusiness. There were few if any antitrust problems. Some industries, such as transportation, communications, and banking, were being deregulated; others, such as oil, metals, and chemicals, went through shakeouts. Opportunities were all over the place. Pension funds and other institutions were investing furiously. Raiders were no longer seen entirely as evil villains—indeed some had become the new heroes of the free market, devoting themselves like modern-day Robin Hoods to the good works of liberating shareholder values by deposing "entrenched" management who only wished to preserve their jobs and status. Investment banking became the most chic of all professions. Even arbitrageurs and money managers were admired. If greed wasn't altogether "good," then it was at least OK. The best and the brightest of America's youth came to Wall Street to become well-paid Yuppies. The capitalistic free-enterprise system had fully recovered the respect and support of the public for the first time in fifty years. You couldn't complain about the air.

There were also a number of improvements in the technology of financial fire building: no longer did you have to strike a soggy match in the dark in the wind and the rain to start your fire, then have to blow gently on the tiny sparks and patiently feed them kindling until the fire was ready for bigger stuff. You could now jump-start the whole process with new technology: front-end-loaded takeovers, leveraged buyouts, and bust-up deals, financed with junk bonds, bridge loans, and cram-down securities gave even the most inexperienced tenderfoot the means to set the woods on fire in no time at all.

And finally, there was the changing character of the fire builder. No longer was he the quiet, trustworthy figure from the backwoods who knew from experience that fires had to last to be really useful, and that patience and care in tending them was the way to assure that they would. New Men had arrived on the scene, changing everything. For them the blaze was the thing. They would start one going, feed it all the easily available fuel, and then lose interest, passing it on to someone else to look after.

In the light of their blazes, the New Men looked wonderful—bold, bright, and beautiful. They were admired and feted as conquerors of a new age.

By the end of the blazing eighties, however, the fires and some of their glory had begun to fade. Some went out altogether. In the cold light of dawn, the magical properties of the fire builders were seen to be only ordinary ones.

Still, some good came of it. The woods were cleaned out: the dry dead wood burned up. The blazes killed off some of the parasites that had been living off the older trees without contributing much, and the heat had stimulated chemical reactions in the soil. Better ways of husbanding the land were discussed and tried. On balance, the fires had probably done more good than harm. Certainly, those companies whose share prices consistently hung at levels well below their restructuring values were taken out. Certainly, companies came to know that they could not continue just to trudge along changelessly in the face of vastly different business and economic conditions. Certainly, the heat and the light enabled some industries to become totally restructured, presumably on a sounder basis, and certainly too the blazes forced many companies to think through what an optimal balance of management and ownership might be.

314 UNDERPINNINGS OF THE NEW ORDER

But equally certain, the blazes did some damage. Great and noble companies, the product of generations of toil and effort by hundreds of thousands of people, were broken into pieces and the pieces sold away. Managements became so distracted by the need to play in the game, either on offense or on defense, that they lost sight of their long-term strategies. Everything was financed with debt, debt, and more debt; dangerously so, many thought. And there was so much action and opportunity that many people lost sight of the difference between right and wrong or began believing their own press: "Brilliant rock-star banker does it again to the acclaim and reward of millions." Certainly the 1980s were a time of great distortion and abuse, just as they were a time of great invigoration and renewal. That's the way these things are. It's always like that.

Although the eighties are over, the elements that started the blazes—the fuel, the heat, and the air—are still with us. However, after a decade of heavy burning in the United States, the easily available fuel has been consumed, the air has started to contain impurities, and the heat to sputter. Undervalued companies are hard to find. The regulatory climate has turned again, this time looking for ways to get the fires under control. These are likely to continue but less fiercely than before—only as slow burners. The brightest, most voracious flames will have jumped to places where the elements are better. To Europe, perhaps, where the fuel is virginal and abundant and the air is full of 1992, perestroika, and free-market socialism. There, only the heat of the market has to be turned up. Perhaps this can be done with some of the new blow-torch technology imported from the United States.

Already two of our most renowned raiders, Sir James Goldsmith and Asher Edelman, have migrated to Europe in search of better opportunities. Goldsmith wasted little time before organizing a raid on giant BAT Industries (Britain's third-largest industrial corporation, a multi-industry company based on a global tobacco business) with a proposed $20 billion junk bond–financed, hostile LBO, the first of its kind in the United Kingdom. Goldsmith mercilessly bashed BAT's management for underperformance (despite a very respectable record by U.K. standards) and announced that in his hands

BAT would be subject to radical surgery: BAT's insurance, retailing, and paper businesses would be sold off, the debt retired with the proceeds, and the tobacco business run for cash. The exercise, analysts suggested, would generate gross values of about $24 billion, which after expenses, interest, and some capital losses on disposals might net Goldsmith and his partners a billion or so for their contribution to the enhancement of the shareholders' value.

At first, BAT treated the proposal derisively, but when it became apparent that Goldsmith had won the ear, if not yet the vote, of BAT's major institutional shareholders, BAT embarked instead on a well-crafted self-restructuring: the group would slim down to just tobacco and financial services, and the rest would be sold or spun off to shareholders; a large share-repurchase program would be undertaken and dividends increased. The reaction to the restructuring was blurred by the market drop on Friday October 13, 1989, which mainly signaled a halt in the availability of high-risk takeover financing. The BAT share price began to reflect both the benefits of the self-restructuring and the fact that Goldsmith probably would no longer be a danger to BAT because of the lesser availability of takeover financing to him. Goldsmith, however, has indicated that he will be around to harass the company for some time to come. Still the largest European restructuring ever had occurred because market forces had been brought to bear against management, which otherwise would never have voluntarily broken up the group. Such a success is bound to breed others.

The BAT deal follows along a trail of greatly increased merger-and-acquisition activity in Europe, activity that has been building steadily during the decade and that reflects long-overdue industrial restructuring, increased market liquidity, and the appearance on the scene of a number of competent and aggressive corporate raiders, the New Men of Europe.

Carlo Benedetti is a quintessential Euro–New Man. An energetic and colorful Italian industrialist (he is chairman of Olivetti), he also operates outside the company, on his own. For some years Benedetti has been seen in his own country as a leader among the growing population of successful wheeler-dealers who have taken control of established companies and made themselves considerable fortunes at the same time. Benedetti is now branching out over the rest of Europe. In 1988 he launched a surprise unfriendly takeover offer for Belgium's largest and most prestigious industrial-financial holding company, La Générale, which controlled (among many other companies) Belgium's largest bank, Société Générale de Banque. Belgium was not prepared for raiders. Laws were inadequate, no protective shields were thought necessary: a takeover of La Générale was unthinkable.

Benedetti had formed a complex alliance with some French partners, bought into the stock secretly (there were no laws requiring disclosure of newly acquired positions in Belgium at the time) until he had about 20 percent, then sprung his announcement on the market. The board of La Générale panicked, attempting several methods of escape, some of which were later declared illegal in court. The Benedetti bid attracted a sort of white knight, the French holding company Indo Suez, which ultimately succeeded in taking control of the company. In the end, old management had been turned out, and La Générale, whose stock price had doubled during the process, began a series of restructuring steps. Benedetti, a new vice chairman of Générale, claims that every time he goes to Belgium now he is greeted by crowds yelling, "Thank you, Carlo" for liberating shareholders' values everywhere from oppression by the social-industrial elite.

European merger-and-acquisition transactions nearly doubled in 1989 from the level of two years earlier. Many deals, including more than a few opposed transactions, took place in France, Italy, Spain, and of course the United Kingdom, long the most active merger market in Europe. Additional transactions also occurred in Switzerland, in Scandinavia, and in Germany, where mergers have traditionally been fairly rare. Some transactions were structured as "management buyouts," a more timid European version of the LBO, and many involved acquisitions of "stakeholdings," or minority interests, instead of outright acquisitions. The scene has become very active. Most observers in Europe believe that it will remain so for several years. Having a few more billion-dollar players like Goldsmith and Benedetti ought to add something to the flames starting to build in Europe.

Most of the major investment banks and law firms have now set up mergers-and-acquisitions specialists in Europe to pry their way into the intra-European takeover business, at which they have been remarkably successful so far. They, of course, are highly experienced in the takeover business, accustomed to its rigors and daring enough to call people they hardly know on the phone in the middle of the night. Though some U.S. and U.K. merchant banks have been successful in participating in intra-European deals, most Continental banks have yet to appear on the scene in advisory capacities.

Lessons from the Eighties

Abraham Lincoln once told a story of an Eastern monarch who asked his wise men to give him one inspirational sentence, or lofty motto, that would be "true and appropriate in all times and situations." The wise men struggled with this, Lincoln reported, until finally they succeeded. They came back to the king and gave him this sentence: "And this, too, shall pass away." The king was disappointed as the sentence was hardly inspirational, and not of much use in a motto. But he realized that the expression was nevertheless what he had asked for and applicable both in times when things are great and humility is required and in terrible times when courage is needed. Surely, the statement applies to these blazing events in the world of finance during the past decade.

But Lincoln disputed the statement. Let's hope, he said, that by experience and effort we can retain the good parts of each of the cycles we go through to build a better world. This seems to be what actually happens in our world of business and finance. The bad parts are paid for through bankruptcies and loss of control, new additions to loan-loss reserves, radical changes in management and manning levels, increased regulation by governments, and even convictions and jail terms. But the best parts, culled from the various laboratories of financial and organizational experimentation, remain intact. Much was learned during the eighties about default rates, the management of free cash flow, the advantages of unbundling companies, the benefits of increased leverage, the many different intrinsic properties of securities, the value of employee ownership as an incentive to boost performance, and many other by-products of the extraordinary financial activities of the times.

Starting with the fuel, that is, all of corporate America, we have learned a number of lessons during the past decade. First, we have recognized that a lot of corporations really did need to be restructured, either because fundamental changes in their business economics had not been addressed or because the company itself was a compilation of businesses that make no particular sense but was the result of the follies of previous managers. These companies had not been held to as high a standard as we thought. Whether this was because management of major companies had become too bureaucratic or too comfortable with their diminished accountability for their actions is hard to say. But many companies, particularly those in fully mature industries and conglomerates, clearly fell into this category in 1980. The public took a while to understand this condition, and to a large extent opponents of hostile raids are still able to attract large and sympathetic audiences. But, nevertheless, challengers emerged, obtained financing from reputable quarters, and gradually made their case.

In time, restructuring became the watchword of American industry. Most companies thought restructuring was necessary to avoid raiders—the most effective way to do so was to get the company's stock price up to a level equal to its breakup value—and sometimes companies had to do some of the restructuring themselves, through cutting costs, making disposals, increasing leverage, and buying back their own stock. Companies in distressed industries, such as steel, felt that diversification into other lines of business was necessary. Some companies simply need to be bigger, or better situated, in order to compete effectively in the emerging global markets for their products. Many such companies, however, themselves adopted the tactics of the raider to accomplish their own objectives, forcing restructuring on their targets. Philip Morris's acquisitions of Kraft and General Foods were initially hostile. The conservative, old-line Bank of New York undertook one of the decade's most vicious and drawn-out battles when it tendered for Irving Trust. Georgia Pacific's offer for Great Northern Nekoosa was also vigorously rejected at first. Most of the restructuring that has occurred has not been the result of hostile, leveraged acquisition attempts by financial entrepreneurs but of industrial corporations operating on themselves or each other.

Usually the restructuring occurred when one large company decided to take on a new line of business through acquisition, for one of several different reasons: excess cash flow, need for diversification, consolidation of market position, or positioning of the company for global consolidation. The board of USX was not trying to act as a financial entrepreneur when it went into the oil business, a move that drew Carl Icahn out to oppose it. Time's long-planned combination with Warner, touted for reasons of globalization in the media and entertainment industry, may have been a wise move, but it wasn't triggered by a raider's attack. Nor were most of the other large acquisitions that took place during the eighties. They were, however, the consequence of a higher standard of performance that was introduced into corporate board rooms by the knowledge that a raider would almost surely put one's company in play if it didn't perk up a bit. All companies had to restructure somewhat during the 1980s, even such huge, well-managed firms as IBM, General Electric, and Proctor & Gamble, all of which did so through rigorous self-evaluation, acquisitions, divestitures, and stock repurchases. These steps are what Michael Jensen meant when he said that the real value of the merger movement in the 1980s was not the $400 billion in added value to those stockholders of companies that were acquired but the internally generated restructuring and standards raising that took place throughout all of the rest of American industry. For this, all American shareholders should be grateful. Perhaps we too, like the Belgians, should hang out banners saying, "Thank you, Carl."

Still the data have not been particularly kind to industrial acquirers. Study after study demonstrates that the shareholders of acquiring companies usually do not benefit from the acquisitions. Most of these studies have focused on short-term stock price movements and have not had suitable opportunity to take into account the longer-term results of the mergers. In general, the academic literature on the value added to acquiring shareholders has built a pretty strong consensus around the idea that there isn't much of it, unless the acquirer itself becomes the target of a subsequent takeover. Most observers wonder, when looking over these results, why industrial acquirers acquire at all.

"Long-term strategic value," the industrial acquirer replies, "plus the fact that we can run that company better than those other fellows. Their costs are too high, their products aren't in the right stores, and their R & D is weak. In the right hands, though, the company could be dynamite. Just give us a little time with it. In three or four years the strengths of the combined companies will far exceed what they were separately."

In some cases this has been so, though the academics have a lot of trouble measuring such things; so they don't, sticking instead with what they can measure, namely changes in short-term stock prices. In a lot of other cases, however, the mergers have turned out to be nightmares for the acquirers, as well as for those acquired.

First, top management of the acquired company leaves, either because individuals are fired or because their jobs are downgraded or eliminated. Many, counting the money they have just put into the bank, decide that if working here isn't fun anymore they'll just split.

Second, the acquirers invariably decide that their top people know more about the way to run the acquired company than its executives do. Things are changed, new ideas put into place, often without much consultation with the old guard. "Why haven't you people at Bloomingdale's recognized the potential that's sitting there right in front of you to put up a store in Moscow?" asked Robert Campeau before ordering it done. Whatever the business, no matter how much it was admired before acquisition, the new people always seem to be tempted to interfere in it and to run things differently once they get control. The result is that often the acquirers spoil whatever was good in the company they bought.

Third, the acquired company now has to be valued as part of a much larger whole. PepsiCo and Philip Morris can get away with making investors believe that Pizza Hut and Jell-o, for example, will be better run as brands under their respective leadership than they would on their own, but lacking the extraordinary credibility that those two companies have, most have to face the fact that investors believe that acquired properties tend to be smothered under layers of bureaucracy after they have been taken in and therefore they are worth less acquired than they were independent. Look at what happened to O. M. Scott and Maidenform once they were released from their bureaucratic parents. The marketplace, therefore, has come to take a cynical view of acquisitions that it did not have, for example, during the merger boom in the 1960s.

So why do corporations acquire others when they know all this?

"Well," the industrialist replies, "we've got to do something with the money coming in. Once we get through paying all our interest and taxes and making capital expenditures to keep our plants up to date, we've still got surplus cash flow. If we just pay it out to stockholders they'll have to pay taxes on it, and besides, in this market stock prices don't go up when you increase the dividend; they often go down.

"Of course we could use some of the money to buy back stock in the market, though that always seems to us to be self-defeating. The shareholders didn't put us here to shrink or liquidate the company: they put us here to make the company grow and become more profitable. Or we could pay off debt, but hell, then we'd just be deleveraging just when everybody's telling us that we ought to be increasing our leverage—not to dangerous levels, but utilizing our borrowing capacity as an advantage.

"Now I know that some of my predecessors have said much the same thing and then gone out and made some dreadful acquisition that didn't work out. My colleagues and I are determined not to make that mistake. We have developed a great management team here and are capable of growing and changing with the times. To do so we will have to acquire some companies to fit into our existing businesses and some companies to move us into the businesses we need to be in. We are perfectly prepared to sell off companies we own that no longer fit into our strategy, including some very profitable ones.

"Look, we've got a winning team here. The market doesn't fully appreciate us just yet, but what do those paper shufflers in Wall Street know about anything? We're out to prove what we can do, to grow this company, and serve the shareholders as best we can."

In short, managers of companies think of themselves as growers and builders. They aren't where they are because they lack confidence, strength of character, or resolve. They believe what they say. Statistics are all about the past and the other guy anyway.

In the final analysis, though, managers know they are vulnerable to being taken over, no matter how well they seem to be running their own businesses. Their greatest dread is to be taken over by another company in the same industry, which will simply swallow their company right up, probably eliminating the entire management team. An LBO, however, could be very different: then the management team not only becomes an essential part of the deal but also becomes substantially richer. But, for an LBO to work, two things have to happen: financing has to be provided for the entire deal, which is very expensive and exposes the new company to a great deal of financial risk; and any counterbidder who might appear has to be fought off. Ross Johnson didn't fight off KKR; nor could the Macmillan group prevent Maxwell from putting forth a higher bid and winning the right to make it from the courts. LBOs can be tricky.

"But there has got to be a way for us to reorganize the ownership of this company so as to include maximum incentives for management and employees to make the most of it," says the industrialist. "LBOs were fine while they lasted, but even I can see how some of the guys got a little greedy. Anyway, they're a lot harder to get done now so we have to look for something else. Polaroid's deal was very interesting—both an ESOP and a 'white squire'—but United Airlines' attempt to give 75 percent of the votes to the employees may have been going a bit too far."

Market Energy

Financial markets generated an extraordinary amount of heat during the eighties, probably more than in the twenties. Stock prices rose 3.5 times in about five years, from mid-1982 until just before the crash in October 1987. But during this period the markets were also digesting a torrent of U.S. government and agency securities, municipal securities, corporate bonds, mortgage-backed securities, junk bonds, and contracts in financial futures and options. Much of this activity had been necessary to finance the growing federal deficit, which loomed ominously over the markets.

The deficit, however, had a curious feature. It was accomplished by the large Reagan tax cut in 1981, which in effect represented a transfer of wealth from the government to the private sector. During the eighties the government was getting poorer and poorer while the private sector, that is, individuals, corporations, and institutions, were getting richer and richer, though not evenly across the citizenry. The new private sector riches were sent back into the markets to swirl around there, adding substantially to the supply of liquidity and, thus, to the heat.

A result was a proliferation of innovative financial products and securities. The market had divided the basic risk-reward spectrum into a hundred parts, each designed to give an investor a security with precise characteristics. These characteristics were defined in terms of a whole new terminology: "spreads over Treasuries," "duration," "convexity," "volatility," "betas," "embedded options," "default rates," "mortality," and so on. The idea was to offer investors exactly what they wanted and to charge them more for it. It worked, as it always had, as far back as the recapitalization of the Sugar Trust in the late nineteenth century.

A financial marketplace so active and specialized must prove to be pretty efficient, claimed a number of academicians at the University of Chicago. All the investors in the market being sophisticated institutions, they all had the same goals and objectives and access to the same information. Price data, for example, were instantly available on television screens in everyone's office. Prices were thought to discount accurately any and all information that the market had about a company. Computers scanned the prices to look for temporary mismatches—and bang, they were closed as soon as they were found. When a takeover bid was announced, arbitrageurs would immediately buy up the stock of the target company, closing the gap between the bid price and the market and providing sellers with an assured high-priced exit. Everything was very efficient.

Still, however, some insidious imperfections remained. There was often a large gap between the cash-flow value of a company (as another company might see it) and its market value. Some of these gaps were closed by takeovers, but several years passed before the market began to work on the gaps still remaining in companies that had not been taken over. And there were the perennial gaps between the market value of junk bonds and their intrinsic value adjusted for default risk. The market still had prejudices, no matter what the University of Chicago said, and these were gold mines to such people as Michael Milken, who learned how to exploit them.

The composition of investors in the eighties was also different from that of prior years. Financial institutions dominated, as usual, but their makeup was different. Pension funds were selling stocks from 1986 onward; mutual funds were more active; foreigners had become major buyers of fixed-income securities and had begun to build up their equity portfolios, despite the crash. The main difference by the end of the eighties, though, was the extent of purchases of shares by corporations, those buying other companies or repurchasing their own shares. Their appetites created a shortage of common stocks, which caused institutional investors to take notice and try to anticipate their next moves.

"Yeah, the eighties were pretty amazing," says a weathered institutional investor. "A lot of money was made, but most of us took a lot of grief too. Our clients don't care whether they make money or not as long as they can point to good performance *relative* to the market. If the S & P 500 index doubles in a two-year period, say, but their portfolio goes up only 95 percent, they're very unhappy. If the market drops by 50 percent, but their portfolio falls only 45 percent they're happy. When they're unhappy they fire you, or put you on notice, or shift to index funds so they can always tie the market, thus being neither happy nor unhappy.

"Beating the averages is very difficult when you are big. We have $15 billion under management, which makes us pretty big. We attracted this money because we were successful as money managers when we were smaller. Now we're somewhat unwieldy. We can't move $2 or $3 billion around quickly without killing the market, so we make up for this by trying to have a lot of smaller, more specialized portfolios, and we buy some different stuff, like foreign stocks or LBOs or whatever looks like it's going to outperform the S & P. But it's tough.

"Corporations bitch about us all the time, saying we'd dump them in an instant to capture a merger premium. Some we would, but some not. Still, they want it both ways: they want us to be more actively involved as holders of their stock (meaning just that, to hold it, not to sell it), but they don't like it much when we vote against them on stockholder proposals or try to tell them how to run their companies, though as large investors we are certainly entitled to do that."

Many institutional investors are trying to shed the short-term beat-the-market performance pressure by specializing in a series of single-purpose off-market portfolios, such as for arbitrage, leveraged buyouts, junk bonds, or (the latest thing) bankruptcy workouts. Some, too, would like to increase their exposure to foreign securities or simply to be like Warren Buffet, the sage of Omaha (and chairman of Berkshire Hathaway), who has hung on for years to the same four or five key investments, though lately he has become the king of white squires. The major pension funds and other institutional investors appear to be putting an increasing percentage of their funds into off-market investments, which does tend to reduce the buying support for shares in the market. However, much of this money is deal-oriented and tends to pop back into action as soon as mergers, recapitalizations, and restructurings are announced. As far as mergers and related transactions are concerned, the market ought to be able to keep much of its heat well into the nineties.

Even at the end of the decade the air quality of the financial transaction environment was pretty good. It was still highly combustive.

There has been very little regulatory interference in transactions, either of an antitrust nature or in the area of takeover regulation. Indeed the absence of the latter accounts for the rising role of the courts in deciding which takeover procedures are acceptable and which are not. There are threats, however, from Washington and various state capitals that action will be taken if unseemly, that is, excessively leveraged, transactions do not subside. Pennsylvania has enacted a new and generally protective amendment to its corporation law; some others have followed suit, but most are not under any immediate pressure to do so.

Congressional interest in reforming the takeover game, though seemingly ongoing, appears to have subsided for the time being—largely because of the fact that market conditions have changed and the number of new LBOs and junk issues has fallen off to a trickle. Recent LBO performances have disappointed many investors, and the junk-bond market has begun to differentiate between "good junk" and "bad junk" and to discount future bankruptcies much more aggressively. Without substantial amounts of junk financing, LBO operators have difficulty putting together financing for high-priced bids, and as a result the field is left open for "friendly" industrial mergers and for self-restructuring with ESOPs and squires.

The courts have helped the latter, too, in ruling in the *Polaroid* and *Time* cases that longer-term corporate plans have to be respected in takeover disputes. Thus by the end of 1989, both the market and the legal atmosphere were tilting back toward large, old-fashioned industrial deals, of which there were several in 1989, including the friendly mergers of Beecham and SmithKline (creating a new $16 billion corporation) and of Bristol-Myers and Squibb ($12.3 billion). Meanwhile UAL's controversial, highly leveraged management-and-pilots-union–led $7 billion LBO was unable to attract financing and had to be abandoned, though efforts continue to resurrect it.

Nevertheless, as financing techniques, LBOs and leveraged re-capitalizations had enormous impact during the eighties. Though these have come off the boil, the principles behind them have been demonstrated to be sound, and therefore we can expect to see them in the future. What we will see less of are the junk bond–financed bids for large corporations in desperate competition with other bidders. Probably, too, there will be much less use of the LBO technique for inappropriate, cyclical businesses. Jerry Kohlberg, proved right after all, must be smiling.

We should also see less of the "merchant banking" technique of bridge financing in light of the serious disappointments that some of the providers of these loans have experienced. First Boston, in particular, suffered a lot of damage from a $1 billion portfolio of bridge loans to such ill-fated deals as Campeau's purchase of Federated Department Stores and the Ohio Mattress buyout. Shearson Lehman Hutton and Merrill Lynch also had large merchant banking exposures. First Boston experienced a major management change in September 1989 in connection with the merger of the firm into CS-First Boston, which was controlled by the Swiss bank, Credit Suisse. The incoming team must have been somewhat horrified by what it found in the way of bridge loan positions, all deteriorating rapidly in the slumping markets after the October 13 mini-crash. In the end, Credit Suisse had to take some of First Boston's positions on its own books to insure the solvency of the firm. Bridge loans also contributed to Shearson Lehman's sudden disintegration toward the end of 1989, which resulted in the acquisition of 100 percent of its shares by American Express, its parent. Without such parents, First Boston and Shearson might well have followed the uphappy path of Drexel Burnham into Chapter 11.

The idea behind bridge lending was that the high level of fees and interest earned for providing the finance and handling all the other transactions involved with a large, multifaceted LBO would provide a profit pool sufficient to absorb normal risks from delays in securing permanent financing. The concept, used moderately to support credit-worthy transactions, generally proved sound, but not when used immoderately or in connection with shaky deals. Once again, at the end of the period, the market was driven to excess.

LBO and merchant banking activities, however, possess a certain staying power because of the money-making energy and talents that they encompass. Whatever the next twist in the market, the same players will be found on the scene. Their activities will continue

to aid corporate restructuring and recapitalization efforts. The sophisticated financial technologies of the eighties won't be forgotten.

Rethinking the Corporation

I spent my business career in a partnership, one that is now the last
of its kind in Wall Street. Partnerships do not have stock; they are
not tradable. They are not efficient forms of organizations. There
are certain tax benefits that derive from the fact that your earnings
are taxed only once, but there are also unlimited liabilities that the
partners must bear individually for the actions of the firm. Partnerships operating in capital-intensive businesses also suffer a grave
disadvantage in having to pay out capital to retiring partners: they
do not have shares that can be sold to the market instead. Except
for small businesses and legal and accounting practices (which are
not capital-intensive), partnerships are almost extinct in the United
States and in most of Europe (Germany excepted).

Modern businesses abandoned the partnership form of enterprise organization in the early twentieth century. Most had simply
so outgrown their partners' ability to provide capital for the enterprise that they had to incorporate and sell shares. Also partnerships
lacked hierarchy—partners were all treated more or less equally—
and too many had descended to effete members of the second or
third generation who were not trained in professional management
science. Yet one large partnership remained in the financial services
field: Goldman, Sachs & Co.

At Goldman Sachs the partnership (established in 1869) has
always had a certain mystique, which possibly explains why it has
survived many attempts to vote it out. The mystique, however, had
some solid backing. In the firm, from your first day as an employee,
you knew that your goal was to become a partner, as tough as that
was. The financial rewards of being a partner were extremely attractive, as were the social recognition and prestige that went with
them. Partnerships were obtained strictly on the basis of merit: you

didn't need any capital of your own if you didn't have any, and absolutely no favoritism was shown to (or against) relatives of other partners. If you were good enough you could make it. There were a lot of partners, about 40 when I became a partner (there are 140 or so now), so you didn't have to wait forever as in a big corporation for one of a handful of top jobs to open up. The number of partners increased over the years, but so did the number of partners who retired (generally in their early fifties) to make room for those on the way up. Over the years the ratio of partners to total employees declined, but the quality, ambitiousness, and self-confidence of the new employees rose steadily nevertheless.

You also realized right away that the firm was run day to day by its owners. Money wasn't spent unnecessarily, but necessary investments were well understood and approved. When times were tough, things were cut back; but when times were good, the extra earnings were spent on bonuses to employees and increased partnership earnings. Overhead was tightly controlled, at least as compared to that of publicly owned firms, and frills were few and far between. Everyone understood: we were in business to make money, not to put on a show.

There was a very flat hierarchy; if you were a permanent professional employee, you were either an associate, a vice president, or a partner. Teamwork, interaction, and intradepartmental communication were stressed. The firm developed its own culture, based on management by owner-producers and a highly charged, intensely meritocratic environment. We believed we were the financial world's equivalent of a team of professional athletes. We were very competitive and worked and trained hard. We were good at what we did and wanted to be the best, the world champions.

Much of this spirit and dedication would be lost in a corporation, an organization that in a generation or two would pass from owners who worked in the firm to owners who did not: institutional and other investors who bought or sold our stock more on the basis of market conditions and modern portfolio theories than on performance. With such absentee owners, the firm would have to form a managerial hierarchy—ostensibly to protect the rights and powers of professional management from the harassment of stockholders, but equally to take advantage of their indifference.

In the late 1960s the New York Stock Exchange changed its rules, allowing member firms to give up partnerships, incorporate, and to sell their shares to the public. The first to do so was Donaldson, Lufkin & Jenrette, a research boutique that prospered and was ultimately bought out by Equitable Life. One of the earliest firms to go public after DLJ was Merrill Lynch. Between then and now, Merrill Lynch has become a company in which the employees, who once owned 100 percent of the company, now own a very small amount of the stock, like a bank. The character of the firm cannot have but changed. It has become a dull institution. Its nickname is the "thundering herd." What champion athlete wants to identify with a thundering herd?

The vast majority of large American companies have also become publicly owned institutions run by cautious, risk-averse mandarins. They have boards of directors made up of a majority of nonexecutives (necessary to prevent management from unduly entrenching itself, though many of these directors, not being businessmen, probably wouldn't know whether management was entrenching itself or not), managements that are reluctant to pay out dividends so as to invest further in building up the size (rather than the productivity) of the empire they command, and shareholders who are indifferent to their businesses, being devotées of modern portfolio theory.

Thus "institutional corporations" came into being. These were often made up of several different businesses that were worth more apart than together, like the closed-end investment companies managed by institutional investors. The institutional corporations were evolving into proxy money managers for their shareholders, the investor institutions, whose own managers had settled back on autopilot. Infected by an extra layer of money managers the system was fast becoming a bureaucracy, a performance-stifling nightmare.

The nightmare had other sides to it, too. Large corporations have been an embarrassment to Americans equally as often as they have been a source of pride. Bribery and political payoffs in the

1970s, toxic waste and pollution, nuclear overbuilding without adequate provision for safety and disposal of radioactive waste, fraud in the defense industries, and other abuses have since become common newspaper reading. These abuses might be more tolerable if American-managed companies led the world in efficiency, competitiveness, and market capitalization. But they don't. Instead, they are being overtaken by foreign competitors, are hesitant to invest in new technologies, and in some cases have become bloated "corpocracies," to use the term coined by Richard Darman, a former investment banker who now serves as President Bush's budget director. Are these creatures so beneficial to society and so worth preserving that America should take a page out of recently abandoned European economic history and cry for protectionism against imports and foreign investment? Or to put the lid on natural forces of competition at home by clamping down on raiders, LBO operators, and junk bond salesmen?

Michael Jensen, the Harvard professor who has studied the current merger and LBO phenomena more perhaps than anyone, has concluded that the "publicly held corporation, the main engine of economic progress in the United States for a century, has outlived its usefulness in many sectors of the economy and is being eclipsed." He particularly points to slow-growing, mature industries that generate more cash than they need, those industries that are naturally appropriate for LBOs or other forms of organization.[1]

"He's got a point there," says one weary industrialist. "I sure would like to get rid of those cold-fish institutional investors as my primary shareholders. Those bastards will sell you out in a minute for just a nickel more. They make the whole idea of a public corporation seem very unstable, which in time makes them uncompetitive."

An alternative idea is to have a small number of involved shareholders (or partners) working with management to maximize the performance of the company. This way the company could be protected from a blindside raid but not protected from incompetence and useless empire building—the nonmanagement owners would be too sharp and too involved to let any of that happen. Such a structure, though, would be a completely new approach to how a business is organized, one that would have been unthinkable at the beginning of the eighties but that might be just the ticket for the nineties.

Institutions ought to be interested, too. Each one could set aside, say, a third of the money it otherwise invests in the stock market to invest in white squire positions, just as Warren Buffet, one of the country's most successful long-term investors, has been doing for several years. Institutions can train or hire competent executives to sit on the boards of the companies they are squires to and get involved and help make things happen. In the end, such off-market investments may be the only way to beat the indices regularly.

Some say that large public companies have a social responsibility that smaller ones do not and that corruption and cheating in business are more prevalent in small businesses than in large ones, for example, in the savings and loan industry. I'm not so sure. Problems arise, and occasionally people get into trouble, but on the whole the people who work for themselves know that the best solution to a business problem is the one that makes the greatest amount of money over the long run, those who, like Goldman Sachs's late senior partner Gus Levy, claim to be "long-term greedy."

The financial marketplace has come to discover that deinstitutionalizing corporations is a profitable business. Partnerships such as KKR, Clayton & Dubilier, Wesray and Gibbons Green and van Amerongen have been successful in buying companies with their own money- or credit-raising potential and in using their own management, differently to be sure, to revalue the companies they acquired. This is a natural process and will continue, according to the theorists, until the opportunities for revaluation are exhausted. In their place will be left a trail of smaller, owner-manager organizations, such as O. M. Scott, trying to make the most money over the long run. Some will still be publicly held corporations, but others will have metamorphosed into partnerships, limited partnerships, closely held corporations, restructured entities owned by ESOPs and/or white squires, and other vehicles yet undiscovered. Some will have liquidated back into a proprietorship form; others (maybe quite a few) will have bitten off too much and failed, probably then being bought out of bankruptcy by a group of "turnaround artists" wanting to give the basic business one last try. But if all this gets us out of the brain-numbing institutional lockstep that we found ourselves a part of in the early 1980s—away from one set of bureaucratic institutions being owned by another with all the rest of us having to accept the valuations put on them by the "perfect market"—we're all better off.

On balance, the eighties were among the most dynamic of all of the thousands of years of financial history. Markets soared, and new wealth was created in abundance, especially by the New Men who stepped forward as innovators and entrepreneurs. New concepts have been forced on us, and these have not always been welcome. New ways of thinking about leverage and default risk, forced takeovers, and the duties and responsibilities of corporate directors have emerged. Change has been everywhere: whole industries have been transformed, markets altered irretrievably. Lawyers and bankers have prospered, too, but only in proportion to their many contributions to these exhausting and explosive times, and much less so than their more successful clients. Still their professions will never be the same. The quiet, scholarly, pipe-smoking Wall Street lawyer of the past has been displaced by a charged-up, overaggressive, workaholic streetfighter, whose brilliant, innovative, and devious mind has been just right for the many intense battles in the courthouse. The old, well-broken-in, client service–oriented investment banker, skilled in bond and stock offerings for AA-rated companies, has also disappeared. He has been replaced by a nerveless, glib, combative individual who has been thoroughly trained in the new ordnance of his trade: leverage, engineering of restructurings, and analysis of risk taking, which often are the final determinants in business getting. If the white-hot era of the eighties slows down, as "it, too, passes away," and clients go back to the old mundane financings of the past, many of these guys will go crazy.

Hardened combat veterans often make poor peacetime soldiers. They, too, will have to be replaced by New Men.

NOTES

INTRODUCTION:
RISE AND FALL OF AN ERA

1. Walter Bagehot, *Lombard Street. A Description of the Money Market* (London: Henry S. King & Co., 1873), pp. 1–20.
2. Bernard M. Baruch, *Baruch: My Own Story* (New York: Henry Holt, 1957), pp. 165–76.

1
MORGAN'S LEGACIES

1. Frederick Lewis Allen, *The Great Pierpont Morgan* (New York: Harper & Row, 1948), pp. 30, 69–71.
2. Thomas R. Navin and Marian V. Sears, "The Rise of a Market for Industrial Securities, 1887–1902," *Business History Review* (June 1953), pp. 105–38.
3. Ralph W. Hidy and Muriel E. Hidy, *Pioneers in Big Business, 1882–1911 (History of the Standard Oil Co. of New Jersey)* (New York: Harper & Brothers, 1955), p. 40.
4. Navin and Sears, "Rise of a Market," p. 120.
5. Alfred Chandler, "The Beginnings of 'Big Business' in American Industry," *Business History Review* (Spring 1959), pp. 1–31.
6. In the period 1898–1902, the dollar value of mergers identified by Nelson ($6.3 billion), divided by the 1900 U.S. GNP ($18.7 billion), was 33.7

percent; for 1984–88, the dollar value of all completed mergers, acquisitions, tender offers, merger-tenders, divestitures, and leveraged buyouts involving at least one U.S. company, as reported by Securities Data Corp. ($1.06 trillion), divided by the 1986 U.S. GNP ($4.2 trillion), was 25.2 percent.

7. Ralph L. Nelson, *Merger Movements in American Industry, 1895–1956* (Princeton: Princeton University Press, 1959), pp. 1–120.

8. John A. Hobson, *The Evolution of Modern Capitalism*, 4th ed. (London: Allen & Unwin, 1926), pp. 180–215, 235.

9. Allen, *Great Pierpont Morgan*, pp. 140–45.

10. Vincent P. Carosso, *Investment Banking in America* (Cambridge, Mass.: Harvard University Press, 1970), pp. 73–74.

11. Allen, *Great Pierpont Morgan*, p. 146.

12. Ibid., p. 145.

13. Most of the recounting of the transaction is based on the article by Thomas R. Navin and Marian V. Sears, "A Study in Merger: Formation of the International Mercantile Marine Company," *Business History Review* 28 (December 1954), pp. 291–328.

14. Allen, *Great Pierpont Morgan*, pp. 207–12.

2
ROARING TWENTIES

1. Frederick Lewis Allen, *The Big Change, America Transforms Itself, 1900–1950* (New York: Harper & Brothers, 1952), pp. 63–108.

2. *The New York Times*, December 11, 1911.

3. Ralph W. Hidy and Muriel E. Hidy, *Pioneers in Big Business, 1882–1911 (History of the Standard Oil Co. of New Jersey)* (New York: Harper & Brothers, 1955), p. 713.

4. Alfred P. Sloan, Jr., *My Years at General Motors*, ed. John McDonald with Catherine Stevens (Garden City, N.Y.: Doubleday, 1964), pp.5–10.

5. Robert Lacey, *Ford: The Men and the Machine* (Boston: Little, Brown, 1986), pp. 80–84.

6. Allan Nevins and Frank Hill, *Ford: Expansion and Challenge, 1915–1933* (New York: Charles Scribner's Sons, 1957), pp. 86–111.

7. Ibid., p. 109.

8. *The New York Times*, July 12, 1919.

9. *Moody's Industrial Manual*, 1919.

10. Forrest McDonald, *Insull* (Chicago: University of Chicago Press, 1962), pp. 50–52.

11. M. L. Ramsey, *Pyramid of Power* (New York: Bobbs-Merrill, 1937), pp. 51–52.
12. Ibid., pp. 225–29.
13. Ibid., pp. 219–30.
14. John Kenneth Galbraith, *The Great Crash, 1929* (Boston, Houghton Mifflin, 1954), p. 46.
15. Ibid., p. 60.
16. Dow Jones Industrial Index quotations from *The Wall Street Journal.*

3
CHINESE MONEY

1. Sidney Homer, *A History of Interest Rates* (New Brunswick, N.J.: Rutgers University Press, 1963, 1977), p. 335.
2. Robert Sobel, *Panic on Wall Street* (New York: Truman Talley Books/ E. P. Dutton, 1988), p. 400.
3. "Adam Smith," *The Money Game* (New York: Random House, 1967), p. 24.
4. Ibid., p. 212.
5. Brock Stokes, much liked and admired, continued to rise in his firm, and later, in another firm. Soon afterward, though, he died as a result of an accident, without seeing the end of the market that gave him his break.
6. Robert Sobel, *The Rise and Fall of the Conglomerate Kings* (New York: Stein & Day, 1984), pp. 23–46.
7. Anthony Sampson, *The Sovereign State of ITT* (New York: Stein & Day, 1973), p. 73.
8. The entire section about James Ling draws heavily on material published in Stanley H. Brown, *Ling* (New York: Atheneum Publishers, 1972).

4
THE MERGER WARS

1. There have been many academic studies concerning the efficiency of acquisitions. Michael Jensen and Richard Ruback summed up thirteen separate studies in "The Market for Corporate Control: The Scientific Evidence" 11 *Journal of Financial Economics* 5 (1983), and Jensen has produced many additional studies of his own. See also David Ravenscroft and Frederick Scherer's book *Mergers, Sell-offs and Economic Efficiency*, (Washington, D.C.: The Brookings Institution, 1987); Gregg Jarrell, James Brickley, and Jeffry Netter, "The Market for Corporate Control: The Empirical Evidence Since 1980," 2 *Journal of Economic Perspectives* 49 (1988); Mark Mitchell and Kenneth Lehn, "Do Bad Bidders Become Good Targets?" Working Paper No. 16, Center for the Study of American Business,

Washington University (May 1989); and "Do Merger's Work," *The Economist* (December 17, 1988).

2. Bryan Burroughs and John Helyar, *Barbarians at the Gate* (New York: Harper & Row, 1990), pp. 497–98.

3. Ibid., pp. 179, 485.

4. Michael Jensen, Steven Kaplan, and Laurie Stiglin, "The Effect of Leveraged Buyouts on Tax Revenues of the U.S. Treasury", *Tax Notes* 42, no. 6 (February 1989).

5. *Pensions and Investment Age* (December 12, 1988), pp. 1, 42.

6. Alan Greenspan, Statement before the Senate Finance Committee of the U.S. Congress, January 26, 1989.

7. Carl C. Icahn, "The Case for Takeovers," *The New York Times Magazine*, January 29, 1989, p. 34.

8. Michael C. Jensen, Statement before the House Ways and Means Committee of the U.S. Congress, February 1, 1989. The $400 billion of restored value is a figure that he has provided, one that some other observers dispute.

9. Kohlberg, Kravis, & Roberts, "Leveraged Buy-Outs," *Journal of Applied Corporate Finance* (Spring 1989).

5
BATTLEFIELD TACTICS

1. Martin Lipton, "Paying the Price of Takeover Money," *Manhattan Inc.* (May 1989).

2. J. W. Van Gorkom, "The 'Big Bang' for Director Liability: The Chairman's Report," *Directors & Boards* (Fall 1987).

3. *Smith* v. *Van Gorkom*, 488 A.2d 858, Del. Supreme Court, 1985).

4. Stuart L. Shapiro, "Judicial Business Judgment: The Investment Banker's Role," unpublished paper presented at a Salomon Brothers Center Conference on Corporate Governance, Restructuring and the Market for Corporate Control, May 1989.

5. *Unocal Corp.* v. *Mesa Petroleum Co.*, 493 A.2d 954, Del. Supreme Court, 1985.

6. Shapiro, "Judicial Business Judgment."

7. The Macmillan episode was based on articles appearing in *The Wall Street Journal* from May to October 1988 by Johnnie L. Roberts, Peter Norman, Lauro Lauro, Cynthia Crossen, et al., and on various filings by Macmillan, KKR, and Maxwell with the SEC.

8. *Robert M. Bass Group* v. *Evans, et al.*, Court of Chancery of Delaware, 552 A.2d 1227, 1988.

9. Ibid.

10. SEC filings by Shamrock and Polaroid, 1988, 1989. See also Stephen Quickel, "Will the ESOP Defense Survive?" *Corporate Finance* (April 1989).

6
THE AMAZING LBO MACHINE

1. Source: Goldman, Sachs & Co., and Security Data Co.
2. Connie Bruck, "Billion-Dollar Mind," *The New Yorker* (August 7, 1989).
3. *Mergers and Acquisitions* (November/December, 1988), p. 50.
4. James Sterngold, "Buyout Pioneer Quitting Fray," *The New York Times*, June 19, 1987.
5. Sterngold, Ibid.
6. Steven Kaplan, "The Effects of Management Buyouts on Operations and Value," *Journal of Financial Economics* (Spring 1989). The paper includes a substantial bibliography of other studies on LBOs conducted by academics.
7. The O. M. Scott story is based on an article by George Anders from *The Wall Street Journal*, "Leveraged Buy-Outs Make Some Companies Tougher Competition," September 13, 1988.
8. Michael C. Jensen, "The Free Cash Flow Theory of Takeovers: A Financial Perspective on Mergers and Acquisitions and the Economy," in Lynn E. Browne and Eric S. Rosengren, eds., *The Merger Boom*, The Federal Reserve Bank of Boston, October 1987.
9. Carol J. Loomis, "Buyout Kings," *Fortune* (July 4, 1988).
10. *The Economist* (September 30, 1989).
11. Loomis, *Op. Cit.* Also, SEC filings by KKR in conjunction with its acquisition of Beatrice Foods, 1986; Ford S. Worthy, "Beatrice's Sell-Off Strategy," *Fortune* (June 23, 1986); and James Sterngold, "Shaking Billions from Beatrice," *The New York Times*, September 6, 1987.
12. Sterngold, *Op. Cit.*
13. David Hilder, "Kohlberg Kravis Is Sued by Founder over Stake in Firms," *The Wall Street Journal*, August 30, 1989.
14. Source: Goldman, Sachs & Co.
15. Cooperman's comment is quoted in John Liscio, "The Buyout Bubble," *Barron's*, October 31, 1988.
16. Michael Cook, unpublished paper, September 1988.
17. Sarah Bartlett, "Cracks in the House that Debt Built," *The New York Times*, August 17, 1989.
18. Sarah Bartlett, "Wall Street's Treacherous Slide," *The New York Times*, November 6, 1989.
19. Kohlberg Kravis Roberts & Co., "Leveraged Buy-Outs," *Journal of Applied Corporate Finance* (Spring 1989).

7
TREASURES IN THE JUNKYARD

1. Connie Bruck, *The Predators' Ball* (New York, The American Lawyer/ Simon & Schuster, 1988), pp. 23–39.

2. Howard Rudnitsky, Allan Sloan, and Richard Stern, "A One-Man Revolution," *Forbes* (August 25, 1986). See also Marie Brenner, "Michael Milken, the Man Who Would Be King," *Vanity Fair* (August 1989), and William Meyers, "Down But Not Out in Beverly Hills," *Institutional Investor* (August 1989).

3. *United States* v. *Michael Milken et al.*, indictment, quoted in *The New York Times*, March 30, 1989.

4. Bruck, *Predators' Ball*, p. 14.

5. Edward I. Altman, "The Anatomy of the High-Yield Bond Market," *Financial Analysts Journal* (July–August 1987).

6. Abraham J. Briloff, "Drexel's Greediest Deal," *Barron's*, December 5, 1988.

7. Daniel Hertzberg and John D. Williams, "Merrill Lynch Gave SEC Key Lead in Levine Case," *The Wall Street Journal*, June 6, 1986.

8. Brenner, "Michael Milken."

9. New York Federal Reserve Bank estimate as quoted in Kevin Winch, "Junk Bonds: 1988 Status Report," Congressional Research Service, Library of Congress, December 30, 1988.

10. Subsequently published in *Journal of Finance* (Septemer 1989).

11. Source: Lipper Analytical Services.

12. Roger Lowenstein, "Heard on the Street," *The Wall Street Journal*, December 10, 1989.

13. Anise C. Wallace, "Time for Jitters in Junk Bonds," *The New York Times*, August 6, 1989.

14. Linda Sandler, "Junk Bond Defaults Are Spreading," *The Wall Street Journal*, July 20, 1989.

8
ARE THE THEORIES WRONG?

1. Edward Altman, R. Haldeman, and P. Narayanan, "Zeta Analysis: A New Model to Identify Bankruptcy Risk of Corporations," *Journal of Banking and Finance* (June 1977).

2. Franco Modigliani and James Poterba, "A Little Extra Leverage Is No Cause for Alarm," *Financial Times* [London] February 8, 1989.

3. "The Decaying Financial Infrastructure," *Quantitative Viewpoint*, Merrill Lynch Capital Markets (June 6, 1989).

4. See Benjamin Graham and David Dodd, *Security Analysis*, originally published by McGraw-Hill Book Company, in 1934; John Maynard Keynes, "Investment Policy and Insurance," from *The Collected Writings of John Maynard Keynes, Vol. XII*, Donald Moggridge, ed. (New York, 1983), pp. 240–44. John Burr Williams, "The Theory of Investment Value" (Cambridge, Mass., 1938); and Harry Markowitz "Portfolio Selection," *Journal of Finance* (March 1952). All of the relevant articles are included in Charles D. Ellis, ed., *Classics: An Investors Anthology* (New York: Dow Jones-Irwin, 1989).

5. Dean LeBaron and Lawrence S. Speidel, "Why Are the Parts Worth More than the Sum? 'Chop Shop,' A Corporate Valuation Model," in Lynn E. Browne and Eric Rosengren, eds., *The Merger Boom* (Boston: The Federal Reserve Bank of Boston, 1987).

9
REFORMING THE SYSTEM

1. See notes to Chapter 4.

2. In addition to the studies on junk bonds performed by Professor Altman and a group at Harvard Business School, the Alliance for Capital Access commissioned two studies of its own, one by the Wharton Econometric Forecasting Associates (which assessed the risks and returns of various assets held by savings and loan institutions, and which demonstrated that junk bonds, next to credit card loans, were the best performing assets S & Ls had), and the other by Data Resources, Inc., to test the durability of junk-bond portfolios under various recession scenarios.

3. John Brooks, *The Takeover Game* (New York: Truman Talley Books/ E. P. Dutton, 1987), p. 269.

4. Ibid., p. 276.

5. Goldman, Sachs & Co., "Bank Track Report," December 1988.

6. Salomon Brothers, "Leveraged Buyout Transactions—Who Owes What to Whom?" Stock Research Department, November 25, 1989; and Goldman, Sachs & Co., "Learning to Like LBOs," Investment Research Department, December 1988.

7. Jeffrey Birnbaum, "Congressional Action on LBOs Slows to Dragging Feet," *The Wall Street Journal*, March, 9, 1989.

10
THIS, TOO, SHALL PASS, OR WILL IT?

1. Michael C. Jensen, "Eclipse of the Public Corporation," *Harvard Business Review* (September/October 1989).

GLOSSARY

Bootstrap acquisition An early leveraged buyout

Breakup fee A fee paid to a party in a takeover if the party's deal breaks up; often an agreement to pay expenses or a bit more to a losing side in a contest to acquire a company.

Bridge loans Short-term loans made to an acquirer by an investment banker, which expects to manage a junk bond offering after the acquisition is completed and thus repay the loans. Lucrative but risky.

Business-judgment doctrine Long-standing legal doctrine giving the benefit of the doubt to a board of directors with respect to the exercise of business judgments; this doctrine no longer applies automatically to ownership matters where an "enhanced" standard now has to be met.

Chinese money The name given to convertible securities of dubious quality issued in connection with acquisitions in the 1960s.

Control premium The amount paid to acquire a company over its market value before the offer. The extra amount you have to pay to take control of a company.

343

Crown jewel lockup A takeover defense in which a major producing asset of a company is sold outright to a favored bidder to discourage a nonfavored bidder.

ESOP Employee stock ownership plan.

Fairness letter A letter from an investment banker to a takeover target stating that the offer price is fair. Such letters are commonly requested from directors of target companies who wish to demonstrate that they have received professional advice in making decisions relative to a takeover.

Fallen angel A former investment-grade bond that is currently rated below investment grade, often the result of downgrading following a leveraged buyout.

Front-end-loaded offer A two-tier offer in which the first tier is made more attractive to investors than the second.

Going private Tendering for shares of one's own company to make it a privately owned company again; the opposite of going public.

Golden parachute Compensation for loss of office awarded to management by a board of directors before a takeover threat appears in order to reduce management's innate opposition to such an offer, so it can be viewed objectively.

Greenmail The process common in the early 1980s (but no longer) of acquiring a 10 or 15 percent investment in a company with the intention of threatening a takeover so as to frighten management into buying the shareholding back at a premium over the market price.

Gunslinger An aggressive money manager of the 1960s.

Highly confident letter A letter, once commonly issued by an investment banker, in which the banker states that it is highly confident that a particular offer of junk bonds scheduled to take place after an acquisition is doable. Banks and other lenders want such letters even though they do not purport to be guarantees.

Hostile deal A takeover proposal opposed by management and/or the board of directors of the target company.

Inadequate value When an offer is deemed to be less than the maximum value obtainable in an auction, it may be called inadequate.

Insider trading Trading illegally in stock based on nonpublic information that has been misappropriated.

Investment-grade debt Debt rated at least Baa by Moody's or BBB – by Standard & Poor's, rating levels that presume risks of default that are the maximum tolerable to prudent investors.

Just say no A takeover defense in which the directors declare that the company is not for sale and make no effort to create an alternative to a takeover offer. This works only when company has a poison pill in place.

Junk bonds High-yield bonds, rated below "investment grade" by Moody's and Standard & Poor's because of their lower quality and greater risk of default.

Leverage The use of borrowed money (or other scarce commodities, such as talents and ideas) to increase the amount of assets under one's own control. The British call it "gearing."

Leveraged buyout The acquisition of a company that is financed almost entirely by money borrowed against the assets or cash flow of the company being bought, without recourse to any other security. When the acquirers are principally members of management, the transaction is called a "management buyout."

Liquidity The availability of active trading markets or credit facilities so as to be able to raise cash quickly.

Merchant banking In the United States, the term applies to sophisticated transactions in which an investment bank takes a principal position in order to facilitate the completion of a deal or for investment.

Pac Man defense A takeover defense in which a company tenders for the company tendering for it.

PIK securities High-yield securities the interest or dividends on which are paid-in-kind, that is, paid in the form of additional securities for a number of years to conserve cash. These securities have little value when issued, but even *some* value later on means a big percentage increase.

Poison pill A program in which shareholders are permitted to purchase additional shares in the company at very low prices if any other shareholder should acquire an interest greater than a specified amount. Any such shareholder would be excluded from the share-purchase plan. The poison pill has the effect of slowing down the takeover process and requiring negotiations with the target company's board of directors.

Put in play When a company is the subject of a real or rumored takeover offer that causes it to attract a great deal of interest from other potential buyers, who otherwise would not have stepped forward.

Raider One who initiates a hostile offer or threat of one.

Restructuring A substantial change in a company's business mix and/or financial structure so as to alter its investment appeal.

Risk arbitrage Stock speculation based on whether a rumored or announced merger or related transaction will actually occur.

Saturday night special A first-come, first-served, short-lived cash tender offer popular in the 1960s, before the Williams bill was enacted.

Self-tender When a company attempts to purchase its own shares through a tender offer to its shareholders.

Senior debt Bank debt or debt securities that, in bankruptcy, rank ahead of subordinated debt or shareholder's equity.

Standstill agreement An agreement sought by a company under threat of a takeover with a party that has acquired an interest not to increase that interest above a specified amount.

Subordinated debt Debt that is taken on by an acquirer in order to complete an acquisition, which is to be repaid relatively soon afterward out of the proceeds of asset sales.

Tender offer An offer to purchase shares of a company for cash or securities that is made directly to stockholders.

Two-tier offer A takeover offer that is divided into two parts: an immediate offer for a controlling interest in the company—usually in cash—and a later offer—usually not in cash—for the remainder of the outstanding shares.

White knight An alternate buyer for a company, one invited to bid for it to prevent the company's being sold to an unwanted first bidder.

White squire A company or investor that will purchase a substantial minority interest in a company in play and agree to vote with management in order to protect the company from being taken over.

SELECTED ANNOTATED BIBLIOGRAPHY

This book is for the general reader, who, in my experience, does not have much appetite for slogging through serious works of history, economics, or financial theory. So in preparing a short bibliography for those general readers who wish to explore the subject matter further, and to be amused and entertained as they do, I have eliminated all scholarly titles. Only best-seller material is mentioned, but of the sort that most readers will find as edifying as they find enjoyable.

PART I

Allen, Frederick Lewis. *The Great Pierpont Morgan*. New York: Harper & Row, 1948. Allen's compelling biography of the great man is an excellent companion to his classic *Only Yesterday*. Morgan has been the subject of many biographies, few as well written and insightful as this one.

Baruch, Bernard. *Baruch: My Own Story*. New York: Henry Holt, 1957. Baruch's autobiography is fascinating, not only as one of the first rags-to-riches stories, but also for its descriptions of the times and characters of his career.

Brooks, John. *Once in Golconda*. New York: Truman Talley Books/E. P. Dutton, 1985. The first of three books by John Brooks in this bibliography, a writer for *The New Yorker* who has brought wit and style to American financial history, is about the twenties and thirties. It was a smash hit when it came out, especially with the Wall Street crowd, for its combination of detail and poignant explanation of what was going on.

——. *The Go-Go Years.* Truman Talley Books/E. P. Dutton, 1984. Brooks's tale of the 1960s, equally as good as *Once in Golconda.*

Galbraith, John Kenneth. *The Great Crash, 1929.* Boston: Houghton Mifflin, 1954. Galbraith's classic story of the crash is short, sardonic, highly readable, extremely interesting, provocative, and thoughtful, even if you think Galbraith is an over-the-hill liberal gone to seed. The absolute best of the crash books.

"Smith, Adam." *The Money Game.* New York: Random House, 1967. The bible of institutional investors, and how they thought and acted, in the go-go years of the sixties. It was an instant success when it came out and later it begat several follow-on books, none as good as the original, and the television series "Adam Smith's Money World."

PART II

Auletta, Ken. *Greed and Glory on Wall Street.* New York: Harper & Row, 1986. Auletta's friendless story of the fall of Lehman Brothers after years of savage infighting and behavior people didn't brag about. The first of the heavy Wall Street exposés, very detailed and interesting.

Brooks, John. *The Takeover Game.* New York: Truman Talley Books/ E. P. Dutton, 1987. Here is Brooks on the 1980s. I think this book is so good I use it as a textbook in my investment-banking class. The students love it.

Bruck, Connie. *The Predators' Ball.* New York: Simon & Schuster, 1988. Bruck, a reporter for *American Lawyer,* stalked Mike Milken and Drexel for years before publishing this "unauthorized biography" of the man and the firm, which both tried to prevent. Though published long before the indictment and the settlement, its portrait of Drexel before its fall is both carefully detailed and incredulous.

Burrough, Bryan, and Helyar, John. *Barbarians at the Gate.* New York: Harper & Row, 1990. The story of the RJR-Nabisco buyout, in graphic detail, from the very beginning to the bitter end, by the two *Wall Street Journal* reporters who covered the story as it broke.

Lewis, Michael. *Liar's Poker.* New York: W.W. Norton, 1989. A trading-room view of the world of Salomon Brothers through the eyes of a highly amusing third-year bond salesman, Michael Lewis. Salomon says it's entertaining and a bit overblown, but not all that inaccurate. Of all the Wall Street books, this one may be the most shocking: do they really do those things?

Train, John. *The Money Masters.* New York: Harper & Row, 1980. Train is a money manager who writes about other professional money managers skillfully and insightfully. Many Wall Streeters regard this book as a classic of its type. He published a sequel, *The New Money Masters*, in 1989 (New York: Harper & Row).

Wolfe, Tom. *The Bonfire of the Vanities.* New York: Farrar, Straus & Giroux, 1987. This novel about the life of a bond trader in New York in the middle 1980s brought the same huge acclaim to Wolfe that he received for his nonfiction works. A tale of "manners" that reflects the times we live in, its message is nasty. He savages all of his characters, none survives his disapproval. If you don't happen to be identified with any of them, you'll think his descriptions of people, places, and events are very amusing.

PART III

Drucker, Peter. *The New Realities.* New York: Harper & Row, 1989. There aren't many books that are helpful when trying to learn about our financial future, which will be shaped more perhaps by international forces than anything else. To understand these and many of the other larger forces of our times, one can always turn to Peter Drucker, whose latest set of essays on government, politics, and economics and business this is. There is something in this book for everyone.

Smith, Roy C. *The Global Bankers.* New York: Truman Talley Books/ E. P. Dutton, 1989. Some may find my book on international investment banking in the United States, Europe, and Japan useful, too, in considering our future in global markets.

ACKNOWLEDGMENTS

A book of this kind is a daunting undertaking for a salt-and-peppered investment banker, who only late in life has sought the paths of total objectivity in the guises of professor and author. Making this particular era in our financial history comprehensible and indeed educational to the general reader requires that it contain mixtures rare in any one individual's experience, so I have relied on many individuals to provide shape, meaning, and interest to this book.

As always, one must start with those who provide the support, encouragement, and argumentation to get it going and to see it through. In first place among these is my wife, Marianne, and not far behind, my incredulous children, Kelley and Peter, Andrew and Allison. Next comes my publisher Truman "Mac" Talley, who talked me into the project and offered useful suggestions and criticisms throughout.

My colleagues on the faculty of the Stern School of Business at New York University have been of enormous help, especially Professors Edward Altman and Ernest Bloch, both experts on much of the subject matter treated, who painstakingly read through the manuscript with many helpful ideas. I have had much help also over the years from many others who taught me what I know about corporate mergers and restructuring: my partners and colleagues at Goldman, Sachs & Co. including in particular Stephen Friedman, Geoffrey Boisi, Willard Overlock, Peter Sachs, and Richard Herbst, some of the long-lasting champions in the field, and too many lawyers, accountants, and public relations experts to count.

To research the book I have continued to have the incomparable assistance of the All-American library team from Goldman Sachs, headed by Kathy Cray, Mary Elizabeth Poje, Mary Anne Reilly, and Elizabeth Mason. I have also had, as usual, the invaluable help of my secretary, Mary Allen, from beginning to end.

I also want to thank the students of the Fall 1989 Corporate Mergers and Acquisitions course B40.3196 at the Stern School for letting me practice on them, scanning their eyes for the light of understanding. As is always the case, their teacher learned more than they did.

Notwithstanding all this, the errors and omissions are my own alone as are all of the opinions expressed.

New York
March 1990

INDEX